H. H. Richardson
Complete
Architectural Works

The MIT Press
Cambridge, Massachusetts
London, England

H. H. Richardson
Complete
Architectural Works

Jeffrey Karl Ochsner

This book was set in Sabon by Graphic
Composition Inc. and printed and bound
by Halliday Lithograph in the United
States of America.

**Library of Congress Cataloging in
Publication Data**

Ochsner, Jeffrey Karl.
    H. H. Richardson, complete architectural
works.

    Includes indexes.
    1. Richardson, Henry Hobson,
1838–1886—Catalogs.
I. Title.
NA737.R5A4 1982   720'.92'4   82–6603
ISBN 0–262–15023–9   AACR2

H. H. Richardson,
17 December 1879;
Society for the Pres-
ervation of New
England Antiquities
(Codman family
papers).

Contents

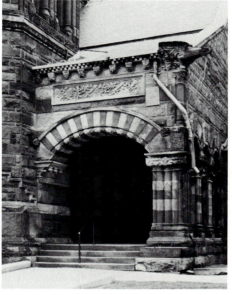

Acknowledgments

In the eight years during which I assembled *H. H. Richardson: Complete Architectural Works*, I was aided by scholars, art historians, librarians, photographers, friends, and family. I hope they will all accept my grateful thanks.

Three art historians made significant contributions to the work, without which it would have been incomplete. Each read the catalogue in manuscript form, offered constructive criticisms, and pointed out necessary revisions. James F. O'Gorman, in particular, thoroughly annotated a draft manuscript with his comments, noting designs which had been missed, sources for additional information, and individuals who had original photographs. John Coolidge graciously gave access to his extensive files of Richardson research material; he also noted some omitted designs and suggested additional photographs. Henry-Russell Hitchcock provided valuable new information and suggested sources for additional visual materials, as well.

In addition, I received valuable assistance from several other individuals who answered my requests with patience and understanding. Of particular importance were Eleanor Garvey, David Becker, and Roger Wieck at the Houghton Library; Jack Jackson at the Boston Athenaeum; and Ellie Reichlin at the Society for the Preservation of New England Antiquities. The completeness of the sections on Richardson's work in Buffalo is due to the generous assistance of Francis Kowsky, who also pointed out several lesser known designs in other cities. Mickey Lutz provided invaluable assistance, searching many hours through materials held by the Library of Congress.

I owe the coherent structure of this catalogue, in large part, to the editorial guidance of the MIT Press, which saw in my initial efforts the possibility of the catalogue which emerged.

Mr. and Mrs. Oliver F. Ames graciously gave financial support toward the book's publication.

I received photographic assistance at various times from Donald Gordon, Providence, Rhode Island; Tom Gates, New York, New York; Jeff Sledge, Cambridge, Massachusetts; Joseph Paskus, Madison, Wisconsin; and Greg Nowicki, Houston, Texas.

The University of Wisconsin, Madison, and Rice University, Houston, allowed me to use their research library facilities. The School of Architecture at Rice University also allowed me to use their photographic facilities.

The typing of various drafts of the manuscript was performed by Catherine C. Alexander, Madison, and Jo Monaghan, Houston.

Finally, I must thank my parents, Mr. and Mrs. R. S. Ochsner, and my wife, Sandra Lynn Perkins, for their patience, understanding, support, and encouragement.

The following organizations and individuals provided valuable information and assistance:

Berenice Abbott
Albany Institute for History and Art (Christine W. Ward, James R. Hobin)
Mr. and Mrs. Oliver F. Ames
Albany Public Library (Michael Catoggio)
Albany Rural Cemetery Association (William H. Kelly, Jr.)
All Souls Unitarian Church, New York
Ames Free Library, North Easton (Margaret Meade)
Anderson, Notter, Finegold, Inc., Boston
Wayne Andrews
Archives of American Art
Art Institute of Chicago (John Zukowsky)
Avery Library, Columbia University (Adolf K. Placzek)
Baptist Home of Rhode Island
The Bettman Archive, Inc., New York
Beverly Public Library (M. Dunklee, Robert Calder)
Geoffrey Blodgett
Boston Athenaeum (Jack Jackson, Sally Pierce)
Boston College Jesuit Community
Boston Public Library (Theresa Cederholm, Sinclair Hitchings)
Bostonian Society (Mary Leen)
Brookline Public Library (Judith Jackson Long)
Buffalo and Erie County Historical Society (William Roberts, Martin King)
Buffalo and Erie County Public Library (William H. Loos)
Buffalo Psychiatric Center (Eileen F. Berntsen)
Cambridge Public Library (Richard Pennington)
Carnegie Library of Pittsburgh (Ann M. Loyd, Audrie Furcron)
Cathedral of All Saints, Albany
Center for Connecticut Studies, Eastern Connecticut State College
Chicago Architectural Photographing Company
Chicago Historical Society (Jane Stevens)
Chicago Public Library (Rose E. Duffy)
Chicago School of Architecture Foundation
Church of the Incarnation, New York (Margaret Morgan)
Cincinnati Historical Society (Mrs. Elmer S. Forman)
Public Library of Cincinnati and Hamilton County (R. Jayne Craven)
Society of the Cincinnati, Washington (John D. Kilbourne)
Cohasset Historical Society (Robert Fraser)
Columbia Historical Society, Washington (Elizabeth J. Miller)
Commission of Fine Arts, Washington (Jeffrey R. Carson)

Connecticut General Life Insurance Company, corporate library (Marian G. Lechner)

Connecticut Historical Society, Hartford (Melancthon W. Jacobus)

Connecticut State Library (Kristin Woodbridge, Ann P. Barry)

John Coolidge

Crystal City Public Library (Alberta Crowe)

Danforth Museum, Framingham (Leah Lipton)

Dartmouth College Library (Kenneth C. Kramer)

Detroit Chapter, AIA

Detroit Public Library (Alice C. Dalligan)

Dover Publications

Public Library of the District of Columbia (Marcie Rickun)

Easton Historical Society (Duncan B. Oliver)

Elizabeth Taber Library, Marion (Ellen Block)

Equitable Life Assurance Society, library (Veronica Viger, Arline Schneider)

Essex Institute, Salem (Mary Ritchie)

First Unitarian Church, Springfield

Fondren Library, Rice University (Kay Flowers)

Stephen Fox

Framingham Historical and Natural History Society (Stephen W. Herring)

Framingham Public Library (Sherry Piselli)

Paul R. Goldberger

Grace Episcopal Church, Medford (Mrs. Burgess C. McCracken)

Samuel L. Guiffre

Hartford Architecture Conservancy (Merle Kummer)

Hartford Public Library (Beverly A. Loughlin)

Harvard University Archives (William Whalen, Rhonda Cooper)

John Hay Library, Brown University (Clifton Jones, Mark Brown)

Henry-Russell Hitchcock

Holyoke Daily Transcript–Telegram (Ella Merkel DiCarlo)

Holyoke Public Library (Mary Kates)

Houghton Library, Harvard University (David Becker, Roger Wieck, Eleanor Garvey)

Hoyt Public Library, Saginaw (Anna Mae Thompson)

International Harvester, Inc., archives (Greg Lennis)

Richard Janson

Francis W. Kowsky

Ellen W. Kramer

Library of Congress, Prints and Photographs Division (Mary Ison)

Lutheran Council in the United States, Washington

Mickey Lutz

Malden Public Library (Irving S. Cole, Dina Malgeri, Jane Lawless)

Massachusetts Historical Society (Ross Urquhart)

Medford Historical Commission (Patricia J. Lawrence, Paul Barter)

Medford Historical Society (Joseph V. Valerani)

Missouri Historical Society, St. Louis (Kathleen Schoene, Anthony Crawford)

Museum of Fine Arts, Houston

Museum of Modern Art, New York

National Capital Planning Commission (Tanya Beauchamp)

National Monuments Record, London, England (Stephen Croad)

National Trust for Historic Preservation

New London County Historical Society

New London Public Library (Elizabeth P. Whitten)

New York Historical Society (Erin Drake)

Museum of the City of New York

New York Public Library

New York State Education Department, State Archives, Albany

Beaumont Newhall

Newport Historical Society (Mrs. Edmund Wordell)

Newport Public Library (Maureen Rooney)

Newton Free Library (Catherine Garoian, Margaret J. Snider)

James F. O'Gorman

Jean Baer O'Gorman

F. L. Olmsted National Historic Site (Mary J. Tynan)

Palmer Public Library (Jane E. Golas)

Peter C. Papademetriou

Pittsburgh History and Landmarks Foundation (Arthur P. Ziegler, James D. Van Trump)

Preservation Press

Prothman Associates, New York

Railway and Locomotive Historical Society (Gregg Turner)

Rice University School of Architecture (O. Jack Mitchell)

Henry H. Richardson III

Steve Rosenthal

Rye Historical Society (Goddard Light)

Rye Presbyterian Church (Mildred R. Cordtz)

Saint-Gaudens National Historic Site, Cornish, N.H. (John H. Dryfhout)

St. Louis Public Library (Martha Hilligoss)

Joseph E. Seagram & Sons, Inc. (Carla Caccamise Ash)

Shepley, Bulfinch, Richardson & Abbott, Inc., Boston

Society for the Preservation of New England Antiquities (Ellie Reichlin)

Springfield City Library (Ellen M. Coty, Joseph Carvalho)

Staten Island Historical Society (Marjorie O'Brien Rapaport)

Stowe-Day Foundation, Hartford (Page Adams Savery)

Sugarman, Alberts, Rogers & Barshak, Attorneys, Boston
Thomas Crane Public Library, Quincy (Dorothy E. Newton)
Anderson Todd
Drexel Turner
United States Postal Service
University of Vermont
City of Waltham Planning Department (Alan McClennen)
Waltham Public Library (Elizabeth D. Castner, Lorena P. Weatherly)
Washington Metropolitan Chapter, AIA
Wayne State University Press
Wellesley Free Library (Marian K. Boring)
Wessell Library, Tufts University (Jean F. Butt)
Historical Society of Western Pennsylvania (Ruth S. Reid)
Weston Historical Society (Harold G. Travis, Greaton H. Dickson)
Willimantic Chronicle
Woburn Public Library (Christina M. DiNapoli)
Worcester City Hospital (Mary Ann Toner)
Worcester Historical Museum (William D. Wallace, Jessica S. Goss)
Worcester Public Library (Nancy E. Gaudette)
Worcester Public School System
Worcester State Hospital, library (Virginia McSweeney)
Worcester Telegram-Gazette, library (Ruth R. Merrill)
Wyoming State Archives, Museums and Historical Department (Paula West,
Philip J. Roberts)
Yale University Library (Patricia Bodak Stark)

H. H. Richardson:
Biographical Note

Henry Hobson Richardson (1838–1886), a great-grandson on his mother's side of Joseph Priestley (the discoverer of oxygen), was born in Louisiana on September 29, 1838. He spent his early life on the Priestley plantation and in New Orleans. Because a speech impediment prevented him from entering West Point, he spent a year at the University of Louisiana and then entered Harvard College in February 1856. He spent four academically undistinguished but socially successful years at Harvard, where he was a member of the Hasty Pudding and Porcellian clubs and the Pierian Sodality. The friendships he made in these years would serve him well in his professional life. Although Richardson had initially intended to pursue a career in civil engineering, while at Harvard he chose architecture instead. After graduation in 1859 he traveled to Paris, where he spent the next five years. He enrolled in the Ecole des Beaux-Arts in November 1860, but he attended only intermittently after the American Civil War cut off his family's support.

Richardson returned to the United States in 1865 and settled in New York. After some months working with a local builder and then as a designer of lamps, he entered practice on his own on May 1, 1866. He won his first commission in November, for Unity Church in Springfield, Massachusetts. In January 1867 he married Julia Gorham Hayden (1837–1914), daughter of Dr. John C. Hayden of Boston, and for the next seven years they lived on Staten Island, first in a rented cottage and later in a house of Richardson's design. Richardson frequently worked at home, as various chronic ailments often left him too sick to commute (by ferry) to his Manhattan office.

In 1867 Richardson entered a partnership with Charles Dexter Gambrill (1834–1880). Gambrill served primarily as the business manager of the firm, Gambrill and Richardson, and was responsible for only a few designs over the next ten years. Richardson, in turn, was free to develop his design talents.

When Richardson entered architectural practice, American architecture was dominated by the Victorian Gothic (English) and Second Empire (French) styles. Richardson's earliest buildings follow the conventions of these styles and are generally indistinguishable from the works of his contemporaries. Only in the early 1870s did he begin to develop his own approach to design; he did not achieve complete maturity as an architect until 1878.

Several buildings stand out in the development of Richardson's personal style. The commissions for the Brattle Square Church, Boston, and the New York State Hospital, Buffalo, of 1870, and the Hampden County Courthouse, Springfield, of 1871, were important steps toward Richardson's successful 1872 entry in the competition for Trinity Church, Boston. The success of his design and the publicity it received during construction propelled Richardson to the front ranks of the architectural profession. The Trinity commission also determined the course of the remaining years of his career.

H. H. Richardson in monk's habit (one of a series of photographs, ca. 1883 by George Collins Cox); Society for the Preservation of New England Antiquities.

H. H. Richardson, in Paris, December 1860; Society for the Preservation of New England Antiquities (Codman family papers).

Portrait of H. H. Richardson by Sir Hubert Herkomer, 1886 (see no. 144); Henry H. Richardson III.

When construction of Trinity Church began in 1874, Richardson moved to the Boston area and settled in the suburb of Brookline, where he resided for the next twelve years. He rented a house from Edward William (Ned) Hooper, Treasurer of Harvard University. As he received a continuing series of commissions from other Harvard acquaintances and friends, Richardson's career prospered. He entered a circle made up of the leading artists, scholars, and intellectuals of the time. The invitations Richardson received to join the Wintersnight and Saturday dining clubs confirmed his acceptance as a prominent member of the community.

Even after the move to Brookline, Richardson continued his partnership with Gambrill for four more years. Each week Richardson would prepare sketches for various projects, which were hand-carried to New York by a member of the staff, there to be translated into architectural drawings. After the dissolution of the partnership in 1878, Richardson brought his office staff to Brookline. Over the last eight years of his career, Richardson ran his practice in the studio additions at the back of the Brookline residence.

Richardson's professional maturity was marked by a series of projects beginning in 1878: Sever Hall, Cambridge; the John Bryant House, Cohasset; the Ames Monument, Wyoming; and the Crane Library, Quincy. In these projects Richardson began to simplify form and to eliminate archeological detail. He turned instead to basic shapes, continuous surfaces, and the innate qualities of brick, stone, and shingles to create the distinctive architectural quality of his buildings.

By 1882 Richardson was recognized as the leading architect in America; even in Europe he had few rivals. In the last years of his career he was besieged with commissions.

Richardson's health deteriorated markedly in the later years of his life. During his visit to Europe in the summer of 1882, he consulted with Sir William Gull concerning his illness, a chronic case of Bright's disease, a renal disorder. Although Gull warned Richardson to be careful, he continued his practice at the same pace on returning to Brookline. He died four years later on April 27, 1886 at the age of 47. His grave may be found in the Walnut Hill Cemetery in Brookline.

The practice of architecture in Richardson's office followed his experience in the Paris ateliers. For each project Richardson provided small sketches, which were given to his draftsmen to be developed in drawing form. A senior draftsman would know all aspects of each design and Richardson's intentions at each stage. When the project was ready for construction, this draftsman was fully prepared to supervise. In this way Richardson maintained his involvement in a large number of projects without becoming overwhelmed in detail.

Two individuals outside the office played important parts in Richardson's career. Orlando Whitney Norcross (1839–1920), the leading partner in Norcross Brothers, general contractors, of Worcester, Massachusetts, was responsible for the construction of a large portion of Richardson's work, including most of his major projects. Richardson first became involved with Norcross in 1870. Thereafter, he relied on Norcross for his knowledge of materials, costs, and construction techniques. Norcross in turn executed such a large portion of Richardson's work that he came to know exactly what Richardson sought in his designs.

Even more significant in Richardson's career was the role played by his close friend and neighbor, America's leading landscape architect, Frederick Law Olmsted (1822–1903). Neighbors initially on Staten Island and later in Brookline, the two men became extremely close. Olmsted was responsible for several of Richardson's commissions and Richardson brought Olmsted into collaboration on a number of others. Even on projects where there was no formal collaboration, Richardson often turned to Olmsted for advice. The evident theoretical consistency of Richardson's mature work may in some part be due to the influence of Olmsted, who in the course of his career developed a broad vision of the place of architecture in the American landscape.

At Richardson's death, the control of his office passed into the hands of his three chief assistants: George Foster Shepley (1858–1903), Charles Hercules Rutan (1851–1914), and Charles Allerton Coolidge (1858–1936). They changed the name of the firm to Shepley, Rutan and Coolidge, and continued in practice. Nearly all of the projects unfinished at Richardson's death were completed under their supervision.

Textual References

The following references are related to Henry Hobson Richardson on a general level and not specifically to any single building or project. (References for each building or project are cited at the end of each catalogue entry.)

Anderson, Robert L. "The Brown Decades Revisited." *Journal of the Society of Architectural Historians* 2 (July 1942): 14–25.

Andrews, Robert D. "The Broadest Use of Precedent." *Architectural Review* 2 (May 15, 1893): 31–36.

Blackall, C. H. "Boston Sketches—the Churches." *Inland Architect and News Record* 12 (Dec. 1888): 77–78.

———. "Boston Sketches—Suburban Work." *Inland Architect and News Record* 13 (Mar. 1889): 40–41; (Apr. 1889): 53–54.

Bosworth, Welles. "I Knew H. H. Richardson." *American Institute of Architects Journal* 16 (Sept. 1951): 115–127.

"Buildings Designed by the late H. H. Richardson, Architect." *American Architect and Building News* 20 (Sept. 11, 1886): 122.

Chaffee, Richard. "Richardson's Record at the Ecole des Beaux-Arts." *Journal of the Society of Architectural Historians* 36 (Oct. 1977): 175–188.

Coolidge, Charles A. "H. H. Richardson." In *The Later Years of the Saturday Club, 1870–1920*, edited by M. A. DeWolfe Howe. Boston: Houghton Mifflin, 1927.

"Death of Henry H. Richardson, Architect." *American Architect and Building News* 19 (May 1, 1886): 205–206.

Eaton, Leonard K. *American Architecture Comes of Age: European Reaction to H. H. Richardson and Louis Sullivan.* Cambridge, Mass.: MIT Press, 1972.

———. "Richardson and Sullivan in Scandinavia." *Progressive Architecture* 47 (Mar. 1966): 168–171.

Elzner, A. O. "A Reminiscence of Richardson." *Inland Architect and News Record* 20 (Sept. 1892): 15.

Flagg, Ernest. "Influence of the French School on Architecture in the United States." *Architectural Record* 4 (Oct.–Dec. 1894): 211–228.

Forbes, J. D. "Shepley, Bulfinch, Richardson and Abbott, Architects: An Introduction." *Journal of the Society of Architectural Historians* 17 (Fall 1958): 19–31.

Hitchcock, Henry-Russell. *The Architecture of H. H. Richardson and His Times.* New York: Museum of Modern Art, 1936; 2d ed. Hampden, Conn.: Archon Books, 1961; rpt. ed. Cambridge, Mass.: MIT Press, 1966.

———. "An Inventory of the Architectural Library of H. H. Richardson." *Nineteenth Century* 1 (Jan. 1975): 27, 31; (Apr. 1975): 18–19.

———. *Richardson as a Victorian Architect.* Baltimore: Smith College by Barton Gillet Co., 1966.

Koch, Robert. "American Influence Abroad, 1886 and Later." *Journal of the Society of Architectural Historians* 18 (May 1959): 66–69.

Langton, W. A. "The Method of H. H. Richardson." *The Architect and Contract Reporter* 65 (Mar. 9, 1900): 156–158.

———. "On the Architect's Part in His Works, as Exemplified in the Methods of H. H. Richardson." *Canadian Architect and Builder* 13 (Feb. 1900).

Lewis, Arnold. "Hinckeldyen, Vogel and American Architecture." *Journal of the Society of Architectural Historians* 31 (Dec. 1972): 276–290.

"Mr. Richardson and the Royal Gold Medal." *American Architect and Building News* 23 (Mar. 24, 1889): 139.

Mumford, Lewis. *The Brown Decades: A Study of the Arts in America 1865–1895*, pp. 114–132. New York: Harcourt Brace, 1931.

———. *The South in Architecture: The Dancy Lectures, Alabama College, 1941*, pp. 79–110. New York: Harcourt Brace, 1941.

———. *Sticks and Stones: A Study of American Architecture and Civilization*, pp. 44–48. New York: Boni & Liveright, 1924.

O'Gorman, James F. *H. H. Richardson and His Office—Selected Drawings.* Boston: David R. Godine, 1974.

———. "Henry Hobson Richardson and Frank Lloyd Wright." *The Art Quarterly* 22 (Autumn 1969): 308–311.

———. "O. W. Norcross, Richardson's 'Master Builder': A Preliminary Report." *Journal of the Society of Architectural Historians* 32 (May 1973): 104–113.

———. "On Vacation with H. H. Richardson: Ten Letters from Europe, 1882." *Archives of American Art Journal* 19 (Jan.–Mar. 1979): 2–14.

"O'Gorman, James F. *Selected Drawings—H. H. Richardson and His Office*" (book review). *Journal of the Society of Architectural Historians* 34 (Dec. 1974): 319–324.

Orth, Myra Dickman. "The Influence of the 'American Romanesque' in Australia." *Journal of the Society of Architectural Historians* 34 (Mar. 1973): 2–18.

Overmire, Edwin P. "A Draftsman's Recollection of Boston." *The Western Architect* 3 (Feb. 1904): 18–20; (Mar. 1904): 18–21; (May 1904): 6–8; (Aug. 1904): 4–6; (Sept. 1904): 4–6.

Pickens, Buford L. "H. H. Richardson and Basic Form Concepts in Modern Architecture." *Art Quarterly* 3 (Summer 1940): 273–291.

Progressive Architecture 46 (July 1965): cover photograph.

"Proposal to Erect a Memorial to the Late Mr. Richardson." *American Architect and Building News* 19 (June 5, 1886): 265.

"Proposed Memorial to H. H. Richardson." *American Architect and Building News* 20 (July 24, 1886): 43.

"Railway Stations at Wellesley Hills, Waban, Woodlands, Auburndale, Brighton, South Framingham, Palmer, Holyoke and North Easton, Mass." *American Architect and Building News* 21 (Feb. 26, 1887): 103.

Reinink, A. W. "American Influences on Late 19th Century Architecture in the Netherlands." *Journal of the Society of Architectural Historians* 29 (May 1970): 163–174.

"Richardson v. Richardson." *The Architect and Engineer* 124 (Mar. 1936): 60.

Schuyler, Montgomery. "The Romanesque Revival in America." *Architectural Record* 1 (Oct.–Dec. 1891): 151–198.

———. "The Romanesque Revival in New York." *Architectural Record* 1 (July–Sept. 1891): 7–38.

Scully, Vincent J., Jr. *The Shingle Style*. New Haven: Yale University Press, 1955; *The Shingle Style and the Stick Style*, rev. ed. New Haven: Yale University Press, 1971.

"Some Incidents in the Life of H. H. Richardson." *American Architect and Building News* 20 (Oct. 23, 1886): 198–199.

Tallmadge, Thomas E. "Holographs of Famous Architects." *American Architect* 143 (Mar. 1933): 8–12.

"Those Who Will Complete Mr. Richardson's Buildings." *American Architect and Building News* 19 (May 8, 1886): 218.

Tselos, Dimitri. "Richardson's Influence on European Architecture." *Journal of the Society of Architectural Historians* 29 (May 1970): 156–162.

"The Uniform Rate of Compensation of Architects." *American Architect and Building News* 23 (Jan. 14, 1888): 14.

Van Rensselaer, Marianna Griswold. *Henry Hobson Richardson and His Works*. Boston: 1888; rpt. ed. New York: Dover, 1969.

"Van Rensselaer, Marianna Griswold. *Henry Hobson Richardson and His Works*" (book review). *American Architect and Building News* 24 (July 7, 1888): 10–11.

Warren, H. Langford. "The Use and Abuse of Precedent." *Architectural Review* 2 (Feb. 13, 1893): 11–15; 2 (Apr. 3, 1893): 21–25.

Waterhouse, Alfred. "Waterhouse on Richardson." *American Architect and Building News* 24 (Dec. 1, 1888): 253–254.

Wight, P. B. "H. H. Richardson" (obituary). *Inland Architect and News Record* 7 (May 1886): 59–61; rpt. *Inland Architect* 15 (Sept. 1971): 47.

Wyatt, J. B. Noel. "Modern Romanesque Architecture." *Architectural Review* 6 (Aug. 1899): 103–107.

Introduction

In the nearly one hundred years since Richardson's death, only a few major texts have appeared on his work. Of the four giants of American architecture—H. H. Richardson, Louis Sullivan, Frank Lloyd Wright, and Louis Kahn—Richardson has received the least attention. Nowhere has there appeared complete photographic coverage of Richardson's buildings or a complete chronology of his designs, built and unbuilt. Other than Hitchcock's monograph of 1936, there have been few interpretive studies. This catalogue partially fills this gap by providing for the first time a complete listing of all of Richardson's known designs.

About 150 designs of Richardson's have been documented, including about 85 built structures and 65 unexecuted designs. These date from the twenty years of Richardson's career, 1866 to 1886.[1]

Any catalogue of Richardson's designs must begin with the three major studies published since his death in 1886. *Henry Hobson Richardson and His Works*, a monograph by Marianna Griswold Van Rensselaer, was published in 1888.[2] Van Rensselaer worked from Richardson's office books and compiled a list of Richardson's structures with a date for each.[3] However, her account omitted projects not listed in the office books, such as personal projects for which no fees were charged.[4] Nor did she discuss any of Richardson's unexecuted projects other than the Albany Cathedral.[5] Nonetheless, these flaws must be regarded as minor, especially in light of Van Rensselaer's pioneering efforts, on which all later Richardson scholarship has been based.

In 1936, just fifty years after Richardson's death, Henry-Russell Hitchcock's monograph, *The Architecture of H. H. Richardson and His Times*, was published by the Museum of Modern Art in conjunction with an exhibition of Richardson's work.[6] Hitchcock made minor revisions to Van Rensselaer's list of built structures. He also discussed in detail most of Richardson's unexecuted projects for which drawings remained in the offices of Coolidge, Shepley, Bulfinch and Abbott, the firm of Richardson's successors.[7] Charles A. Coolidge, who began his architectural career with Richardson, other living members of Richardson's office, and Henry Richardson Shepley, H. H. Richardson's grandson, all aided Hitchcock's research. Since publication in 1936, Hitchcock's book has been reissued twice, with additions, corrections, and annotations.[8]

The third major text on Richardson, *H. H. Richardson and His Office—Selected Drawings*, by James F. O'Gorman, was published in 1974 in conjunction with an exhibition of Richardson's drawings at Harvard University.[9] While this book concentrated largely on drawings, it did provide new information on some of Richardson's structures and many of his unexecuted designs. O'Gorman worked extensively with primary sources, including letters and archives. His work established exact dates for design and construction of many of the projects included in the catalogue.

The second major resource for a complete catalogue of all of Richardson's designs is the Richardson drawing collection, now held by the Houghton Library at Harvard University.[10] For many years these drawings had been preserved in storage files by his successors. In 1942 Henry Richardson Shepley donated the bulk of the collection—largely the same material which had been studied by Hitchcock in the 1930s[11]—to Harvard University. Since that time other documents, including Richardson's early sketch book[12] and an extensive photograph album,[13] have been placed on deposit at Houghton Library by Richardson's successors. The drawing collection of more than 15,000 items was organized and indexed in the early 1960s by Charles Price.[14] This has made it more easily accessible to researchers.

These basic resources were the foundation for a dual approach to the field research necessary for an accurate and complete catalogue. In the course of several years, I paid visits to all of Richardson's remaining structures and to most of the sites of those which have been destroyed. At the same time, I corresponded with local libraries, historical societies, and other similar institutions, to verify basic information on the origins, clients, development, construction, and demise of the various designs. This correspondence over several years yielded a wealth of new information, which has given this catalogue a level of completeness and accuracy not otherwise achievable.

Other resources I used at various times in the compilation of the catalogue included Richardson's office books[15] and personal as well as professional correspondence, both available on microfilm through the Archives of American Art,[16] various scholarly articles and research papers published in leading art and architectural history journals, and several unpublished dissertations on aspects of Richardson's work.[17]

Finally, from 1978 to 1980, with the assistance of the MIT Press, I was able to contact and correspond with various authorities in architectural history: Hitchcock, O'Gorman, Coolidge, and Kowsky, each of whom pointed out some lesser known designs which had been omitted. Their assistance made possible a catalogue documenting all of Richardson's known designs.

The catalogue lists designs in basically chronological order. Since it is often very difficult to date a building design exactly, the order may not be completely accurate. This problem of order is complicated by the various dates attributed to each of them. Van Rensselaer's list of dates, based on Richardson's office books, follows the order in which project contracts were received by the office. But the designs were often developed before agreement on a contract, particularly in the case of competition entries; the Van Rensselaer sequence consequently requires analysis and revision.[18] Further, the addition of unbuilt projects, for which contracts were never received, makes the determination of a completely accurate chronological sequence nearly impossible. In some cases information gleaned from local sources has clarified project dates. In other cases

Van Rensselaer's dates are the only ones available, so the order of projects must be inferred. Dates for some projects known only from undated drawings in the Houghton collection, for which no correlative material could be developed, remain problematic. Approximations by architectural historians for some projects are used in this catalogue. In the few cases where dates remained completely undetermined, the designs were placed where they seemed most appropriate in relation to designs of known date.[19]

Each design has been assigned a number in the order of its appearance in this catalogue. The only deviation from this system occurs when Richardson designed minor adjuncts or additions to his own work, such as the Trinity Church porch or the Bryant stables. These few projects are indicated only by a letter suffix to the major design number and are included at the end of the text for the major design.

Each catalogue entry is organized in the same format. The number of each design precedes its name, generally the one used by Richardson scholars, although in a few cases a correction appears. The name is followed by the date or dates of the design. In the case of built structures, the first date marks Richardson's first involvement with the project, and the last is the completion of its construction. For unbuilt projects the date or dates correspond to the time when the project was known to be under consideration in the office. Designs from the period of Richardson's partnership with Gambrill are noted by the "G&R" after the date. The next lines give the address for the design. For some unbuilt projects only a city or town is listed, and in a few cases no address is given. Addresses which have not been definitively established are omitted, but the speculations of scholars for the possible locations of some unbuilt projects are noted in the text. Following the address, buildings which have been demolished are so noted. The descriptive text for each entry generally presents the information available in the following order:[20]

clients
how the commission was received (if in competition, other competitors)
history of design, construction, alteration, demolition
collaborators
architectural description
historical/architectural significance.

Biographical information is provided for most of Richardson's clients. In the case of Richardson's patrons such as William Dorsheimer, James Rumrill, and F. L. Ames, who were involved in several commissions, biographical information is provided with the first design for which each was responsible; subsequent reference is made to that entry. In the building descriptions I have used stylistic terminology only when a clear stylistic designation has been agreed upon by architectural historians. Frequently, I have omitted discussion of historical significance because not every work can be said to have been significant either for Richardson's career, for the architectural profession of the time, or for the history of architecture in general. Otherwise, information omitted for any design was simply not available.

At the end of each catalogue entry is a list of selected resources. The selected bibliography of the most significant references to each project in print precedes a listing of other resources for the design, including drawings, photographs, archival materials, letters, and other documents. I have limited the selected bibliography to architectural and scholarly periodicals and omitted popular periodicals and newspaper references.

Almost all of Richardson's known structures are shown in photographs. Omissions include many of Richardson's little known New York City remodelings, and possibly the Boston & Albany Railroad dairy building (see no. 97). In many cases I have used contemporary photographs obtained from the general collections at the Houghton Library, the Boston Athenaeum, and the Society for the Preservation of New England Antiquities;[21] from local sources such as historical societies and public libraries; or from contemporary publications.[22] The contemporary photographs are supplemented by more recent photographs from a variety of sources. In a few cases, only recent photographs were available. I have included at least one overall view for each structure; unusual views, interiors, and significant details appear whenever they were available.

Richardson's unexecuted projects are shown in drawing form. In most cases I have included only a single drawing, but for a few particularly significant designs I have presented several drawings. These drawings were found either in the Houghton Library collection, in the Richardson sketchbook now held by Houghton Library, or in contemporary publications.[23] In the case of projects for which no visual material is presented, I have been unable to find what probably does not exist.

Unfortunately plans could not be included for every Richardson design. They are unavailable for most of the early designs, and limitations of space prevented the inclusion of more than a sampling for the later works. Plans which are included provide an indication of the development of Richardson's spatial concepts.

The catalogue includes all of Richardson's known designs within certain limits. There are projects on which Richardson played a minor role, but which are not considered truly his. I have omitted these designs of several types. Prior to Richardson's entry into practice, he made contributions to the work of other architects in whose offices he was employed.[24] These works actually belonged not to Richardson but to the offices. During Richardson's partnership with Gambrill, the office produced several buildings which Van Rensselaer and Hitchcock credit to Gambrill.[25] Although Richardson may have offered advice on these projects, they are Gambrill's and not included here. However, those

Gambrill and Richardson designs whose authorship is uncertain are included, since they may have been Richardson's. Moreover, Richardson may have acted as a consultant to landscape architect Frederick Law Olmsted on a number of projects, such as the design of the Hubbard Estate, Weston, Massachusetts.[26] Whenever Richardson's specific architectural contributions cannot be identified, I have omitted these projects; they must be accepted as Olmsted's.

These distinctions were easily made, but several other omissions were more difficult. The transition from projects by Richardson to those by his successors, Shepley, Rutan and Coolidge, is a subtle one. This catalogue follows Hitchcock and O'Gorman by adding the I. H. Lionberger house and the Potter house to Van Rensselaer's list. Richardson's correspondence clearly indicates that he designed these before his death.[27] However, some of the unexecuted projects in the Houghton Library collection cannot be assigned clearly to Richardson or to Shepley, Rutan and Coolidge. Thus, this catalogue includes the project for the Hampton house, although it may be an early work of Shepley, Rutan and Coolidge. A number of projects included in the Houghton Library drawing collection are definitely the work of Shepley, Rutan and Coolidge;[28] they are not included here. Moreover, the Houghton Library drawing collection also has 45 drawings for domestic projects and 134 for other projects, all unidentified and undated.[29] While most of these are detail studies, a few are plans, elevations, sections, or sketches of entire buildings, but I could infer no project name or date and consequently omitted them. Nevertheless, I have included a few of these, tentatively dated by Hitchcock in his 1966 publication, *Richardson as a Victorian Architect*.[30] Finally, Richardson was responsible for furniture and decorative arts design for many of his buildings. This work constitutes a separate study, so I have omitted it from this catalogue.[31]

A series of appendixes, which provide additional information in the form of maps, charts, and tables, follows the catalogue.

Much work remains to be done on Richardson. This study is only an initial step, but it does provide the most complete guide to Richardson's work now available and makes it more accessible to all interested individuals—students, architects, or scholars.

Unfortunately, even this record of Richardson's work is already incomplete. After the book was in press, too late to alter the project sequence, three additional Richardson designs were uncovered: the Boston & Albany Railroad suburban cars (1881), the Boston & Albany Railroad Station alterations, Boston (1881), and the Algonquin Club alterations, Boston (1885).[32] Further research may uncover additional unknown Richardson works which have not been included here.

Travelers using this catalogue as a guide should respect the privacy of individual owners of Richardson's residences. The inclusion of addresses in this catalogue in no way implies the public's right of entry to any property.

Notes

1. The period of Richardson's career can be dated exactly. Richardson's letter of April 25, 1866 (Archives of American Art Microfilm Roll 643) stated that he would go into business by himself on May 1, 1866. His active career ended with his death, April 27, 1886.

2. Marianna Griswold Van Rensselaer (Mrs. Schuyler), *Henry Hobson Richardson and His Works* (Boston: Houghton Mifflin, 1888; New York: Dover Publications, 1969). Mrs. Van Rensselaer was a unique Victorian as well as an art and architectural critic. Educated by private tutors and European travel, she began publishing works of art and architectural criticism, history, and poetry after her husband's death in 1884. She later served as an inspector of New York City Schools and as president of the Public Education Association of New York. Moreover, she was an honorary member of the American Institute of Architects and the American Society of Landscape Architects. Two of Richardson's closest friends, Frederick Law Olmsted and Charles Sprague Sargent, urged Van Rensselaer to write a memorial to Richardson. Drawing on her extensive personal knowledge of Richardson and his work, she compiled a nearly complete list of his buildings and illustrated her work extensively with drawings and photographs. Although Richardson's shingled houses were mentioned, Van Rensselaer concentrated on the stone and brick designs. The only unexecuted design discussed in detail was the Albany Cathedral.

3. Van Rensselaer, *Works*, pp. 139–140. This list has been the beginning for all later research on Richardson's buildings. Most of its omissions date from early in Richardson's career when the office books from which Van Rensselaer worked were presumably sketchy.

4. The chief omissions of this type were Richardson's own house (no. 10) and the Hayden Building (no. 56).

5. Van Rensselaer did include sketches of several unbuilt Richardson projects but failed to identify them (*Works*, pp. 86, 111, 117). Most of these have been identified only recently by architectural historians (see nos. 79, 141, 143).

6. Henry-Russell Hitchcock, *The Architecture of H. H. Richardson and His Times* (New York: Museum of Modern Art, 1936; Hampden, Conn.: Archon Books, 1961; Cambridge, Mass.: MIT Press, 1966). Hitchcock wrote in his 1936 introduction that his monograph complemented the Museum of Modern Art exhibition of photographs and drawings. The exhibition has long since disappeared, so the book now stands alone. It is a detailed historical coverage of all of Richardson's work. O'Gorman has noted that the monograph is permeated with a particular viewpoint, which tends to demonstrate that Richardson was a precursor of the modern movement in architecture, still in its infancy in the United States when Hitchcock wrote in 1936. It remains the only significant interpretive text on Richardson's contribution to architecture.

7. See J. D. Forbes, "Shepley, Bulfinch, Richardson and Abbott: An Introduction," *Journal of the Society of Architectural Historians* 17 (Fall 1958): 19–31. Richardson's practice was continued by his three chief assistants at the time of his death, George Foster Shepley (1858–1903), Charles Hercules Rutan (1851–1914), and Charles Allerton Coolidge (1858–1936). Shortly after Richardson's death, Shepley married H. H. Richardson's daughter Julia. Since that time many of the principals of the firm have been related. The name of the firm has changed several times:

Gambrill and Richardson, New York	1867–1878
H. H. Richardson, Brookline	1878–1886
Shepley, Rutan and Coolidge, Boston	1886–1915
Coolidge and Shattuck, Boston	1915–1924
Coolidge, Shepley, Bulfinch and Abbott, Boston	1924–1952
Shepley, Bulfinch, Richardson and Abbott, Boston	1952–1972
Shepley, Bulfinch, Richardson and Abbott, Inc., Boston	1972–present

8. The later editions of *The Architecture of H. H. Richardson and His Times* include 30 pages of detailed notes added at the end of the text. These provide new information and correct some errors that Hitchcock had made in the 1936 edition. The revised editions also include different photographs from the first edition, but neither edition provides full photographic coverage of all of Richardson's buildings.

9. James F. O'Gorman, *Henry Hobson Richardson and His Office—Selected Drawings* (Boston: David R. Godine, 1974). The Richardson drawings, exhibited at the Fogg Museum on the centennial of Richardson's move to Brookline (1874), comprised forty-two projects from the period 1874–1886. This catalogue contains a wealth of previously unpublished material on Richardson and his practice. O'Gorman's introductory essay, "The Making of a 'Richardson Building' 1874–1886," describes in detail Richardson's Brookline practice, the atelier style of his office, his method of design, and his collaboration with O. W. Norcross and F. L. Olmsted. The text of the catalogue discusses many of Richardson's unexecuted designs which were ignored by Van Rensselaer and only briefly mentioned by Hitchcock.

10. Houghton Library at Harvard University is a repository of rare books, papers, and other documents, all held under tight security. However, most of the Richardson drawings are on microfilm and are available to visitors. Researchers wishing to use the actual Richardson materials must write to make arrangements with the curator of the collections.

11. Unfortunately, some of the drawings studied by Hitchcock may not now be found in the Houghton Library collection. Examples include the Dorsheimer house (Albany) drawings, the Stoughton house plans, and the Equitable Life Assurance Building project elevations and sections, among others.

12. Richardson's sketchbook (1869–1876) is an album of sheets now bound in more or less chronological order, recently placed on deposit at the Houghton Library by Shepley, Bulfinch, Richardson and Abbott, Inc. O'Gorman, *Selected Drawings* includes a complete transcription of this sketchbook, with annotations (pp. 211–216).

13. The Richardson photo album, including photographs of buildings and presentation drawings, covers the period 1866 to 1876. For a few Richardson designs the photographs in this album are the only known visual materials.

14. The Price index organizes and numbers all of the drawings in the collection. Fortunately, this massive index is cross referenced in several ways, including alphabetically, chronologically, and by location.

15. The four office account books now held by Shepley, Bulfinch, Richardson and Abbott, Inc., generally date from the period 1884 to 1894. They cover the end of Richardson's practice and the first years of Shepley, Rutan and Coolidge.

16. H. H. Richardson Papers, Archives of American Art Microfilm Rolls 643, 676, and 1184. Roll 643 contains some of Richardson's own correspondence. Roll 676 includes the four office account books: two drawing lists books, one office ledger, and one receipt book. Roll 1184 includes correspondence between Richardson's wife Julia and her family.

17. The most important of these are Larry J. Homolka, "Henry Hobson Richardson and the 'Ames Memorial Buildings'" (Ph.D. dissertation, Harvard University, November 1976) and Cynthia Ridgway Zaitzevsky, "Frederick Law Olmsted and the Boston Park System" (Ph.D. dissertation, Harvard University, June 1975).

18. The Allegheny County Buildings, Pittsburgh, are a typical example. Van Rensselaer lists only the February 1884 contract date. Richardson was notified of the competition on September 28, 1883, and presented plans on January 1, 1884. Thus, the design must precede, not follow those for the Adams, Hay, and Paine houses.

19. The author approximated dates only for the Holyoke church project (no. 17), the Mrs. Hyde house project (no. 37), the Borland cottage project (no. 72), the William James house project (no. 99), and the Hampton house project (no. 151).

20. This organization was suggested by James F. O'Gorman.

21. The collection of photographs held by Houghton Library was donated by Henry Richardson Shepley in 1942 with the Richardson drawing collection. It includes about 125 photographs of different Richardson buildings. More recently, Shepley, Bulfinch, Richardson and Abbott placed a large photographic album on deposit at Houghton (see note 12). The Society for the Preservation of New England Antiquities (SPNEA) and the Boston Athenaeum both hold extensive photographic collections organized by location. The SPNEA collection covers all of New England, while the Athenaeum collection is restricted to Boston and the surrounding areas. The Athenaeum also has a portfolio of loose photographs of many of Richardson's buildings.

22. A major source, *American Architect and Building News* (AABN), a weekly periodical devoted to architecture and construction, first appeared in 1876. Although it was published in Boston, it covered architectural practice throughout the United States and rapidly developed national circulation. Beginning in 1877, this periodical appeared in several editions. The more expensive Imperial and International editions were illustrated with excellent plates of buildings of significant interest, including, between 1876 and 1899, many of Richardson's major projects. Van Rensselaer's 1888 monograph is the other major source for published contemporary views. Both Van Rensselaer and *AABN* failed to cover any of Richardson's shingled houses, a conspicuous lapse. Consequently, American architects working solely from these publications must have known only Richardson's work in brick and stone.

23. Fortunately, Richardson's mature career coincided with the appearance of the first significant American architectural periodicals. The publication of *The Architectural Sketchbook* (1873–1876) and *The New York Sketchbook of Architecture* (1874–1876) provided a forum in which Gambrill and Richardson publicized their work. Richardson was editorially connected with *The New York Sketchbook*, which may explain why so many of the firm's projects appeared there.

From the time Richardson opened his own office in Brookline until his death, he was totally averse to the publication of unbuilt projects. During these years none of his work was published in drawing form. With the publication of Richardson's Young Men's Association Library project (no. 121) in *AABN* in 1887, however, the editors explained that Richardson had restricted publication of his unbuilt projects because he believed he could improve them significantly during construction. (O'Gorman amply documents Richardson's penchant for changes during construction: see *Selected Drawings*, pp. 26–27).

24. Beginning in July 1862, Richardson worked for Theodore Labrouste in Paris on the Hospice des Incurables at Ivry. Later Richardson worked for Jacques Hittorf on various railroad stations in Paris, including the construction supervision of the Gare du Nord. On returning to America in 1865, Richardson evidently worked for a Brooklyn builder named Roberts, then for Tiffany's designing gas fixtures. See Hitchcock, *Richardson*, 1936, pp. 37–60.

25. Van Rensselaer lists three houses by Gambrill: Edward Stimpson house, Dedham, Mass. (1868); Jonathan Sturges House, New York, N.Y. (1869); and Dr. J. H. Tinkham House, Oswego, N.Y. (1874). Hitchcock notes that the house project for Mary F. King— drawings are in the Houghton Library collection—was also the work of Gambrill (Hitchcock, *Richardson*, 1936, p. 79). It now appears that the Sturges House was by Richardson.

26. Albert Fein, *Frederick Law Olmsted and the American Environmental Tradition* (New York: George Braziller, 1972), p. 168. Fein's chronology includes three Olmsted– Richardson collaborations: the Mason estate, Newport, R.I. (1881–1882); the C. J. Hubbard estate, Weston, Mass. (1883); and the Vanderbilt mausoleum, New Dorp, Staten Island, N.Y. (1886).

Hitchcock notes drawings for the Mason house, but they are now lost (Hitchcock, *Richardson*, 1966, p. 252n). Olmsted's drawings, now held by the Olmsted National Historic Site, do not include Richardson's proposed Mason house renovations (see no. 98).

With regard to the Hubbard estate, no drawings of work in 1883 appear in either the Houghton collection or the Olmsted National Historic Site collection, even though plans for the Hubbard estate dated 1910 to 1916 are found in the Olmsted vault.

The Vanderbilts may have considered Richardson as architect for the mausoleum after William Henry Vanderbilt died on December 8, 1885. Richardson also may have aided Olmsted in the mausoleum design. But after Richardson's death in 1886, the architectural design of the mausoleum was developed by Richard Morris Hunt.

27. In the last months of his life Richardson was unable to travel. Consequently, George F. Shepley made several trips to visit Richardson's clients and projects. Richardson's letters to Shepley (Archives of American Art Microfilm Roll 643) describe work in progress in the office in January and March 1886. One letter, dated March 6, mentions the sending of the drawings of the two Lionberger houses and the Potter house to St. Louis and the signing of the Bigelow house construction contract. Another letter of March 13 mentions progress on the Cincinnati Chamber of Commerce and the Herkomer house. Stating that the Gratwick house plan was settled, Richardson adds, "The large railroad station at Springfield is well in hand." This refers to the Boston & Albany Railroad station at Springfield which historians have credited to Shepley, Rutan and Coolidge. Richardson also mentions a commission for an addition to the Billings Library, which was to be among the first designs of Shepley, Rutan and Coolidge.

28. The following designs in the Houghton Library collection are not the work of Richardson or of his office while he was alive:

By Shepley, Rutan and Coolidge:
Huntington Park entrance project, Boston, Mass.
Mt. Vernon Church project, Boston, Mass.
Carnegie Free Library, Cincinnati, Ohio
Nickerson house, Dedham, Mass.
Baptist Church, Malden, Mass.
New London Public Library, New London, Conn.
Stanford University buildings, Palo Alto, Calif.
Hopkins Building project, San Francisco, Calif.
Tudor barn, Buzzard's Bay, Mass.

By Alexander Estey:
Boston and Albany Railroad Station, Boston, Mass.

By Gambrill and Post:
Church project (?)

In addition, Hitchcock credits the Mary F. King house project to Gambrill alone (see note 25).

29. A few examples of drawings of unidentified projects were published by O'Gorman in *Selected Drawings*, pp. 107–108, 184.

30. Henry-Russell Hitchcock, *Richardson as a Victorian Architect* (Baltimore: Smith College at Barton Gillet Co., 1966).

31. Richardson's furniture and decorative arts designs were the subject of an exhibition at the Boston Museum of Fine Arts in 1962. The catalogue of that exhibit was published as *The Furniture of H. H. Richardson* (Boston: Museum of Fine Arts, 1962). Other references to Richardson's furniture and decorative arts designs are found in *19th Century America: Furniture and other Decorative Arts*, exh. cat. (New York: Metropolitan Museum of Art, 1970); in Anne Farnam, "H. H. Richardson and A. H. Davenport: Architecture and Furniture as Big Business in America's Gilded Age," in Paul B. Kebabian and William C. Lipke, eds., *Tools and Technologies: America's Wooden Age* (Burlington: University of Vermont, 1979), pp. 80–92; and in O'Gorman, *Selected Drawings*, pp. 203–210.

32. The Boston & Albany Railroad suburban cars (1881) and the Boston & Albany Railroad Station alterations, Boston (1881) were uncovered in the Boston & Albany Railroad records now in the collection of the Baker Library, Harvard University. Unfortunately, records in the possession of the Baker Library end in 1881, so no additional information is available about Richardson's later Boston & Albany works. However, the ledger entry for the suburban cars makes it clear that Richardson was involved in rail passenger car design several years before the Boston & Albany private car project, tentatively dated 1884 (see no. 128). Richardson's alteration work on the Boston & Albany Station in Boston explains the inclusion of an elevation of that building (originally by Alexander Estey) among his drawings (see note 28).

The Algonquin Club alterations, Boston (1885) are known only from a single entry in Richardson's receipts book (see note 15) indicating the payment of the fee for the project.

Abbreviations

AABN	*American Architect and Building News*
AF	*Architectural Forum*
AIAJ	*American Institute of Architects Journal*
ARec	*Architectural Record*
JSAH	*Journal of the Society of Architectural Historians*
Hitchcock, *Richardson*, 1936	Hitchcock, Henry-Russell. *The Architecture of H. H. Richardson and His Times*. New York: Museum of Modern Art, 1936.
Hitchcock, *Richardson*, 1961	*Ibid*. Hampden, Conn.: Archon Books, 1961.
Hitchcock, *Richardson*, 1966	*Ibid*. Cambridge, Mass.: MIT Press, 1966.
Hitchcock, *Victorian*	Hitchcock, Henry-Russell. *Richardson as a Victorian Architect*. Baltimore: Smith College at Barton-Gillet Co., 1966.
O'Gorman, *Selected Drawings*	O'Gorman, James F. *H. H. Richardson and His Office—Selected Drawings*. Boston: David R. Godine, 1974.
PA	*Progressive Architecture*
Scully, *Shingle Style*	Scully, Vincent J., Jr. *The Shingle Style and the Stick Style*. Rev. ed. New Haven: Yale University Press, 1971.
Van Rensselaer, *Works*	Van Rensselaer, Marianna Griswold (Mrs. Schuyler). *Henry Hobson Richardson and His Works*. Boston: Houghton and Mifflin, 1888; rpt. ed. New York: Dover, 1969.

Catalogue of Buildings
and Projects

1866

I
Unity Church, 1866–1869
209 State Street
Springfield, Massachusetts
Demolished 1961

On March 4, 1819, dissenting members of the First Congregational Church of Springfield established a new religious organization with the name Third Congregational Society in Springfield. At that meeting Jonathan Dwight, a local businessman, offered funds for the erection of a new church. A white clapboard structure with a temple front was erected and dedicated on January 5, 1820. By 1866, however, the growth of this Unitarian organization led to a decision to build a new church building.

Among the major supporters of the new building effort were Chester W. Chapin (1798–1883) and James Bliss Rumrill (1812–1885). A leader in the development of the Massachusetts transportation network, Chapin served at various times as president of the Connecticut River Railroad, Western Railroad, and the Western's successor, the Boston & Albany Railroad. He was also president of several Springfield banks and served one term in the United States Congress from 1874 to 1876. James B. Rumrill, on the other hand, was a manufacturer of gold jewelry and gold chains. His son, James Augustus Rumrill (1837–1909), was graduated with Richardson from Harvard in 1859 and remained thereafter his good friend. In 1861 James A. Rumrill married Anna Chapin, the daughter of Chester Chapin. He later served as secretary and attorney for the Western Railroad, and after its consolidation with the Boston & Worcester, as executive vice president of the Boston & Albany. It was through the efforts of the two Rumrills and Chapin that Richardson was allowed to submit a design in competition with several local architects.

The church commission was awarded to Richardson November 6, 1866, a little more than six months after he had entered business for himself. Since it had been won in competition, he must have been working on the project for some months in New York where he practiced alone, sharing space with another architect, Emlin Littell. Construction documents were completed during the winter and ground was broken March 1, 1867. The building was dedicated February 16, 1869.

The Unitarian Society used the building for almost one hundred years until 1957, when the congregation voted to move to new facilities. The building was then sold and razed in 1961. Only a John La Farge window, "Rebekah at the Well," remains and is now in the George Walter Vincent Smith Museum, Springfield.

Richardson's first building was composed of four elements—the southwestern tower and spire, the western narthex, the central nave, and the eastern Sunday school—in an asymmetrical arrangement. The central nave with side aisles was oriented perpendicular to the street. The chancel, not required by Unitarian services, was eliminated, and a bank of organ pipes provided a background for the pulpit. The open hammerbeam timber roof sloped down to a clerestory which provided light to the interior. A rose window at the west end provided additional light. At the east end of the composition, in place of the chancel, Richardson located the Sunday school room with its axis perpendicular to that of the nave. Entry to the church was through doors at the base of the tower, which led to the narthex across the front of the nave. The square tower was topped by an octagonal spire. Longmeadow stone laid up in

1a
Unity Church,
Springfield, Massa-
chusetts, 1867–
1869, under con-
struction; Hough-
ton Library,
Harvard University.

random ashlar was the chief building material. The windows, doors, and other openings were trimmed in cut Monson granite.

The chief importance of Unity Church is as Richardson's first building. Through his success in its design and construction, Richardson assured himself of continued support from Chapin and Rumrill, who were instrumental to his other Springfield commissions. This commission also gave Richardson a sound financial basis for his next year of practice. As a direct result of this early success, Richardson married Julia Gorham Hayden (1837–1914) of Boston in January 1867 after a long engagement. Thereafter the young couple established their home in Clifton, Staten Island.

Textual References

Guiffre, Samuel L. "A Documentation of Grace Episcopal Church, Medford, Massachusetts, by Henry Hobson Richardson: A Study of His Gothic Revival Period." Master's thesis, Tufts University, 1975.

Hitchcock, Henry-Russell. "Catalogue of an Exhibition of Photographs Illustrating Springfield Architecture 1800–1900 at the Springfield Museum of Fine Arts." Typescript, Springfield City Library, 1934.

Hitchcock, *Richardson*, 1966, pp. 61–67.

Hitchcock, *Victorian*, pp. 6–7.

King, Moses, ed. *King's Handbook of Springfield*. Springfield: J. D. Gill, 1884, pp. 184–185.

Kirkham, Guy. *The Church of the Unity*. Springfield: The Church of the Unity, 1929.

Tower, James E., ed. *Springfield Present and Prospective*. Springfield: 1905.

Van Rensselaer, *Works*, pp. 18, 47–49.

Williams, Talcott. "A Brief Object-Lesson in Springfield Architecture." *AABN* 10 (Nov. 12, 1881): 227–231.

Miscellaneous Resources

Photographs: Houghton Library, Harvard University; Library of Congress (Historic American Buildings Survey); Springfield City Library.

Letters: Archives of American Art Microfilm Rolls 643 and 1184.

1b
Unity Church; Library of Congress (Historic American Buildings Survey, photo by Cervin Robinson, 1959).

1c
Unity Church; Library of Congress (Historic American Buildings Survey, photo by Cervin Robinson, 1959).

1d
Unity Church, view of nave looking toward entry; Library of Congress (Historic American Buildings Survey, photo by Cervin Robinson, 1959).

1e
Unity Church, view of nave looking toward chancel; Springfield City Library.

1867

2
Chapel (Project ?), 1867
New London, Connecticut

3
Redmond House (Project ?), 1867
Staten Island, New York

The New London chapel is an early Richardson work mentioned briefly in Julia Richardson's letter to her mother, February 10, 1867. Mrs. Richardson stated that her husband was to make a trip to Springfield on business and then to New London for the chapel project. She wrote, "He is building a chapel there."

It is doubtful whether this chapel was actually under construction at the time, or if it was ever built. All churches in the New London area (and neighboring Waterford) predate 1867, with the exception of the Pequot Chapel (857 Montauk Avenue, New London), a nondenominational chapel incorporated in 1872. The Pequot Chapel building was designed by James Renwick of New York. Although the dates roughly coincide, no evidence has been uncovered to indicate whether Richardson's New London chapel design was for the Pequot Chapel.

Miscellaneous Resource

Letter: Archives of American Art Microfilm Roll 1184.

George and Elizabeth Redmond were Staten Island acquaintances of the Richardsons. In her February 10, 1867, letter to her mother, Julia Richardson states that her husband had been consulting with Mr. Redmond and that Redmond would probably build a Richardson design on Staten Island. Nothing is known of the further development of this project.

Miscellaneous Resource

Letter: Archives of American Art Microfilm Roll 1184.

4a
Cottage project, 1867; *Boston Architectural Club Yearbook*, 1917.

The background of this small Richardson project is completely unknown. A single perspective sketch of the project appeared in the 1917 *Boston Architectural Club Yearbook*.

The drawing shows a house of irregular plan. The steep roof drops all the way down to the second floor and is broken by dormers which continue the wall surfaces vertically. A tower-like element appears in the reentrant angle at the center of the design, and a porch is against one wall. The wealth of ornamental iron work gives the house an almost fanciful appearance. The exterior walls were apparently intended to be wood.

Textual Reference

"Sketch for a Cottage, 1867." *Boston Architectural Club Yearbook*. Boston: Boston Architectural Club, 1917, unpaginated.

5
Western Railroad Offices, 1867–1869
236 Main Street
Springfield, Massachusetts
Demolished 1926

Richardson's success in the Unity Church competition led to a series of Springfield commissions. Chester W. Chapin, president of the Western (later the Boston & Albany) Railroad and a leading member of the Unity Church congregation (no. 1), was undoubtedly responsible for Richardson's selection as architect for the Western Railroad Offices.

The project evidently came to Richardson early in 1867, because Julia Richardson's letter to her mother in mid-March mentions that her husband had taken the plans to Springfield. Construction, however, was not completed until 1869. Shortly thereafter the Western Railroad was absorbed by the Boston & Albany, but the offices remained in use until the 1920s. After the building was vacated in 1926, conversion into stores and offices for lease was not economically feasible, so it was demolished.

Richardson's design was a three-story building with a full basement and attic. The basement, a half level below grade, was marked by rusticated stonework. The first floor was reached by a double flight of steps. Its stonework, like that of the next two floors, was local smooth-faced Monson granite. The attic story was enclosed by a mansard roof, typical of contemporary American commercial architecture and evidence of Richardson's French schooling. Hitchcock notes that the treatment of the window details corresponds closely to the palace architecture of Rome and Florence of the early sixteenth century as published in Letarouilly's *Edifices de Rome moderne* and Grandjean de Montigny's *Architecture toscane*, both of which Hitchcock suggests Richardson may have brought back from Paris.

Although a minor structure in Richardson's total oeuvre, the Western Railroad offices are significant as his first response to the problem of commercial office space.

Textual References

Hitchcock, Henry-Russell. "Catalogue of an Exhibition of Photographs Illustrating Springfield Architecture 1800–1900 at the Springfield Museum of Fine Arts." Typescript, Springfield Public Library, 1934.

Hitchcock, *Richardson*, 1966, pp. 71–75.

Hitchcock, *Victorian*, p. 8.

Van Rensselaer, *Works*, pp. 19, 49.

Miscellaneous Resources

Photographs: Springfield Public Library.

Letter: Archives of American Art Microfilm Roll 1184.

5a
Western Railroad
Offices, Springfield,
Massachusetts,
1867–1869;
Springfield City
Library.

6
Grace Episcopal Church, 1867–1869
160 High Street
Medford, Massachusetts

Medford Episcopalians first met in 1847, organized as a parish in 1849, and built their first church in 1850. In 1866 under the direction of the rector, Rev. Charles Learoyd (1834–1909), an 1858 graduate of Harvard, a committee to consider expansion of the existing church met and proposed the construction of an addition. At this point Mrs. Gorham (Ellen Shepherd) Brooks (1809–1884) and her two sons, Peter Chardon (1831–1920) and Shepherd (1837–1922), proposed to contribute as much toward the erection of a new church as all other parishioners combined. Moreover, they offered to donate a parcel of land on High Street for the new building. The offer was accepted, and $15,000 was raised. (Peter Chardon and Shepherd Brooks played a major role in later architectural history as developers of the Monadnock Building and other Chicago office buildings.)

In February 1867 the building committee asked several architects to submit designs, which were received from William R. Potter of New York, Alexander R. Estey of Cambridge, and Richardson. Richardson was possibly invited to compete through the efforts of Shepherd Brooks, whom he had known at Harvard, although Julia Richardson's letter of mid-March 1867 suggests that another Richardson classmate, Josiah Bradlee (1837–1902), may have made the initial contact. Richardson's design was accepted, although it was modified in an attempt to bring it within the budget.

The cornerstone and foundation were laid in 1867. By August 1868, with the project far under construction, it was evident that the budget would be exceeded considerably. The Brooks family then absorbed all cost of the church ($42,000) and leased it to the parish on completion in 1869. But under Episcopal law it could not be consecrated: it was now the private chapel of the Brooks family. When in 1873 the Brooks family turned the church over to the parish for a nominal sum, it was consecrated by the bishop of Maine.

Modifications to the church began almost immediately. In 1882 a Sunday school of incompatible design was added to the south. In 1883 the interior was redecorated. Major changes began in 1957 with another addition to the south. The chancel was modified in 1962. Richardson's altar was then given to the Department of Decorative Arts of the Brooklyn Museum in New York. The original dark stained wood of Richardson's nave was replaced in the early 1970s in an effort to create a brighter interior. Only the original pulpit remains.

From the north the church still appears as Richardson designed it. The nave, oriented parallel to the street, has low walls and a massive slate roof. Attached to the east wall of the nave is the smaller five-sided apse. On the north side near the junction of nave and apse is the 90-foot-tall tower with a square base and octagonal spire. The walls and tower are constructed of glacial boulders said to have been suggested by Mrs. Brooks. The rusticity of this material is balanced by the trim of cut granite. The church is entered through a porch and vestibule at the center of the north side of the nave. The original interior was poorly lit—Richardson's proposed clerestory was eliminated, probably for reasons of cost. The interpenetration of the chancel and nave spaces was emphasized by the projection of the chancel floor into the nave.

The central window in the south wall of the nave was designed by John La Farge. It was given by Peter and Shepherd Brooks in memory of their mother, though it is not known if Richardson had anything to do with the selection of La Farge. The window probably dates from 1884 or 1885, soon after Ellen Shepherd Brooks's death.

Textual References

Brooks, Charles and Usher, James M. *History of the Town of Medford, Middlesex County, Massachusetts, from its First Settlement in 1630 to 1885*. Boston: Rand, Avery, 1886, pp. 273–274.

"Episcopal Church, West Medford, Mass." *AABN* 27 (Feb. 8, 1890): 94.

"Episcopal Church, West Medford, Mass." *American Buildings, Selections*, no. 3: pl. 1.

French, Francis J. "The Ecclesiastical History of Medford," In *Medford, Past and Present*. Medford: Medford Mercury, 1905, pp. 72–73.

Guiffre, Samuel L. "A Documentation of Grace Episcopal Church, Medford, Massachusetts, by Henry Hobson Richardson: A Study of His Gothic Revival Period." Master's thesis, Tufts University, 1975.

Hitchcock, *Richardson*, 1966, pp. 68–69.

Hitchcock, *Victorian*, pp. 8–9.

Hollis, Benjamin P. "Grace Church, Medford: An Historical Monograph." *The Medford Historical Register* vol. 5, no. 2 (1902): 23–43.

Perry, Marguerite C., ed. *Grace Church, Medford, Massachusetts: 100th Anniversary, 1848–1948*. Medford: [Grace Church?], 1948.

Van Rensselaer, *Works*, pp. 49–50.

Miscellaneous Resources

Photographs: Medford Public Library.

Letters: Archives of American Art Microfilm Rolls 643 and 1184.

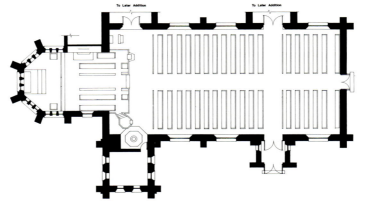

6a
Grace Episcopal
Church, Medford,
Massachusetts,
1867–1869, plan
ca. 1975; redrawn
by author from
Guiffre, Samuel L.
"A Documentation
of Grace Episcopal
Church, Medford,
Massachusetts, by
Henry Hobson
Richardson: A
Study of His Gothic
Revival Period,"
1975.

6b
Grace Episcopal
Church; *AABN* 27
(Feb. 8, 1890).

6c
Grace Episcopal
Church; photo by
Berenice Abbott
(ca. 1934).

6d
Grace Episcopal
Church, entrance
vestibule.

7
Equitable Life Assurance Building Project (Competition), 1867
120 Broadway
New York, New York

The Equitable Life Assurance Society was organized in 1859 and soon became one of the largest life insurance companies in the United States. By 1869 it was writing more new policies than any other company, and by 1886 it was the largest life insurance company in the world. In December 1865 the board of directors authorized erection of a new home office building. Lots at Broadway and Cedar Street were purchased as the site in 1865 and 1867. Designs were solicited from architects in 1867.

The architects Arthur Gilman and Edward Kendall won the competition. Their building was erected in 1868–1870, was expanded substantially in 1887 by George B. Post, but burned in 1912. In 1915 it was rebuilt from a design by Ernest R. Graham, successor to D. H. Burnham.

Richardson's entry in the Equitable Building competition is in the Richardson collection at the Houghton Library. Richardson's early response to the large urban commercial office block, the irregular quadrilateral plan shows office and similar major spaces arranged along the two exterior walls with stairs and support spaces along the two party walls. A large central court allows light to reach the interior. The side elevation of the six-story building is Richardson's first known use of windows vertically grouped under arches and between piers. The corners and basement are heavily rusticated, but the rest of the wall surfaces are flat. The mansard roof recalls Richardson's French training.

Textual References

Buley, Roscoe Carlyle. *The Equitable Life Assurance Society of the United States: One Hundredth Anniversary History, 1859/1959.* New York: Appleton-Century-Crofts, 1959.

Hitchcock, *Richardson*, 1966, pp. 76–78.

Miscellaneous Resources

Drawings: Houghton Library, Harvard University. (Note: Houghton now holds only the plan of the main floor of the building. Elevations shown and discussed by Hitchcock have evidently been misplaced.)

Archives: Equitable Life Assurance Society.

7a
Equitable Life As-
surance Building
project, New York,
New York, 1867,
main floor plan;
Houghton Library,
Harvard University.

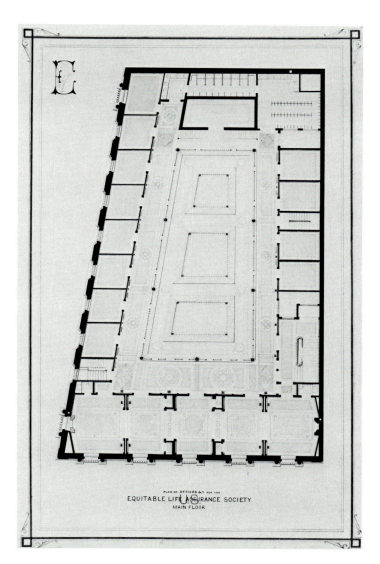

PLAN OF OFFICES &c FOR THE
EQUITABLE LIFE ASSURANCE SOCIETY
MAIN FLOOR

7b
Equitable Life Assurance Building, side elevation; Hitchcock, *Richardson*, 1936.

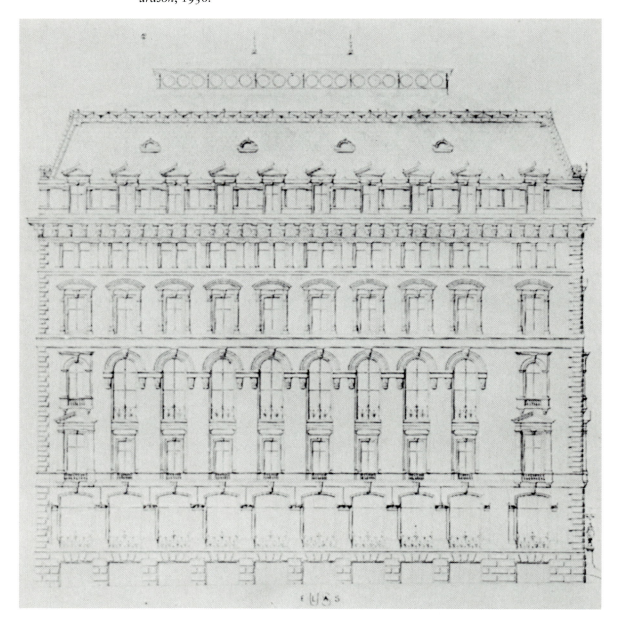

8
Century Association
Alterations, 1867–1869,
1878 G&R
42 East Fifteenth Street
New York, New York
Demolished 1891

In October 1867 Richardson entered a partnership with Charles D. Gambrill (1834–1880), whose previous partnership with George B. Post had just been dissolved. Gambrill's role in the partnership with Richardson appears to have been largely as business manager. During their eleven years of business together Richardson was responsible for almost all of the design work produced by the firm. Van Rensselaer identifies only three projects during that time as the work of Gambrill. The partnership benefited Richardson: it provided the sharing of space and the expansion of an office force.

Like Gambrill, Richardson was a member of the Century Association. Richardson's acceptance into the club in 1866 showed recognition of his social position and artistic promise. The Century Association had been founded in 1846 by authors, artists, and talented amateurs in the New York area who wished a permanent place for meeting socially. Leaders in law, medicine, finance and politics—the "amateurs"—also became members. The Century became a prestigious organization of men of distinction and wealth in the second half of the nineteenth century. (It may have been through the Century Association that Richardson first became acquainted with Frederick Law Olmsted, who had become a Centurion in 1859.)

The Century Association initially established club rooms on Clinton Place, but in 1857 it purchased for $24,000 a residence on East Fifteenth Street for use as a clubhouse. Remodeling was done at that time by New York architect Joseph C. Wells. In 1867, however, Gambrill and Richardson began designing an art gallery addition. It may have been Gambrill's project initially, since he is the architect of record in the Century archives. But research by Ellen Kramer in the archives of the New York City Building Department (see no. 18) shows that a permit for the $21,000 addition was issued only in 1869 with the firm Gambrill and Richardson listed as the architects. Therefore, the project was evidently in the office for all of 1868, and it seems likely that Richardson had a role in its design.

The addition was completed by the end of 1869. When the Century Association moved to new quarters on Forty-third Street in 1891, the Fifteenth Street property was sold and the building demolished.

Unfortunately nothing is known of the design. The only photographs in the Century Association archives are of the front of the clubhouse, not the art gallery addition to the rear.

According to Kramer's research a building permit for additional minor remodeling, designed by Richardson alone, was issued in 1878.

Textual Reference

Hitchcock, *Richardson*, 1966, pp. 307–308 (see note iv–1, quoting Kramer).

Miscellaneous Resource

Archives: Century Association.

1868

**9
Benjamin W. Crowninshield
House, 1868–1870   G&R**
164 Marlborough Street
Boston, Massachusetts

Benjamin William Crowninshield (1837–1892) probably knew Richardson at Harvard, where he graduated in 1858. After the Civil War, he became a member of Sprague, Colburn and Company, drygoods commission merchants in New York, and may have renewed his acquaintance with Richardson at that time. In 1869, Crowninshield moved to Boston to join Wheelwright, Anderson and Company, another drygoods firm. Later he became president of the Realty Company, which was involved in land speculation in the American West.

Van Rensselaer dates the Crowninshield commission April 1868, when it entered Richardson's office. The house was completed in 1870, and Crowninshield lived there until his death in 1892. Since then the house has passed through a succession of owners. Since 1960 it has been owned and operated by Garden Halls Dormitories as a residence for college women. Although the interior has been modified to serve this use, much of the woodwork and paneling remains in its original condition.

Richardson's design occupies a corner site in Boston's Back Bay area. The exterior of the four-story house is marked by three floors treated in flat red brick and the fourth enclosed by a mansard roof. The rectangular entry projects forward from the mass of the house and is reached by a short flight of steps. The windows are topped with stone lintels with a minor amount of decorative carving. Blue, green, and white tiles are inset into the surface of the brick wall. Two unusual twisted columns of uncut bricks are found at the corners of the entrance bay. In 1871 two houses of similar design were constructed on adjacent lots on Dartmouth Street, but there is no evidence to indicate that they were designed by Richardson.

Textual References

Bunting, Bainbridge. *Houses of Boston's Back Bay: An Architectural History, 1840–1917*. Cambridge, Mass: Belknap Press of Harvard University Press, 1967, pp. 212–213.

Harrell, Pauline C., and Smith, Margaret S., eds. *Victorian Boston Today: Ten Walking Tours*. Boston: New England Chapter, Victorian Society in America, 1975, p. 49.

Hitchcock, *Richardson*, 1966, pp. 81–82.

9a
Benjamin W.
Crowninshield
house, Boston,
Massachusetts,
1868–1870; Hitch-
cock, *Richardson*,
1936.

9b
Benjamin W.
Crowninshield
house (1972).

10

H. H. Richardson House,
1868–1869   G&R
45 McClean Avenue
Clifton, Staten Island,
New York

After Richardson's marriage to Julia Gorham Hayden in January 1867, the couple moved into a small rented cottage on Staten Island. Once Richardson entered partnership with Gambrill, he began work on a house of his own. Although the project initially may have been a response to the growth of the practice, Richardson's father-in-law, Dr. John Cole Hayden, may well have paid for the house or contributed much of the financing. Traditionally, many fathers gave their daughters houses as wedding presents. However much the elder Hayden contributed, the house cost more than Richardson expected.

Evidently the house was in design by early 1868, because construction was completed in January 1869. Julia's letter to her mother on January 31 stated that they hoped to complete moving in within another week. Dr. Hayden visited the family in March 1869, and reported in a March 21 letter to his wife that the house was "very handsome" and had "every convenience." Even though gas was not available in McClean Avenue at the time of construction, Richardson had provided gas piping in anticipation of that utility. Consequently Dr. Hayden confided to his wife in a letter of April 18 that Richardson had probably overextended himself in the construction of the house; only by strict budgeting could he meet the payments.

Richardson and his family lived in the house until 1874, when they moved to Brookline during the construction of Trinity Church. The house subsequently passed through several owners. Today it serves as doctors' offices. The exterior has been covered in white stucco so the original appearance is completely lost. The project had remained unknown to architectural historians until Wayne Andrews discovered it. Because it was a personal project, it had not been carried on the office books and thus was missed by Van Rensselaer when she compiled her list.

Richardson's design was sheathed entirely in clapboard siding contained within flat boards to indicate major elements of the structural frame. The roof is an angular mansard. The house, Scully writes, generally follows conventions of the later phases of the stick style. Because of subsequent interior remodelings and the absence of drawings, the original interior arrangement remains a matter of conjecture.

Textual References

Hitchcock, *Richardson*, 1966, p. 310 (see note v–11).

Hitchcock, *Victorian*, p. 9.

Scully, *Shingle Style*, pp. 4–5.

Wodehouse, Lawrence. "Henry Hobson Richardson's Home at Arrochar." *Victorian Society in America Bulletin* 2 (Sept. 1974):6.

Miscellaneous Resources

Photographs: New York Public Library.

Letters: Archives of American Art Microfilm Roll 1184.

10a
H. H. Richardson house, Clifton, Staten Island, New York, 1868–1869; photo by Wayne Andrews.

10b
H. H. Richardson house, with later alterations (1978).

11
Alexander Dallas Bache
Monument (1867),
1868–1869 G&R
Congressional Cemetery
Washington, D.C.

11a
Alexander Dallas Bache monument, Congressional Cemetery, Washington, D.C. (1867), 1868–1869; photo by Francis R. Kowsky.

Alexander Dallas Bache (1806–1867), a grandson of Benjamin Franklin, was a professor of natural philosophy and chemistry at the University of Pennsylvania from 1828 to 1841 and was superintendent of the United States Coast Survey from 1843 to 1867. During the Civil War he served on the United States Sanitary Commission with F. L. Olmsted.

After Bache's death, C. P. Patterson of the Coast Survey wrote Olmsted requesting his assistance in preparing a monument to Bache, Patterson's former superior. Initially, Patterson estimated that $5,000 could be raised, but by July 1868 he wrote to Olmsted reducing the total to $2,000. Olmsted apparently then turned to Richardson, his Staten Island neighbor and fellow member of the Century Association (see no. 8), with the request that he prepare a design based on Patterson's sketch. On October 13, 1868, Richardson wrote to Olmsted: "I have just risen from a sick bed & have been unable until now to attend to Monument to be erected to Mr. Bache." An elevation and perspective drawing (now lost) of the design were sent to Olmsted on November 14, with a cost estimate of $2,800. Patterson wrote Olmsted on December 8 that the design, which he called "remarkably fine," was trimmed before its acceptance. The granite and marble memorial was subsequently erected over Bache's grave in the Congressional Cemetery.

The Bache monument remained unknown to Richardson scholars until recently when it was first uncovered by O'Gorman and subsequently researched in detail by Kowsky. Its chief importance lies in being the first documented collaboration between Richardson and Olmsted.

Textual References

Kowsky, Francis R. "The William Dorsheimer House: A Reflection of French Suburban Architecture in the Early Work of H. H. Richardson." *The Art Bulletin* 62 (Mar. 1980): 136n.

O'Gorman, *Selected Drawings*, p. 36n79.

Miscellaneous Resources

Letters: F. L. Olmsted Papers, Library of Congress.

Worcester Civil War Monument Project, 1868 G&R
Worcester, Massachusetts

James Barnard Blake (1827–1870) was first elected mayor of Worcester in 1865. His administrations were marked by the construction of major public improvements in the city, including city water, sewerage, new public schools, street railway, and new public monuments.

In 1866 the Worcester City Council appointed a committee to consider the erection of a memorial to Worcester's Civil War dead. Subscriptions were solicited, and by September 1867 a fund of over $11,000 was available. A select committee then solicited plans for a monument.

Gambrill and Richardson submitted a design for a memorial arch which was favored by Blake and selected by the committee. But because of its high cost, estimated at $90,000, it was submitted to the community in a municipal referendum in December 1868. Opposition developed to the design, and it was rejected by the voters.

In 1871 interest in the memorial revived; and the sculptor Randolph Rogers presented a design for a sixty-six-foot column topped by a bronze statue of "Victory" and surrounded by figures representing the branches of the military. This design was accepted and constructed. The memorial was dedicated in 1874.

The Gambrill and Richardson design, based loosely on the Arc de Triomphe in Paris, called for an arch of rusticated stone, above which was a row of medallions and then a heavily corbeled cornice. A similar design was proposed by Richardson for a Civil War Memorial in Buffalo several years later (no. 54).

Textual References

Dedication of the Soldiers' Monument at Worcester, Mass., July 15, 1874. Worcester: Soldiers Monument Committee, 1875.

O'Gorman, James F. "Richardson, Olmsted and the Rejected Civil War Monuments for Worcester and Buffalo." In *Three Centuries/Two Continents: Essays on the Arts . . . in Honor of Robert C. Smith*, edited by K. L. Ames and N. H. Schless. Watkins Glen, N.Y.: American Life Foundation, in press.

Miscellaneous Resource

Drawing: Houghton Library, Harvard University.

12a
Worcester Civil
War Monument
project, Worcester,
Massachusetts,
1868; Houghton
Library, Harvard
University.

This house project is known from drawings dated August 10, 1868, in the Richardson collection at Houghton Library.

The project was marked by an unusual roof with elements of mansard and gambrel construction. The exterior walls were divided into panels by flat wood members in a fashion typical of the stick style. Only the porte cochere was to be of stone. The interior plan shows a moderate-sized entry hall connecting to the entry vestibule, stair, parlor, dining room, and billiard room.

In *Richardson as a Victorian Architect* Hitchcock noted a clear relationship between this project and the Codman House project (no. 16).

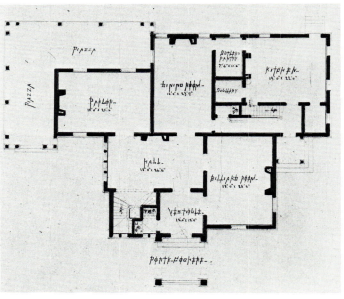

13a
House project,
Aug. 10, 1868;
Houghton Library,
Harvard University.

Textual References

Hitchcock, *Richardson*, 1966, p. 310 (see note v–11).

Hitchcock, *Victorian*, p. 9.

Miscellaneous Resources

Drawings: Houghton Library, Harvard University.

14a
House project, ca.
1868; Houghton
Library, Harvard
University.

This project is known only from a single watercolor perspective view in the Houghton Library collection. Hitchcock has suggested that it dates from about 1868.

The design is another in the series of houses by Richardson with exterior walls of clapboard siding divided by flat wood elements roughly corresponding to structural members. The mansard roof with a high central peak was to be covered with slate.

Textual Reference

Hitchcock, *Victorian*, pp. 9–10.

Miscellaneous Resource

Drawing: Houghton Library, Harvard University.

15

William E. Dorsheimer House, 1868–1871 G&R
438 Delaware Avenue
Buffalo, New York

William Edward Dorsheimer (1832–1888), who attended Harvard from 1849 to 1852 but left because of poor health, received an honorary M.A. from Harvard in 1859, the year of Richardson's graduation. Admitted to the bar in 1854, Dorsheimer was appointed district attorney for northern New York after the Civil War. A leading citizen of the state, Dorsheimer served as lieutenant governor from 1874 to 1880. Originally from Buffalo, he moved to New York City after 1880 and was elected to Congress in 1882. In 1886 he became editor of the New York *Star*.

In August 1868, F. L. Olmsted traveled to Buffalo at Dorsheimer's request to aid in determining a site for a major park. Dorsheimer probably then expressed his desire for a house, and Olmsted, who already knew Richardson, may have recommended him to Dorsheimer. (In addition, Dorsheimer, like Richardson and Olmsted, was a member of the Century Association of New York City.) Richardson's involvement with Dorsheimer proved extremely important; Dorsheimer was instrumental in obtaining major New York state commissions for the architect.

Van Rensselaer dates the commission at Richardson's office in October 1868, but Richardson and Dorsheimer may have discussed it earlier. When the house was completed in 1871, it was the finest then built on the elegant Delaware Avenue. The original rectangular building with a single bay facing the street was enlarged in the late 1870s or early 1880s. Dorsheimer moved to Albany as lieutenant governor in 1874, rented the house in 1876, and sold it in 1881. Today it is the office building of Percival B. Bixby and Company, certified public accountants. While the exterior remains mostly intact, the interior, except for Richardson's staircase, has been completely modified.

Richardson's design for the Dorsheimer house was a simple and dignified treatment within the conventions of the time. The exterior walls are of ochre-colored brick with bands of gray sandstone. The gray slate mansard roof is marked by a line of red tiles near the crest. The formal entry to the house was along the north side, but Kowsky has determined that the major facade was toward the south, a fact particularly evident in the continuation of the stone banding along this side. The stone is marked by minimal carved Neo-Grec detail. As reconstructed by Kowsky, the plan of the house was organized around a traditional central hall. No drawings for the project survive, but Kowsky has noted the correspondence of his plan reconstruction with studies found in Richardson's sketchbook at the Houghton Library.

Textual References

Hitchcock, *Richardson*, 1966, pp. 82–83, 309–310 (see note v–11).

Hitchcock, *Victorian*, p. 9.

Kowsky, Francis R. *Buffalo Projects: H. H. Richardson.* Buffalo: Buffalo State College Foundation, 1980, pp. 6–7.

———. "The William Dorsheimer House: A Reflection of French Suburban Architecture in the Early Work of H. H. Richardson." *The Art Bulletin* 62 (Mar. 1980): 134–147.

Scully, *Shingle Style*, p. 5n.

Miscellaneous Resources

Photographs: Buffalo and Erie County Historical Society; Library of Congress (Historic American Buildings Survey).

15a
William E. Dorshei-
mer house, Buffalo,
New York, 1868–
1871, view of street
and north facade;
Buffalo and Erie
County Historical
Society.

15b
William E. Dorshei-
mer house, view of
street and garden
(principal) facades
with later additions
and alterations;
Buffalo and Erie
County Historical
Society.

16

**Richard Codman House
Project, 1868–1869   G&R**
Cottage Avenue
West Roxbury, Boston,
Massachusetts

The Codman family were friends of both Richardson and his wife. Richard Codman (1842–1928) was a fellow member of the Porcellian Club at Harvard, but as he did not graduate until 1864, this connection to Richardson remains uncertain. After a two-year tour of Europe, Richard Codman and his wife returned in 1867 to Boston, where after 1872 Codman devoted his attention to the design of interiors, a field previously the province of architects. Julia Richardson's mother first mentions Mrs. Codman in a letter to Julia dated January 13, 1867, and the name recurs occasionally thereafter in the Richardson correspondence.

In February 1868 Richard Codman purchased a small house on Cottage Avenue in West Roxbury and moved there in May 1868. According to his *Reminiscences* Codman soon began to plan a larger house with H. H. Richardson. The development of the project took about a year, and the resulting design cost about twice what Codman had hoped. Therefore, Codman abandoned plans for a new house and added to the existing one following a design of his own. He moved into his enlarged house in 1870.

Richardson's Codman project plan showed significant innovations in American domestic planning. The first floor included a large living hall with drawing room to one side and dining room to the other. Besides the kitchen and service spaces, these three rooms are the only plan divisions. The hall was to be the core of the house and combined the elements of entry, stairs, and fireplace. The upstairs bedrooms were arranged conventionally. The exterior had many characteristics of the "stick style" as defined by Scully.

The Codman house project is now recognized as an important departure in American house design. Earlier houses had large central halls, but they were never intended to be the living center or spatial core of the designs. Richardson's Codman design showed the first experiment with an open interior hall for living, with its hearth the true heart of the house. Only dining and secluded activities were assigned separated spaces.

Textual References

Codman, Richard. *Reminiscences*. Boston: North Bennett Street Industrial School, 1923, pp. 29–31.

Downing, Antoinette, F., and Scully, Vincent J. *The Architectural Heritage of Newport, Rhode Island*. Cambridge, Mass.: Harvard University Press, 1952, pp. 141–142.

Hitchcock, *Richardson*, 1966, pp. 95–96.

Hitchcock, *Victorian*, pp. 10, 52n29.

Scully, *Shingle Style*, pp. 5–9.

Miscellaneous Resources

Drawings: Houghton Library, Harvard University.

Letters: Archives of American Art Microfilm Roll 643 and 1184.

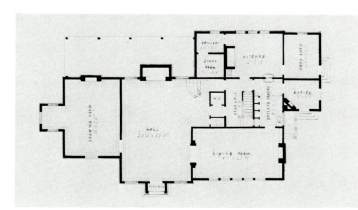

16a
Richard Codman
house project, West
Roxbury, Boston,
Massachusetts,
1868–1869, first
floor plan; Hough-
ton Library, Har-
vard University.

16b
Richard Codman
house project, front
elevation; courtesy
Houghton Library,
Harvard University.

17

**Holyoke Church Project,
ca. 1868–1870(?)   G&R**
Holyoke, Massachusetts

The Holyoke church project is known only from five studies for a church tower in the Houghton Library collection.

The drawings are undated, but the pointed arch over the door suggests that this is an early project dating before 1870. Possibly this project was of Gambrill's design.

The church tower has a square plan in each drawing. Entry doors with steps are indicated at the base, and several of the drawings show a nave with gabled end adjacent to the tower. Various expressions are shown for the tall pointed tower roof.

Miscellaneous Resources

Drawings: Houghton Library, Harvard University.

·Study·for·Church·Spire·
·at·Holyoke·Mass:·

HOC·D·I

17a
Holyoke church project, ca. 1868–1870; Houghton Library, Harvard University.

18

**George E. Stone House
Alterations, 1868   G&R**
12 East Thirty-seventh Street
New York, New York
Demolished

Between 1868 and 1875 the firm of
Gambrill and Richardson did a series
of remodeling and renovation projects
in New York City. It is not known
how much of these project designs is
attributable to Richardson himself.
They are included in this guide in an
effort to be complete, even though
they remain of uncertain attribution.
These projects were uncovered by Ellen W. Kramer during research in the
archives of the New York City Building Department and reported by
Hitchcock in later editions of *The Architecture of H. H. Richardson and
His Times.*

The alterations for George Stone
must have consisted of minor changes,
since the cost was only $3,000.

Textual Reference

Hitchcock, *Richardson*, 1966, pp. 307–
308 (see note iv–1 quoting Kramer).

1869

19
Jonathan Sturges House,
1869–1870   G&R
38 Park Avenue
New York, New York
Demolished 1954

20
Frederick Sturges House,
1869–1870   G&R
40 East Thirty-sixth Street
New York, New York
Demolished 1954

19a/20a
Jonathan Sturges
house and Freder-
ick Sturges house,
New York, New
York, 1869–1870
(note adjacent
house by Hunt
undergoing exten-
sive remodeling);
Museum of the
City of New York.

19b/20b
Jonathan Sturges
house and Freder-
ick Sturges house;
New York Public
Library—Astor,
Lenox and Tilden
Foundations.

Jonathan Sturges (1802–1874) was a leading New York grocery merchant, particularly in the tea and coffee trade. He was also a founder and director of the New York Bank of Commerce and a director of both the Illinois Central and New York, New Haven & Hartford Railroads. Active in the affairs of the Century Association, he undoubtedly knew both Gambrill and Richardson through this connection.

The involvement of the firm of Gambrill and Richardson in the design of these two Park Avenue townhouses was verified by Ellen Kramer in the archives of the New York City Building Department in the early 1950s. They correspond to the pair described by Montgomery Schuyler in an April 23, 1881, *AABN* article, as "two sober and respectable houses by Mr. Richardson." Moreover, Richardson's own work on the design of these two houses is substantiated by a brief notation in his sketchbook, now on deposit at the Houghton Library and transcribed by O'Gorman in *Richardson and His Office*. Dated October 12 (?), 1869, Richardson's notes on fol. 3r state, "J. & F. Sturges and Ross were in —." (Ross remains unidentified.) It is not known why this design was credited only to Gambrill in Van Rensselaer's list in *Henry Hobson Richardson and His Works*.

According to Kramer's research the two house plans for Jonathan and Frederick Sturges, father and son, were filed with the Bureau of Inspection of Buildings on August 14, 1869. Thus, the project was probably under consideration early in 1869. Construction of the two houses, at a cost of $60,000, was completed in November 1870.

Jonathan Sturges lived in his house until his death in 1874. In 1895 the house was considerably enlarged; and the original drawings were apparently discarded by the New York City Department of Buildings, thus making it impossible to verify Richardson as the actual designer. The two townhouses were demolished in 1954, the last of Richardson's New York City work to be destroyed, leaving only Richardson's own house on Staten Island (no. 10). The William H. Osborn House by Richard M. Hunt on the adjacent site at 32–34 Park Avenue was demolished at the same time.

The two 26-foot-wide houses were built as a unit with an exterior of brick and brownstone and a mansard roof.

Textual References

Kramer, Ellen W. "Richardson in New York." Typescript, Scarsdale, N.Y., 1954.

O'Gorman, *Selected Drawings*, p. 211.

Schuyler, Montgomery. "Recent Building in New York III: Dwellings." *AABN* 9 (Apr. 23, 1881): 196.

Miscellaneous Resource

Sketchbook: Houghton Library, Harvard University.

Agawam National Bank,
1869–1870   G&R
233 Main Street
Springfield, Massachusetts
Demolished pre-1935

21a
Agawam National
Bank, Springfield,
Massachusetts,
1869–1870;
Springfield City
Library.

Chester W. Chapin, Richardson's Springfield patron (see nos. 1, 5), was founder and president of the Agawam National Bank. He continued his support of Richardson with this commission.

Van Rensselaer gives April 1869 as the date this project entered the office of Gambrill and Richardson. The structure was completed and occupied by the end of 1870. For many years it was used by the bank, but was demolished by 1935.

The overall arrangement of the Agawam Bank design followed the scheme of the Western Railroad Offices (no. 5) with a half basement, three stories in granite, and a fourth behind a mansard roof. But the detailing was completely different. Heavy voussoirs formed arches over the windows, round on the main floor but segmental pointed on the upper floors. On the front facade these arches appeared to be supported by stubby colonnettes. A string course at the third floor echoed the cornice above.

Textual References

Hitchcock, Henry-Russell. "Catalogue of an Exhibition of Photographs Illustrating Springfield Architecture 1800–1900 at the Springfield Museum of Fine Arts." Typescript, Springfield Public Library, 1934.

Hitchcock, *Richardson*, 1966, pp. 85–86.

King, Moses, ed. *King's Handbook of Springfield.* Springfield: J. D. Gill, 1884, pp. 199–200.

Van Rensselaer, *Works*, p. 50.

Miscellaneous Resources

Photographs: Springfield Public Library.

**Christ Episcopal Church
Project, 1869   G&R**
Delaware Avenue between
Edward and Tupper Streets
Buffalo, New York

Richardson's involvement in the design for a new building for Christ Episcopal Church was discovered by Kowsky. Although drawings for the project do not survive, the vestry's minutes provide a source from which Kowsky reconstructed the history of the commission.

In early 1869 Reverend Orlando Witherspoon, rector of the newly formed congregation, visited New York and Boston, seeking advice on the design of his new church. The building committee, which had rejected a number of plans by local and out-of-town architects, then requested designs from Richardson and from Arthur Gilman of Boston. Both architects were required to fit their designs to a ground plan prepared by Witherspoon.

Although Richardson traveled to Buffalo in the summer of 1869 to defend his design, Gilman's design was selected. Dr. James P. White, a leader in the effort to establish the Buffalo State Hospital (see no. 30), was Richardson's only supporter. Richardson was paid $250 for his drawings on August 2, 1869. Foundation walls for Gilman's church were erected by 1872, but the project proceeded no further because it was too expensive. In 1882, Christ Church parish merged with Trinity Church parish (see no. 40). Cyrus K. Porter, a Buffalo architect, then erected a church on the original foundations.

The ground plan of the Christ Church design consisting of a nave of three bays, a crossing, and a broad monumental apse was found by Kowsky in an 1872 Buffalo city atlas. Kowsky suggests this plan by Witherspoon may have been a source for some ideas developed by Richardson in his later ecclesiastical designs.

Textual References

Kowsky, Francis R. *Buffalo Projects: H. H. Richardson.* Buffalo: Buffalo State College Foundation, 1980, p. 8.

————. "The William Dorsheimer House: A Reflection of French Suburban Architecture in the Early Work of H. H. Richardson." *The Art Bulletin* 62 (Mar. 1980): 139n.

Miscellaneous Resource

Archives: Trinity Church, Buffalo, Christ Church Vestry Minutes.

23
Rye Presbyterian Church
Project, 1869   G&R
Post Road
Rye, New York

The Rye Presbyterian Church was formally organized in 1829, but the third church building constructed in 1841 had become too small by 1869. In March a committee on church accommodation was formed, and by April this committee had received pledges of assistance from nine members of the congregation totaling $42,500, including $10,000 from William P. Van Rensselaer, an elder of the church. A building committee including Van Rensselaer was appointed, and between April 1869 and April 1870 the committee visited churches in Springfield, New Rochelle, Brooklyn, and other cities.

Evidently Richardson's involvement in the project began during these visits. The committee members probably visited Richardson's recently completed Unity Church (no. 1) while they were in Springfield. That Richardson prepared a design for submission to the committee is suggested by two brief notations in his sketchbook. Richardson's notes on fol. 3r dated October 12 (?), 1869, state, "Framing Rye Church drawing—" and "Wm. P. Van Rensselaer called about Rye Church—." But the sketch on fol. 3r may have been for the Narragansett Chapel (no. 24).

Unfortunately church records make no mention of Richardson's involvement. On April 1, 1870, the building committee in the absence of Van Rensselaer resolved to award the commission to R. M. Upjohn of New York. His building was dedicated on December 5, 1872.

Textual References

McKay, Ellen Cotton. *A History of the Rye Presbyterian Church*. Rye, N.Y.: Rye Presbyterian Church, 1957, pp. 112–139.

O'Gorman, *Selected Drawings*, p. 211.

Miscellaneous Resource

Sketchbook: Houghton Library, Harvard University.

24
Narragansett Chapel Project,
1869   G&R
(Narragansett, Rhode Island?)

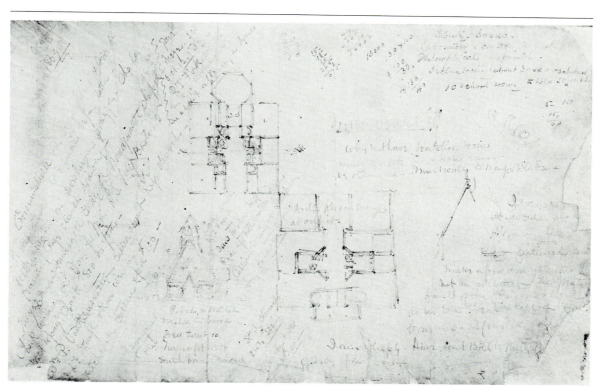

23a/24a
Richardson, sketch-
book, fol. 3r, 1869;
with sketch of
church elevation
which could be
either Rye Presby-
terian Church proj-
ect, Rye, New
York, or Narragan-
sett Chapel project,
Narragansett,
Rhode Island;
Houghton Library,
Harvard University.

The Narragansett chapel project is
known only from a single mention in
Richardson's sketchbook. On fol. 3r,
in notes dated October 12 (?), 1869,
Richardson states, "Meyer made mis-
erable study for Narragansett
Chapel." (Meyer is unidentified.)

This project does not appear in the
Van Rensselaer list and was therefore
probably not executed. The sketch on
fol. 3r may be for this or for the Rye
Church (no. 23).

Textual Reference

O'Gorman, *Selected Drawings*, p. 211.

Miscellaneous Resource

Sketchbook: Houghton Library, Harvard
University.

25
Mrs. R. S. Fay Project (?),
1869 G&R
Boston, Massachusetts

26
Worcester High School,
1869–1871 G&R
Maple Street at Walnut Street
Worcester, Massachusetts
Demolished 1966

The Mrs. R. S. Fay project is known only from a single notation in Richardson's sketchbook. Richardson's notes of fol. 3r dated October 12 (?), 1869 indicate, "Clark working on plans for Mrs. R. S. Fay[,] Boston." Clark is Theodore Minot Clark, one of Richardson's assistants until the late 1870s. Mrs. R. S. Fay is most likely Elizabeth Francis Bowditch (Fay) (1836–1924) of the prominent Bowditch family of Boston. Her husband, Richard Sullivan Fay (1833–1882), was a descendant of a Boston family of judges and statesmen.

Nothing more is known of this project.

Textual Reference

O'Gorman, *Selected Drawings*, p. 211.

Miscellaneous Resource

Sketchbook: Houghton Library, Harvard University.

The first Worcester High School was constructed in 1844 when the population of Worcester was about 10,000. By 1869 the city had grown to 40,000, and the existing high school building had become inadequate. The school report of 1867 first pointed to the need for new facilities, and the next year it was determined that the existing building could not be enlarged. Early in 1869 the school board requested that the city proceed with the project to build the new school, an effort led by Mayor James Blake.

Plans were invited from several architects in the fall of 1869. Notations in Richardson's sketchbook indicate that Gambrill and Richardson were working on the project in October. They were probably invited to compete as a result of their effort the previous year toward a Civil War Memorial (no. 12). Seven architectural firms (five from Worcester, one from Boston, Gambrill and Richardson from New York) actually presented schemes on November 23, 1869. The Gambrill and Richardson design was accepted. Construction documents were evidently prepared over the next few weeks as proposals from builders were received December 28, and a contract for construction was signed with Norcross Brothers on December 30, 1869.

Construction proceeded over the next two years with daily supervision by the local architects Earle & Fuller and occasional visits by Gambrill and Richardson. The building was completed and dedicated December 30, 1871. The entire project including land and furnishings cost $169,690.

The building served as the Worcester High School until 1892 when it became Worcester Classical High

School. In 1914 the Classical High School moved to new facilities, and the Richardson building became part of the Commerce High School. The bell tower was damaged by the 1938 hurricane and then removed to roof level in 1954. In 1966 the site was sold to Paul Revere Life Insurance Company. The school was razed to make room for the office building which now stands in its place.

In overall form the Gambrill and Richardson building was a plain brick box with a mansard roof and an attached bell tower. But within the relatively simple exterior was a complex plan. The basement, a half level below grade, included a "play room" (gymnasium) and boys' and girls' toilets and coat rooms; the first floor included the main entry hall, principal's office, library, chemistry laboratory, and classrooms; the second floor included six large classrooms and men's and women's teachers' lounges; and the third (mansard) floor had a large auditorium and four smaller rooms. Stairs at the center of each end of the building served all four floors. On the first and second floors these stairs were connected by a wide, longitudinally oriented corridor giving access to all other spaces.

The exterior design corresponded only slightly to this interior plan. Windows were grouped and detailed differently on each floor. The corner towers did not relate to any interior features. The entrance porch was reached by a monumental double reverse stair. Above this rose the slender brick shaft of the bell tower topped with a tall spire. The exterior of the entire building was sheathed with red pressed brick accented with Nova Scotia stone trim and decorative black bricks and colored tiles.

The most important aspect of this project may have been the first association of Richardson with Norcross Brothers, general contractors of Worcester. Orlando Whitney Norcross (1839–1920), the active partner of the firm, was a self-trained engineer who was to build many of Richardson's projects over the next two decades. Richardson came to rely on the expertise of Norcross Brothers, particularly in working with stone.

Textual References

Ambler, James A. & Co. *Worcester Illustrated.* Worcester: Lucius P. Goddard, printer, 1875, pp. 26–27.

Hitchcock, *Richardson*, 1966, pp. 89–92.

Illustrated Business Guide of the City of Worcester, Massachusetts. Worcester: Snow, Woodman and Company, 1880, p. 29.

O'Gorman, James F. "O. W. Norcross, Richardson's 'Master Builder': A Preliminary Report." *JSAH* 32 (May 1973): 104–113.

Roe, Alfred S. *Worcester Classical and English High School: A Record of 47 years.* Worcester: Alfred S. Roe, 1892.

Van Rensselaer, *Works*, p. 51.

Worcester High School. Worcester: Press of Edward R. Fiske, 1871.

Miscellaneous Resources

Photographs: Worcester Historical Museum; Worcester Public Library; Houghton Library, Harvard University.

Sketchbook: Houghton Library, Harvard University.

26a
Worcester High
School, Worcester,
Massachusetts,
1869–1871;
Worcester Histori-
cal Museum.

A. P. Nichols House Project,
ca. 1869–1870   G&R
Buffalo, New York

27a
A. P. Nichols house project, Buffalo, New York, ca. 1869–1870, plans of first and second floors; Houghton Library, Harvard University.

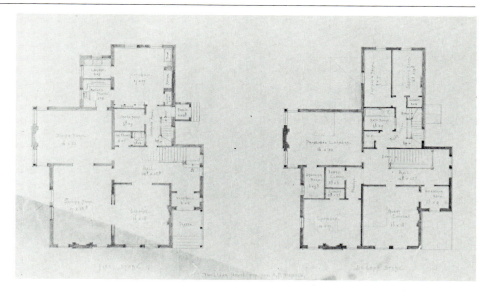

Asher P. Nichols (1815–1880) was a leading Buffalo attorney. In 1868 and 1869 he served in the New York state senate and from 1870 to 1873 was state comptroller. For many years he was also a trustee of the Buffalo State Hospital, the insane asylum. It is certain that Nichols was friendly with Richardson's patron William Dorsheimer. The Nichols house commission may have helped to lead to Richardson's involvement with the Buffalo State Hospital (no. 30).

The A. P. Nichols project is known only from an undated drawing on construction paper in the Houghton Library collection. The location indicated is "Buffalo." Kowsky has suggested that the house may have been intended for the lot which Nichols purchased in 1868 immediately to the south of Dorsheimer's house (no. 15). However, as Nichols owned other lots in Buffalo, this is not certain. The name "Nichols" appears in Richardson's sketchbook fol. 5r an undated page that falls between those dated 1869 and 1870. The design clearly antedates Richardson's important domestic work after 1873.

The Nichols plan was a rectilinear composition resulting in a house with an irregular outline. The main downstairs spaces were a library, drawing room, dining room, and kitchen. Upstairs were bedrooms for the owner's family, guests, and servants. The small stair hall of this design was typical only of Richardson's early work.

Textual References

Kowsky, Francis R. *Buffalo Projects: H. H. Richardson.* Buffalo: Buffalo State College Foundation, 1980, p. 7.

———. "The William Dorsheimer House: A Reflection of French Suburban Architecture in the Early Work of H. H. Richardson." *The Art Bulletin* 62 (Mar. 1980): 139n.

O'Gorman, *Selected Drawings*, pp. 211–212.

Miscellaneous Resources

Drawing: Houghton Library, Harvard University.

Sketchbook: Houghton Library, Harvard University.

General Hospital Project,
ca. 1869–1870   G&R
Worcester, Massachusetts

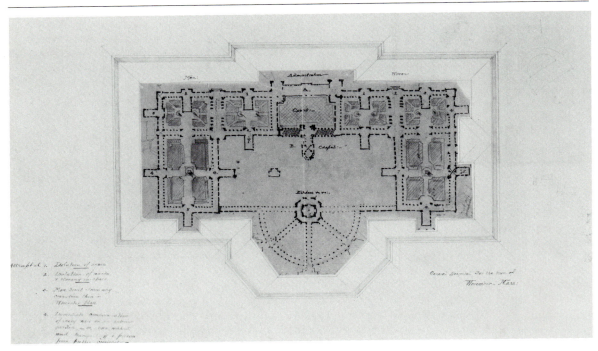

28a
General Hospital
project, Worcester,
Massachusetts, ca.
1869–1870, floor
plan showing distri-
bution of ward
spaces on the pe-
rimeter of the *U*
enclosing private
gardens; Houghton
Library, Harvard
University.

The Worcester general hospital remains among the most obscure of
Richardson's unbuilt projects. No evidence has yet been uncovered to
explain how this project was commissioned or why it was not built.
City physician, Dr. Albert Woods,
called attention to the pressing need of
hospital accommodations for the city
poor in his annual report of 1870. As
Gambrill and Richardson were involved in the high school (no. 26) at
the time, they may have been asked to
prepare sketches for cost estimating
purposes. Ultimately Worcester built a
hospital in 1880 from the designs of
two local architects, but it was called
Worcester City Hospital.

The project is known from a single
plan drawing in the Houghton Library
collection. The design was in the form
of a large *U* with one wing for each
sex and a central administration area.

The wards actually followed the outline of the *U* and as a result enclosed
private garden spaces to which each
ward had direct access.

Textual References

Hitchcock, *Richardson*, 1966, p. 311 (see
note vi–1).

Hitchcock, *Victorian*, p. 12.

Miscellaneous Resource

Drawing: Houghton Library, Harvard
University.

29
Brattle Square Church, 1869–1873   G&R
Commonwealth Avenue at
Clarendon Street
Boston, Massachusetts

The first Brattle Square Congregational (later Unitarian) Church was erected in 1699 on land donated by Thomas Brattle in 1697. This church was demolished in 1772, and a second was constructed on the same property. As Boston developed, however, the Brattle Square area deteriorated; many prominent parishioners felt compelled to move. By 1869 the church had acquired a relatively small but prominent lot in the newly developing Back Bay area. The decision to move to the new site was difficult, requiring at minimum expense a building handsome enough to attract prosperous new members.

In 1869 the congregation apparently invited several architects to submit designs. Richardson may have been suggested to the congregation by Benjamin Crowninshield, a leading supporter of the project, the father of Richardson's Harvard acquaintance, for whom he had already designed a Back Bay house (no. 9). Gambrill and Richardson won the limited competition and, according to Van Rensselaer, received the commission in July 1870. Studies for the church in Richardson's sketchbook may date as early as fall 1869. Moreover, Richardson visited Boston, Beal notes, for estimating purposes as early as August 1869. The project, constructed by Augustus Lothrop between 1871 and 1873, opened December 17, 1873, and was dedicated December 22, 1873.

The building was a disaster acoustically; but the congregation, already overburdened by the higher than expected cost, could not afford the necessary alterations. A combination of several factors, including the depression of the early 1870s, the death of

several prominent parishioners, the loss of members during the move, and the large debt, caused the society to declare bankruptcy in 1876. The mortgage was foreclosed, leaving the building unoccupied until 1882 when it was purchased by the First Baptist Church for $100,000. The First Baptist congregation also bought the adjacent land to the west for a chapel which was designed by another architect and opened in 1883. Galleries were added to the auditorium to relieve the acoustical problems. At a later date the original stenciled interior decoration was painted over. Thus transformed, the building remains in use today.

For the church, Richardson designed a cruciform building with the main axis oriented parallel to Commonwealth Avenue. The upper arm of the cross, traditionally the chancel, was cut so short that the interior of the auditorium is actually a T shape. The Sunday school was located in one reentrant angle of the T, the conspicuous campanile in the other. A monumental composition of pulpit and organ was at the junction of the T. From the study in his sketchbook Richardson planned this space mathematically to accommodate the maximum number of saleable pews.

Richardson had hoped John La Farge would be commissioned to decorate the interior; instead, the walls were richly stenciled. Three immense rose windows were located in each end of the T-shaped auditorium. (Later in the nineteenth century the Baptists added stained glass by Tiffany.) The outer walls are of buff Roxbury puddingstone with cocoa-colored sandstone trim, a typical example of Richardson's use of locally available materials. An arcade on Clarendon Street and all the large windows are round arched, but groups of rectangular windows occur below the rose windows at the ends of the nave and transepts. For the frame of the chapel side window, Richardson used iron.

The 176-foot tower is the most noticeable exterior feature. It rests on four piers connected by four arched openings forming a carriageway. Of unusual design, the tower has a red-tiled pyramidal roof, carved frieze, and multiple belfry arches. The four groups of figures on the frieze, representing Baptism, Communion, Marriage, and Death, were carved *in situ* by Italian craftsmen working from plaster models by the Alsatian Frédéric Auguste Bartholdi, sculptor of the Statue of Liberty. At the four corners four angels blow once-golden trumpets, earning the church the nickname "Church of the Holy Bean Blowers." Incorporated into the tower are quoins and cornerstones from the old Brattle Square Church. One reads "John Hancock, Esq., July 27, 1772," and the other "Jno. Greenleaf, 1772." The bell from the Brattle Square Church, cast in 1809, hangs in the tower.

This church is a significant advance in Richardson's development, perhaps the major breakthrough that Hitchcock regarded it. The recent entry of Charles F. McKim into Richardson's office may have helped to crystallize the design.

Textual References

Back Bay Churches and Public Buildings: An Album of Nineteenth Century Photographs Chiefly from the Collections of the Bostonian Society. Boston: Bostonian Society, 1967, pp. 14, 15.

Beale, Margaret E. "H. H. Richardson's Brattle Square Church: Drawings and Development." Typescript, Harvard University, 1976.

Damrell, C. S. *A Half Century of Boston's Building.* Boston: L. P. Hager 1892, after p. 231.

"First Baptist ('Brattle Square') Church, Clarendon Street, Corner Commonwealth Avenue, Boston, Mass." *AABN* 43 (Mar. 24, 1894): 142.

Hitchcock, *Richardson*, 1966, pp. 110–117.

Hitchcock, *Victorian*, pp. 11–12.

King, Moses, ed. *King's How To See Boston 1895.* Boston: Moses King, 1895, pp. 148–149.

"The Tower of Brattle Square Church, Boston, Mass." *AABN* 3 (June 29, 1878): 225.

Van Rensselaer, *Works*, pp. 19–21, 51–53.

Willard, A. R. "Recent Church Architecture in Boston." *New England Magazine* 1 (Feb. 1890).

Winsor, Justin, ed. *The Memorial History of Boston, Including Suffolk County Massachusetts 1630–1880.* Boston: J. R. Osgood and Co., 1880–1881.

Wood, Nathan E. *History of the First Baptist Church of Boston (1665–1899).* Philadelphia: American Baptist Publication Society, 1899, pp. 339–344.

Miscellaneous Resources

Drawings: Houghton Library, Harvard University.

Photographs: Boston Athenaeum; Boston Public Library; Bostonian Society; Houghton Library, Harvard University; Society for the Preservation of New England Antiquities.

Sketchbook: Houghton Library, Harvard University.

Letters: Archives of American Art Microfilm Roll 643.

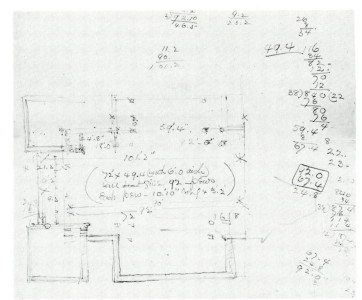

29a
Brattle Square
Church, Boston,
Massachusetts,
1869–1873, Rich-
ardson, sketch-
book, fol. 13r,
showing sketch
plan of church and
Richardson's calcu-
lations of seating
capacity; Houghton
Library, Harvard
University.

29b
Brattle Square
Church; Houghton
Library, Harvard
University.

29c
Brattle Square
Church; *AABN* 43
(Mar. 24, 1894).

29d
Brattle Square
Church, entrance
arcade; Society for
the Preservation of
New England An-
tiquities (ca. 1888–
1892).

29e
Brattle Square
Church, interior
with original sten-
ciled walls, now
painted out; Na-
than E. Wood, *The
History of the First
Baptist Church of
Boston (1665–
1899)*, 1899.

30

Buffalo State Hospital,
1869–1880 (1895)   G&R
400 Forest Avenue
Buffalo, New York

In 1869 the city of Buffalo gave the state of New York a site for the construction of a state insane asylum or mental hospital. Headed by Dr. James P. White, who had for many years urged the establishment of the facility (and who had been a supporter of Richardson's design for Christ Church—see no. 22), a committee of ten managers was selected by New York Governor Hoffman and instructed to proceed with construction. Dr. John P. Gray, head of the state asylum in Utica, consulted on the project. Richardson's selection apparently resulted from his friendships with board members, including Asher P. Nichols, and with a leading Buffalo citizen, William Dorsheimer (see nos. 15 and 27).

According to Van Rensselaer the commission was received by the office in March 1871, but work on the project may have begun as early as 1869. Julia Richardson's letter to her mother December 12, 1869, mentions a Richardson meeting with the consultant, Dr. Gray. Moreover, Richardson's plans were approved August 25, 1870. Early in 1871 Richardson consulted with F. L. Olmsted on the siting of the buildings and the design of the grounds. In March Richardson's elevations were approved, and architect Andrew Jackson Warner of Rochester, who had met with Richardson and Olmsted in January, was named supervising architect.

Ground was broken in June 1871. Stone was ordered, but construction proceeded slowly; significant excavation began only in 1872. The project, the drawings show, was simplified from the initial design before construction actually commenced. The design was finally established by September 18, 1872, and construction proceeded. But the project then became involved in New York politics, dragging on for many years. Richardson received his last payment in 1876 after the decision to construct the three outer pavilions in brick rather than stone.

In 1878 the central pavilion and five wards to the east were largely complete. Patients were admitted in 1880, even though the formal opening was not until November 13, 1881. The west group of five pavilions were erected between 1891 and 1895 after the legislature appropriated sufficient funds. The three easternmost ward buildings were demolished in 1969 to make room for an adolescent treatment facility. The central administration building continues in use, but all seven remaining wards are now empty, their future in doubt. The buildings are now part of the Buffalo Psychiatric Center.

The general plan of the hospital is a flattened V with the central administration building at the apex, five pavilions radiating to the east and west, and four low service buildings in the inner courtyard. The plan is not unusual, but follows the model developed by Samuel Sloan and Dr. Thomas S. Kirkbride. Kirkbride, superintendent of the Pennsylvania Hospital for the Insane, published the plan in *Hospitals for the Insane* in 1854.

With its twin towers the administration building dominates the composition. This three-story building over a basement a half level below grade appears emphatically vertical because of its tall towers with their steep hip roofs and round corner turrets. The end bays of the administration building project slightly forward of the central section and are topped with gables, further adding to the verticality of the design.

The central section is marked by the three round arches of the entrance loggia and three dormers, one large and two small, at the attic level. This central pavilion and the two adjoining wards on either side are constructed of brown sandstone in random ashlar. The three outer wards are of irregularly textured common brick with stone trim. The wards are all connected by quarter circular passages. Interior features were simple and plain, reflecting the use of the buildings. The total length of the complex was about 2,200 feet.

The commission was significant for several reasons. In it Richardson continued lines of investigation and development begun in the Brattle Square Church (no. 29) which led to his mature style. In its own right the building is an oustanding example of nineteenth-century institutional architecture. One of Richardson's largest projects, it provided steady work in the office in the early part of the 1870s, a stable source of income during the severe depression of the period.

Textual References

Hitchcock, *Richardson*, 1966, pp. 117–124.

Hitchcock, *Victorian*, p. 13.

Kowsky, Francis R. *Buffalo Projects: H. H. Richardson*. Buffalo: Buffalo State College Foundation, 1980, pp. 8–11.

Proceedings in Connection with the Ceremony of Laying the Cornerstone of the Buffalo State Asylum for the Insane in the City of Buffalo, September 18, 1872. Buffalo: White and Brayley, 1872.

Van Rensselaer, *Works*, p. 53.

Miscellaneous Resources

Drawings: Houghton Library, Harvard University.

Photographs: Buffalo Psychiatric Center Library; Buffalo and Erie County Historical Society; Buffalo and Erie County Public Library; Library of Congress (Historic American Buildings Survey).

Archives: Buffalo Psychiatric Center Library, Annual Reports of Board of Managers.

Letter: Archives of American Art Microfilm Roll 1184.

Sketchbook: Houghton Library, Harvard University.

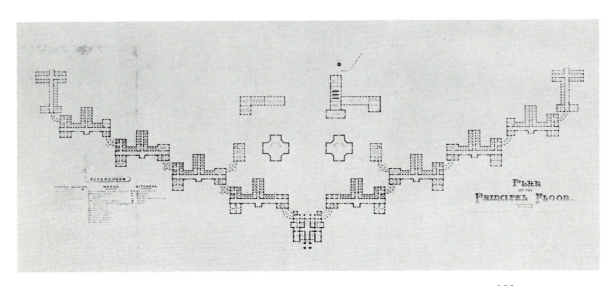

30a
Buffalo State Hospital, Buffalo, New York, 1869–1880 (1895), plan of main floor showing central administration pavilion and attached wards; Houghton Library, Harvard University.

30b
Buffalo State Hospital, with five eastern wards completed; Buffalo and Erie County Historical Society (ca. 1890).

1870

1870

31
Exposition Building,
1870   G&R
Cordova, Argentina
Demolished (?)

32
Brunswick Hotel Alterations,
1870–1871   G&R
225–231 Fifth Avenue
New York, New York
Demolished 1904

Van Rensselaer's list indicates that this project was commissioned in February 1870. It was a temporary exhibition pavilion of wood which was initially assembled on a vacant lot in New York, then disassembled and shipped to Cordova. There it was reconstructed under the supervision of a number of American carpenters who accompanied it in transit.

On February 18, 1873, the Argentine Republic consulate in New York City notified Gambrill and Richardson that they had been awarded a medal in commemoration of the Cordova Exposition.

No descriptive material has been discovered for this project.

Textual References

Hitchcock, *Richardson*, 1966, p. 94.

Van Rensselaer, *Works*, p. 51.

Miscellaneous Resource

Letter: Archives of American Art Microfilm Roll 643.

The Brunswick, a very fashionable hotel catering particularly to European tourists, occupied three adjoining buildings filling the entire block facing Fifth Avenue between Twenty-sixth and Twenty-seventh streets. The property for the hotel was assembled before 1870, and Gambrill and Richardson were commissioned to do renovations. Two building permits were issued—one for $50,000, the other for $10,000—so the project cost a total of $60,000. The hotel opened in 1871 after the completion of the renovation. But in 1885 the hotel went bankrupt after a scandal regarding an 1882 banquet. It was then converted to commercial use, but demolished in 1904 for construction of the Brunswick Building, which occupies the site today.

The hotel was composed of three sections of different height and design. The southern section and southern half of the central section were brownstone, but the rest was brick. Ribner discovered that Gambrill and Richardson added mansard roofs of slate and tin to the southern and central sections as well as doing some interior alterations.

Textual References

Hitchcock, *Richardson*, 1966, p. 94.

King, Moses, ed. *King's Handbook of New York City.* 2d ed. Boston: Moses King, 1893, p. 230.

Ribner, Jonathan Paul. "H. H. Richardson and the Hotel Brunswick." Typescript, New York University Institute of Fine Arts, n.d.

Miscellaneous Resources

Photographs: The Bettmann Archive, Inc., New York.

32a
Brunswick Hotel
alterations, New
York, New York,
1870–1871; The
Bettmann Archive,
Inc.

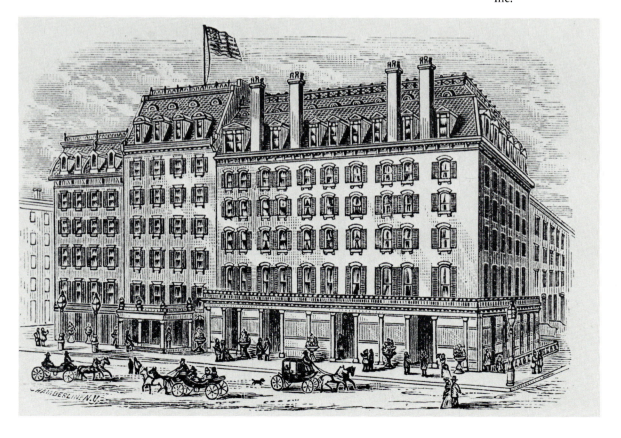

33

Public Building (?) Project (?),
1870   G&R

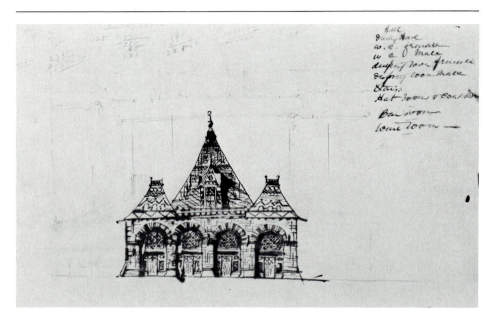

33a
Public building (?)
project (?), 1870,
elevation sketch
from Richardson,
sketchbook, fol. 8r;
Houghton Library,
Harvard University.

This project, which O'Gorman suggests may have been a casino, is known only from notations in Richardson's sketchbook (fol. 8r). The notations indicate a dining hall, restrooms, dressing rooms, hat and coat room, bar, and wine room.

An ink design sketch showed a small building with four round-arched ground floor openings, a high central roof with a single dormer, and two smaller peaked roofs at each end. O'Gorman noted the similarity of this sketch to the competition entry for the Brookline town hall (no. 34), although this building is much smaller.

Textual Reference

O'Gorman, *Selected Drawings*, p. 212.

Miscellaneous Resource

Sketchbook: Houghton Library, Harvard University.

34
Brookline Town Hall Project
(Competition), 1870   G&R
Prospect Street and
Washington Street
Brookline, Massachusetts

34a
Brookline Town
Hall project,
Brookline, Massa-
chusetts, 1870;
Houghton Library,
Harvard University.

At the March 28, 1870 Brookline town meeting, a committee was selected to study the possibility of constructing a town hall. Following a favorable committee report shortly thereafter, the town appropriated $100,000, eventually increased to $150,000, for construction of a new building. The committee invited plans and sketches from architects, and sixteen entries were received.

The winning design by S. F. J. Thayer of Boston was a rectangular building, three stories tall in a Gothic style. The cornerstone was laid May 23, 1871, the building completed and dedicated February 22, 1873.

The Gambrill and Richardson entry is known from a single sketch in reduced form in Van Rensselaer's book and from an etching in the large album at Houghton Library. The use of an etching, first noted by O'Gorman, is unusual. It is likely that other prints were made from the original plate, possibly as part of the competition entry package, but none is known to have survived. The sketch showed a roughly symmetrical design in rugged stone. The low entry loggia had pointed arches, and above these were strongly mullioned windows of a central hall. A corbeled chimney to one side was balanced by a turret to the other. A single central dormer broke the high pyramidal roof.

Textual References

Hitchcock, *Richardson*, 1966, pp. 109–110.

Hitchcock, *Victorian*, p. 11.

Proceedings at the Dedication of the Town Hall, Brookline, February 22, 1873. Brookline: Town of Brookline, 1873.

"Town Hall, Brookline, Mass." *AABN* 5 (Feb. 8, 1879): 45 (S. F. J. Thayer Building).

Van Rensselaer, *Works*, p. 72 (sketch).

Miscellaneous Resource

Etching: Houghton Library, Harvard University.

1871

35
Hampden County Courthouse, 1871–1874 G&R
37 Elm Street
Springfield, Massachusetts

The first Hampden County Courthouse was a frame structure built in 1822. In the 1860s popular pressure developed for a new courthouse, which was resisted by the county commissioners. But in 1869 the commissioners were indicted by a grand jury for official misconduct in neglecting to provide fireproof rooms for the registry of deeds and the safekeeping of public records. When the commissioners initiated construction of a new courthouse in 1871, the indictment was dropped.

In spring 1871 designs were invited from several architects, and that by Gambrill and Richardson was selected. The date the commission was received in the office, according to Van Rensselaer, was July 1871. (Unfortunately Richardson's study in his sketchbook, fol. 20r, is undated.) Norcross Brothers began construction of the courthouse in late 1871, and it was dedicated April 28, 1874. The site cost $75,716, the building $214,068.

Within 35 years the building proved inadequate. In 1907 the probate court and registry of deeds moved to a recently constructed adjacent building. Between 1908 and 1912 a large addition and severe alterations were made by Shepley, Rutan and Coolidge. A new wing was added to house offices for the clerk of courts, county treasurer, and county commissioners. Modifications were also made to the Richardson structure, eliminating the sloping roof and high dormers, adding heavy spandrels to the tall windows,

reorienting the front stairway, and changing the rear entry. In 1930 a new district court building was constructed in Springfield, and district court cases were moved from the courthouse. In 1976 the Hampden County Hall of Justice replaced the Richardson building as the major courthouse of the county. Richardson's building has since undergone a $2 million renovation and houses today the juvenile and housing courts.

Richardson's design for the courthouse occupies a mid–block rectangular site measuring 160 by 90 feet. The two short sides face streets. In plan the building was originally an *I*–shape two stories high, but the original high hipped roof added another full floor to the central mass of the building. The overall composition of the main facade on the base of the *I* was emphatically vertical with tall windows and two tall dormers flanking the central bell tower. At the first floor a central three arched loggia was originally approached by a wide double flight of stairs. At the second floor a double window was located over each of the three arches. The symmetry of the facade was broken by a balcony at the north corner and a counterbalancing narrow slit window at the opposite corner. All of the facades were constructed of light gray Monson granite in rough-faced random ashlar with smooth faced trim. Unfortunately the modifications by Shepley, Rutan and Coolidge were so severe that the building's original design is difficult to visualize.

The Hampden County Courthouse reflects Richardson's continued evolution as a designer. Lines of investigation begun in the design of the Brattle Square Church (no. 29) were further developed here.

Textual References

"Court House, Springfield, Mass." *The New York Sketchbook of Architecture* 3 (Oct. 1876): pl. 38.

Hitchcock, Henry-Russell. "Catalogue of An Exhibition of Photographs Illustrating Springfield Architecture 1800–1900 at the Springfield Museum of Fine Arts." Type-script, Springfield City Library, 1934.

Hitchcock, *Richardson*, 1966, pp. 125–129.

Hitchcock, *Victorian*, pp. 13–14.

King, Moses, ed. *King's Handbook of Springfield.* Springfield: J. D. Gill, 1884.

"The New Springfield Courthouse." *The New York Sketchbook of Architecture*, 1 (Jan. 1874): 2.

O'Gorman, *Selected Drawings*, p. 212.

Tower, James E., ed. *Springfield Present and Prospective.* Springfield: Pond and Campbell, 1905.

Van Rensselaer, *Works*, pp. 54–55.

Williams, Talcott. "A Brief Object-Lesson in Springfield Architecture." *AABN* 10 (Nov. 12, 1881): 227–231.

Miscellaneous Resources

Drawings: Houghton Library, Harvard University.

Photographs: Houghton Library, Harvard University; Library of Congress (Historic American Buildings Survey, Seagram County Courthouse Archives); Springfield Public Library.

Sketchbook; Houghton Library, Harvard University.

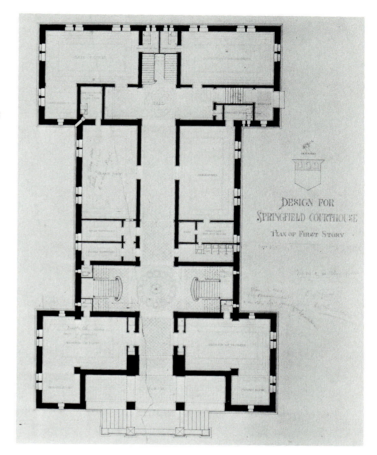

35a
Hampden County Courthouse, Springfield, Massachusetts, 1871–1874, early presentation plan; Houghton Library, Harvard University.

35b
Hampden County
Courthouse, before
alterations; Hough-
ton Library, Har-
vard University.

35c
Hampden County
Courthouse, before
alterations; Hough-
ton Library, Har-
vard University.

35d
Hampden County
Courthouse, with
alterations and ad-
ditions; Library of
Congress (Seagram
County Courthouse
Archives, photo by
Nicholas Nixon).

36
H. B. Hyde House Alterations, 1871 G&R
11 East Fortieth Street
New York, New York
Demolished

Henry Baldwin Hyde (1834–1899) was the founder of the Equitable Life Assurance Company. Richardson had submitted a design in the Equitable Competition in 1868 (no. 7), but it had not been selected.

In 1871 Gambrill and Richardson made minor alterations costing only $700 to the Hyde house. This work remained unknown until discovered by Kramer's research in the New York City Building Department.

Textual Reference

Hitchcock, *Richardson*, 1966, pp. 307–308 (see note vi–1 quoting Kramer).

37
Mrs. Hyde House Project, ca. 1871–1875(?) G&R

The Mrs. Hyde House project is known only from three study plans in the Houghton Library collection. The client is indicated by the notation "Mrs. Hyde's Room" in a downstairs front room. None of the plans is dated, but the overall design appears typical of Richardson's early work.

It is possible that Mrs. Hyde was the wife of Henry Baldwin Hyde of New York for whose house Gambrill and Richardson designed alterations in 1871 (no. 36). It is possible that the Hydes considered building a new house at the time or soon afterward, or that this drawing actually relates to the H. B. Hyde house alterations. A nursery indicated on the second floor might have been intended for any of the Hyde children, Mary (b. 1867), Henry (b. 1872), or James Hazen (b. 1876). On the other hand, the client may have been an entirely different Mrs. Hyde.

The basic plan of the house was square with a full-length porch along one side and a projecting bay at the front. A stair hall occupied the exact center reached by a deep entrance hall at one side. Doors from the stair hall on the first floor opened into the dining room, library, and Mrs. Hyde's room. The only room indicated on the second floor was a nursery.

Miscellaneous Resources

Drawings: Houghton Library, Harvard University.

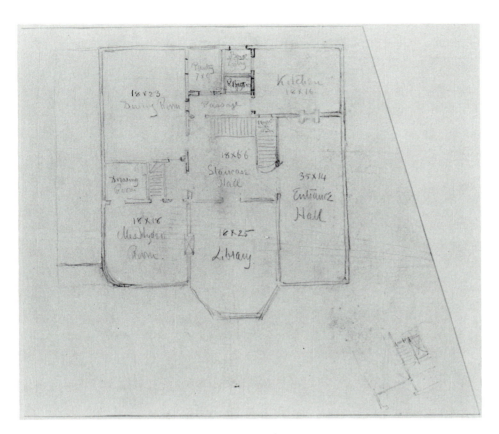

37a
Mrs. Hyde house
project, ca. 1871–
1875, first floor
plan; Houghton Li-
brary, Harvard
University.

38

Connecticut State Capitol Project (Competition), 1871–1872   G&R
Capitol Avenue
Hartford, Connecticut

In July 1871 the Connecticut General Assembly established a special commission and authorized a bond issue and the expenditure of funds to build a new capitol building. The existing (Bulfinch) State House was given to the city of Hartford, and in turn the city gave the site for the capitol to the state. The Board of State House Commissioners invited designs in fall 1871. The first entries were received in January 1872, but all were rejected. New invitations to submit were sent out with a one month deadline. By February 1872 entries had been received from Charles B. Atwood, Batterson and Keller, H. and J. E. Billings, Bryant and Rogers, Emerson and Fehmer, Gambrill and Richardson, William T. Hallett, T. O. Langerfeldt, N. LeBrun, Peabody and Stearns, George B. Post, Sturgis and Brigham, and Richard M. Upjohn.

The Victorian Gothic design by Upjohn was accepted April 18, 1872. James G. Batterson was retained as general contractor later in 1872. Construction proceeded over the next seven years with modifications made in 1873 for fireproofing and replacement of the planned clock tower with a gilded dome. The marble and granite building, costing $2,532,500, was completed and occupied in January 1879.

The Gambrill and Richardson entry was planned as an equal-armed cross. The main entrance was at one end of one arm with the large assembly in the center of the opposite arm on axis with the entry. The central spaces in the cross arms were occupied by the senate to the left and by the supreme court to the right. The center of the cross was to be a vast open space, occupying more area than even the assembly and rising four stories inside the central tower. Rooms for the executive branch of the state government were largely confined to the second floor. The exterior was a composition of symmetrically distributed masses with steep roofs creating an overall pyramidal effect. The exterior was probably to have been brownstone in random ashlar.

Gambrill and Richardson's descriptive brochure on this building was their first. Similar printed documents were used thereafter for other competition designs. (O. W. Norcross collaborated on the competition entry by providing the cost estimate.)

Textual References

Gambrill and Richardson. *Descriptive Report and Schedule for Proposed Capitol Building, State of Connecticut*. New York: 1872.

Hersey, G. L. "Replication Replicated, or Notes on American Bastardy." *Perspecta* 9–10 (1965): 211–230.

Hill, John T. "Photographs of the Connecticut State Capitol, Hartford." *Perspecta* 9–10 (1965): 231–248.

Hitchcock, Henry-Russell, and Seale, William. *Temples of Democracy: The State Capitols of the U.S.A.* New York: Harcourt Brace Jovanovich, 1976, pp. 159–167.

Hitchcock, *Victorian*, pp. 41–43.

"The New State Capitol at Hartford." *AABN* 2 (Sept. 15, 1877): 295–296 (Upjohn design).

Price, Charles. "Henry Hobson Richardson: Some Unpublished Drawings." *Perspecta* 9–10 (1965): 199–210.

Miscellaneous Resources

Drawings: Houghton Library, Harvard University.

Sketchbook: Houghton Library, Harvard University.

Archives: Connecticut State Library.

38a
Connecticut State
Capitol project,
Hartford, Con-
necticut, 1871–
1872, first floor
plan; Houghton Li-
brary, Harvard
University.

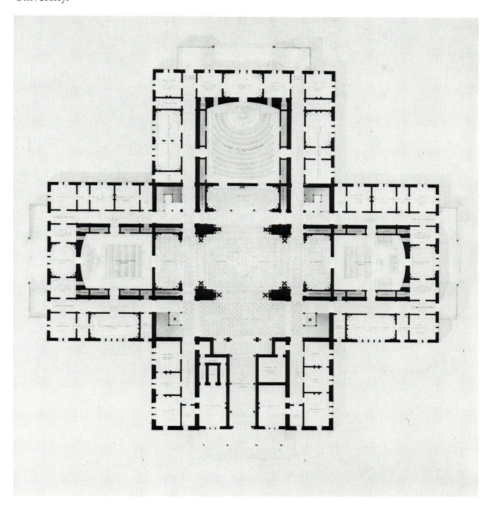

38b
Connecticut State
Capitol project,
main elevation;
Houghton Library,
Harvard University.

38c
Connecticut State
Capitol project,
section; Houghton
Library, Harvard
University.

39
Church and Parsonage Project,
ca. 1871–1872   G&R
Columbus, Ohio

This project is known only from a single drawing in the British magazine *The Architect* (Oct. 5, 1872). Unfortunately no further information on this project has been uncovered.

The Gambrill and Richardson perspective showed the facade of a church in stone whose nave was oriented perpendicular to the street. The gabled end was set slightly in back of two flanking towers of unequal size and height. The tower to the left was somewhat similar to that at Brattle Square Church (no. 29), but here it was topped with a steep pyramidal stone spire. The tower to the right was smaller but with a similar spire. In the *U* formed by the two towers and the end of the nave, Richardson created a small porch. The entire building would have been constructed of stone in random ashlar.

This was the first of Richardson's projects to receive attention in Europe.

Textual References

"Church and Parsonage, Columbus, Ohio." *The Architect* 8 (Oct. 5, 1872): 188.

Hitchcock, *Richardson*, 1966, p. 315 (see note viii–6).

Hitchcock, *Victorian*, p. 39.

Miscellaneous Resource

Drawing: Houghton Library, Harvard University.

39a
Church and parsonage project, Columbus, Ohio, ca. 1871–1872; *The Architect* 8 (Oct. 5, 1872).

40
Trinity Church Project,
ca. 1871–1872 G&R
Delaware Avenue
Buffalo, New York

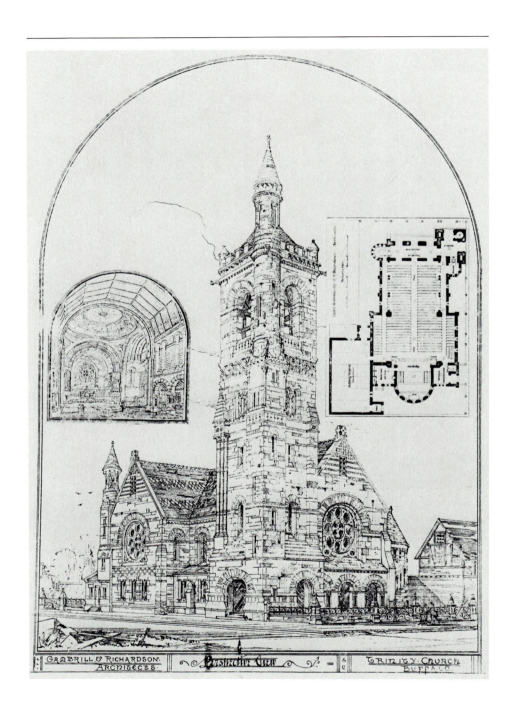

40a
Trinity Church project, Buffalo, New York, ca. 1871–1872; *Architectural Sketchbook* 1 (Oct. 1873).

The Trinity Church project is known only from two drawings: one in the *Architectural Sketchbook* in October 1873, and the other in Richardson's sketchbook dating possibly from early or mid–1872 and identified by O'Gorman. Kowsky's study of the parish history, however, has developed a background for the project.

For nearly two decades Trinity Church had considered moving from a building near downtown Buffalo to new facilities. In 1871 the Reverend Edward Ingersoll finally pushed the parish to take definite steps. A lot was purchased at Delaware Avenue and Park Place, now part of Johnson Park, and a subscription drive was begun. William Dorsheimer (see no. 15), a prominent member of the congregation pledging $500, probably suggested that the building committee contact Richardson. The design must date from this time. But the project went unexecuted for lack of interest and funds. Reverend Ingersoll resigned his position in October 1873, an action which Kowsky suggests led to Richardson's publication of the design. In 1884 Trinity merged with Christ Church (see no. 22), and the enlarged congregation built the present Trinity Church at Delaware Avenue and Tupper Street.

For the church Richardson proposed a cruciform building with three gabled ends and a circular apse. The interior was planned in the form of a nave and aisle church, with the side aisles continued forward parallel to the central aisle across the stubby arms of the transept. The interior perspective shows a sheathed wood barrel vault and a low dome on pendentives over the crossing. A rose window was located in the gable of each end of the transept and nave. The building was to occupy a corner site and would have been dominated by a tall corner tower at the front end of the nave, the main entry to the church leading through arched openings in the base of this tower to a low porch across the front of the nave. The tower design recalls the Brattle Square Church (no. 29), except for a round turret attached to the front corner of the tower. The building would have been executed in buff sandstone in random ashlar with Medina brownstone trim.

Hitchcock suggests that this project may be important historically as the link between the *T*-shaped plan of Brattle Square Church (no. 29) and the later plan for Trinity Church, Boston (no. 45).

Textual References

Hitchcock, *Richardson*, 1966, p. 137n.

Hitchcock, *Victorian*, pp. 39–40.

Kowsky, Francis R. *Buffalo Projects: H. H. Richardson.* Buffalo: Buffalo State College Foundation, 1980, pp. 12–13.

———. "The William Dorsheimer House: A Reflection of French Suburban Architecture in the Early Work of H. H. Richardson." *The Art Bulletin* 62 (Mar. 1980): 139n.

O'Gorman, *Selected Drawings*, p. 213.

"Trinity Church, Buffalo, N.Y." *The Architectural Sketchbook* 1 (Oct. 1873): pl. 16.

Miscellaneous Resources

Drawing: Houghton Library, Harvard University.

Sketchbook: Houghton Library, Harvard University.

41
North Congregational Church, 1868, 1871–1873   G&R
18 Salem Street
Springfield, Massachusetts

The parishioners of the North Congregational Church initially intended construction of a new building on the site of their existing church. Designs were received from several architects early in 1868, and according to Van Rensselaer's list the commission was awarded to Gambrill and Richardson in May 1868. But the project did not proceed: the congregation decided to seek a new site. A corner lot at Salem and Mattoon streets was purchased in 1871 and the building apparently redesigned. Ground was broken for construction in May 1872, and the new church was dedicated September 18, 1873. The cost of the building was about $50,000.

When the North Congregational Society disbanded in 1935, the building was sold and renamed Grace Baptist Church.

Richardson's design is cruciform in plan with the spaces between the arms filled out on the exterior with the lower spaces such as the vestibule. The 100-foot aisleless nave and the 84-foot transept seat over 1,000 people. The ceiling is barrel-shaped, supported by intersecting beams. The treatment of the interior is plain, since no funds were available for decoration. Located at the re-entrant angle of nave and transept, the tower is topped with an octagonal stone spire. The roof descends low over the walls and is broken by a single dormer. The church is constructed of red Longmeadow sandstone in random ashlar.

Textual References

Historic District Study Committee. *Final Report of the Historic District Study Committee.* Springfield: 1972.

Hitchcock, *Richardson*, 1966, p. 83–85, 130.

Hitchcock, *Victorian*, p. 14.

King, Moses, ed. *King's Handbook of Springfield*: Springfield: J. D. Gill, 1884, pp. 194–196.

"'North Church,' Springfield, Mass." *New York Sketchbook of Architecture* 3 (June 1876): pl. 21.

Tower, James E., ed. *Springfield Present and Prospective.* Springfield: Pond and Campbell, 1905.

Van Rensselaer, *Works*, pp. 55–56.

Williams, Talcott. "A Brief Object-lesson in Springfield Architecture." *AABN* 10 (Nov. 12, 1881): 227–231.

Miscellaneous Resources

Photographs: Houghton Library, Harvard University; Springfield Public Library.

41a
North Congrega-
tional Church,
Springfield, Massa-
chusetts, 1868,
1871–1873, under
construction;
Houghton Library,
Harvard University.

41b
North Congrega-
tional Church;
New York Sketch-
book of Architec-
ture 3 (June 1876).

41c
North Congregational Church, door detail (1972).

41d
North Congregational Church, original interior, with Independence Day celebration decorations; Springfield City Library.

1872

42
Phoenix Fire Insurance Company Building, 1872–1873 G&R
64 Pearl Street
Hartford, Connecticut
Demolished 1957

How Gambrill and Richardson received the Phoenix Insurance building commission remains unknown, but the success of their nearby Springfield commercial work (nos. 5, 21) may have been a factor. Van Rensselaer dates the project's entrance into the office March 1872; consequently the schematic design may date from late 1871 or early 1872. The building was completed and occupied in 1873. In 1905 it was occupied by the Connecticut General Life Insurance Company, which made additions to the building in 1907 and 1920, but outgrew these facilities by the 1950s. After Connecticut General moved to its new suburban offices in 1957, the site was sold and the building razed. The site is now occupied by a bank.

Richardson's design was a three-story rectangular building of brick. The five openings at the first floor were arched with polychrome voussoirs, but those of the second floor had stone lintels and at the third floor the two outer windows had both stone lintels and polychrome voussoirs. Additional decorative trim included horizontal stone bands, stone quoins, decorative tile spandrels, and ornamental ironwork at the cornice. The center of the cornice was broken by a small gable. The brick used in the structure was of three colors, red, yellow, and black.

Textual References

Hitchcock, *Richardson*, 1966, pp. 129–131.

Van Rensselaer, *Works*, p. 55.

Miscellaneous Resources

Photographs: Connecticut Historical Society; Hartford Public Library.

Archives: Connecticut General Life Insurance Company library.

42a
Phoenix Fire Insur-
ance Company
Building, Hartford,
Connecticut, 1872–
1873; Connecticut
Historical Society.

43
(Boston & Albany Railroad?)
Clock Tower Project,
ca. 1872   G&R

The clock tower project is among the least known of Richardson's works. A small copy of an ink perspective drawing for this project is found in the large album placed on deposit in the Houghton Library by Shepley, Bulfinch, Richardson and Abbott in 1975. Studies for the project appear on several pages of Richardson's sketchbook; the 1872 date is inferred from these.

The design appears to be an addition to an existing railroad station. At the base is a large arch about three stories high flanked by two much smaller arches. Above the central portion and one end of the arch is a small wood construction of unknown use with a peaked roof. Adjacent to this, over the other end of the arch rises the tall, slender clock tower. The tower is corbeled out to carry the large clock with a face on each side, and this is topped by a sloped roof. The major material in the tower is stone, laid in straight courses at the lower levels and random ashlar in the tower shaft.

Textual Reference

O'Gorman, *Selected Drawings*, p. 213.

Miscellaneous Resources

Drawing: Houghton Library, Harvard University.

Sketchbook: Houghton Library, Harvard University.

43a
Boston & Albany
Railroad clock
tower project, ca.
1872; Houghton
Library, Harvard
University.

44
F. W. Andrews House,
1872–1873
Maple Avenue,
Coddington Point
Newport, Rhode Island
Demolished 1921

Frank Williams Andrews (1826–1903) was a resident of Boston and a summer visitor to Newport. His father, William Turrell Andrews (1794–1879), was a wealthy Boston attorney. The younger Andrews might have known of Richardson through his brother, Edwards Reynolds Andrews, an 1853 graduate of Harvard, even though their years at Harvard did not overlap. According to Van Rensselaer the commission for this summer house entered the office of Gambrill and Richardson in July 1872. Completed in 1873, it was used by Andrews, even after his move to Washington in 1888, as his summer house until his death in 1903. Unfortunately it was destroyed by fire in 1921, though photographs of the house have recently been discovered.

Richardson's plan continued the development of the interior living hall first seen in the Codman house project (no. 16). The Andrews hall was the heart of the house with all other first floor rooms including dining room, library, drawing room, and billiard room clustered around it. The interior space seemed to open up in plan, but this cannot be verified since interior photographs are unknown. The exterior with its high angular roof and skeletal porches followed the conventions of the stick style as identified by Scully, but the exterior surface treatment of clapboards on the first floor and shingles on the second showed a new interest in the surface itself. This was further emphasized by the use of diamond–paned windows in the project drawings, even though the house was actually built with windows with rectangular panes and thin mullions. The overall massing appeared irregular and quite picturesque.

The importance of the Andrews house for American domestic architecture cannot be overestimated. According to Scully, the emphasis on surface treatment and the reintroduction of shingles to American domestic architecture began the transformation from the stick to the shingle style.

Textual References

Downing, Antoinette F., and Scully, Vincent J. *The Architectural Heritage of Newport, Rhode Island*. Cambridge, Mass.: Harvard University Press, 1952, pp. 142–143.

Hitchcock, *Richardson*, 1966, pp. 133–136.

Hitchcock, *Victorian*, p. 45.

Scully, *Shingle Style*, pp. 9–10.

Miscellaneous Resources

Drawings: Houghton Library, Harvard University.

Photographs: Houghton Library, Harvard University.

44a
F. W. Andrews
house, Newport,
Rhode Island,
1872–1873, plan;
Hitchcock, *Rich-
ardson*, 1966.

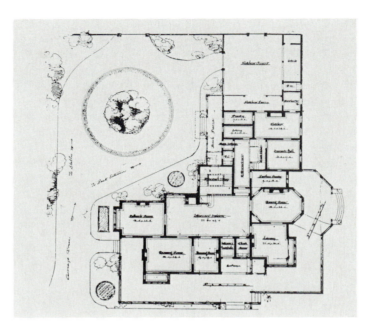

44b
F. W. Andrews
house; Houghton
Library, Harvard
University.

44c
F. W. Andrews
house; Houghton
Library, Harvard
University.

45
Trinity Church,
1872–1877   G&R
Copley Square
Boston, Massachusetts

In 1869 Phillips Brooks (1835–1893) became the ninth rector of Trinity Church, which then occupied a Gothic building on Summer Street. Later the sixth bishop of Massachusetts and the author of the Christmas carol "O Little Town of Bethlehem," Brooks was then a major force behind the decision to build a new church in the Back Bay area. In December 1870 the parish voted to move, and in January 1872 the site at Clarendon Street and St. James Avenue was purchased.

The history of the Richardson project for Trinity is complex. Long the subject of scrutiny, it was studied first by Stebbins, supplemented and corrected by O'Gorman, and then studied again by Ann Adams. The project began with an invited competition among six architects and firms: Richard M. Hunt, Ware and Van Brunt, Peabody and Stearns, John Sturgis, William A. Potter, and H. H. Richardson (the building committee letter was not addressed to Gambrill and Richardson). Other architects who corresponded with the committee included C. Arthur Totten, L. Frère, John Ames Mitchell, and Faulkner and Clark. Invitations were sent out by the committee on March 12, 1872 (Richardson's is included in the Archives of American Art collection) calling for drawings prepared for a rectangular site by May 1, 1872. In the month preceding the selection of Richardson on June 1, the church acquired the additional triangular parcel to the north. Richardson began revisions to his winning scheme by June 13 to fit to the new site configuration. Revisions continued for the next year, delayed apparently by Richardson's illness. Finally in April 1873 Richardson presented completed plans to the committee.

Concern arose over the weight of the structure, particularly of the tower, resting on wood piles in the watery Back Bay soil. Construction firms bid on the revised drawings early in September 1873, but even the low bid by Norcross was too high and further revisions were required. A contract was signed with Norcross Brothers on October 10, 1873 and the final drawings delivered to them in April 1874, though the committee forced abandonment of the octagonal tower. Richardson substituted a square tower and further revised the design during the spring and summer of 1874.

Construction actually began April 21, 1873, involving over 4,000 wood piles driven to prepare the base for the church. Norcross began work on the parish house in March 1874 and the sanctuary in March 1875. The last stone was laid in the tower July 8, 1876. In 1876 Richardson persuaded the church to employ John La Farge to do the interior decorations. The building was consecrated February 9, 1877. The total cost of about $635,000 included the site, pilings, building, and interiors.

After only a few years alterations were begun. The cappings of the west towers were removed by 1886 after damage by fire. Richardson's proposals to finish the west front were never accepted, though an archeologically detailed porch and new towers designed by Richardson's successors, Shepley, Rutan and Coolidge, were built between 1894 and 1897. In 1916 a new pulpit was erected as a memorial to Robert Treat Paine, a warden and vestryman of the church who had served on the building committee as the chief fund-raiser for the project. A temporary altar under a baldacchino, erected in 1914, remained until the chancel was redecorated in 1938 when the present altar and baldacchino were installed. The La Farge decorations were restored to their original brilliance in 1957, but the Richardson-designed "corona," the light fixture central to his conception of the interior, was removed. In the late 1960s the originally trapezoidal site was obscured by the closing of Huntington Avenue and the remodeling of Copley Square. As a result, Richardson's innovative site plan is now almost impossible to visualize.

The design for Trinity Church is a unified composition that includes the parish house and sanctuary. The parish house, which Richardson always called "the chapel," includes on the ground floor a parlor, library, and rector's study and on the second floor a two-story chapel (now altered) with vestibule in the northeast corner. The parish house appears pyramidal in three dimensions, tied to the church by an open cloister, on the west side of which rises the stair to the chapel. The sanctuary, like the parish house, is built of Dedham, Quincy, Westerly, and Rockport granite with Longmeadow brownstone trim. The plan of the building is in the form of a Greek cross with a central tower. There are three galleries, one at each end of the transept and one at the west end of the nave. Inside the semi-circular apse the chancel floor is raised several steps above the main floor of the church. It

was particularly suited to Phillips Brooks, who was generally considered among the finest preachers of his day. Originally he preached from the reading desk in the middle of the chancel. (Bad acoustics later forced the introduction of a pulpit and sounding board set to one side against one of the four tower piers.) In the center of the great space below the tower hung the "corona," the Richardson-designed chandelier, now removed. The ceilings of the sanctuary are in the form of trefoil barrel vaults. A vestibule stretches across the west front between the two west towers. The entire building is dominated by the 211-foot central tower of square design with corner turrets and an octagonal roof covered with red Akron tiles. The overall massing, again, is pyramidal.

Trinity Church is among the most famous of Richardson's designs. It established him as a truly national figure, the dominant architect of his day. He received coverage not only in the new architectural press, but in many other periodicals as well.

Trinity also had a direct personal effect on Richardson's life. In spring 1874, when the construction of Trinity was about to begin, Richardson moved his home and personal office to Brookline. Although his partnership with Gambrill continued and the office staff remained in New York for four years, Richardson became an active member of Boston society. In this move he set the stage for the home–studio which was to serve him so well over the last eight years of this career (no. 70).

45a
**Trinity Church Porch Project,
1878–1886**
Copley Square
Boston, Massachusetts

Richardson's design studies for the porch to complete the west front of Trinity Church are known from drawings held by the Houghton Library and from one drawing published by Van Rensselaer.

Textual References

Adams, Ann Jensen. "Birth of a Style: Henry Hobson Richardson and the Competition Drawings for Trinity Church, Boston." *Art Bulletin* 62 (Sept. 1980): 409–433.

Back Bay Churches and Public Buildings: An Album of Nineteenth Century Photographs Chiefly from the Collections of the Bostonian Society. Boston: Bostonian Society, 1967.

"A Boston Basilica." *The Architect* 17 (Apr. 28, 1877): 274.

Chester, Arthur H. *Trinity Church: An Historical and Descriptive Account With a Guide to Its Windows and Paintings.* Cambridge, Mass.: J. Wilson and Son, 1888.

Consecration Services of Trinity Church, Boston, February 9, 1877, with . . . a Description of the Church Edifice by H. H. Richardson. Boston: Printed by Order of the Vestry, 1877.

Damrell, C. S. *A Half Century of Boston's Building.* Boston: L. P. Hagen, 1892, p. 92.

Graff, Myrtle S. *Guidebook to Trinity Church in the City of Boston.* Boston: Church Service League, 1924.

Harrell, Pauline C., and Smith, Margaret S., eds. *Victorian Boston Today: Ten Walking Tours.* Boston: New England Chapter, Victorian Society in America, 1975, pp. 43–45.

Herndon, Richard. *Boston of Today.* Boston: Post Publishing Company, 1892, p. 49.

Hitchcock, *Richardson*, 1966, pp. 136–148.

Hitchcock, *Victorian*, pp. 39–41, 43–47.

King, Moses, ed. *King's How To See Boston 1895.* Boston: Moses King, 1895, p. 142.

Lawrence, William. *The Life of Phillips Brooks.* New York: Harper and Brothers, 1930.

"The Narthex, Trinity Church, Boston." *Christian Art* 3 (Apr. 1908): 98.

"The New Trinity Church, Boston." *The Architectural Sketch Book* 1 (Aug. 1873): pl. 5.

Norton, Bettina A. *Trinity Church*. Boston: Wardens and Vestry of Trinity Church, 1978.

O'Gorman, *Selected Drawings*, pp. 42–51.

"One Hundred Years of Significant Building: Churches." *ARec* 120 (Dec. 1956): 177–180.

Paine, Robert Treat. "Report of the Activities of the Trinity Church Building Committee 1872–1877." Manuscript, Trinity Church, 1877.

Perry, Thomas Sargeant. "Colour Decoration in America." *The Architect* 18 (Oct. 20, 1877): 210–211.

Romig, Edgar D. *The Story of Trinity Church in the City of Boston*. Boston: The Wardens and Vestry, 1952.

Sargeant, Irene. "Trinity Church, Boston, as a Monument of America Art." *Craftsman* 3 (Mar. 1903): 329–340.

Stebbins, Theodore E., Jr. "Richardson and Trinity Church: The Evolution of a Building." *JSAH* 27 (Dec. 1968): 281–298.

"Study for Tower of Trinity Church, Boston." *New York Sketchbook of Architecture* 1 (Aug. 1874): pl. 32.

"Tower of Trinity Church, Boston, Mass." *AABN* 22 (Dec. 31, 1887): 131.

"Trinity Church, Boston, Mass." *AABN* 2 (Feb. 3, 1877): 36.

"Trinity Church, Boston, Mass." *AABN* 3 (Feb. 17, 1877): 49.

Trinity Church, Boston, Mass." *American Buildings, Selections*, no. 3: pl. 21.

"Trinity Church, Boston, Mass." *Monographs of American Architecture* 5. Boston: Ticknor, 1888.

"Trinity Church, Boston, Mass., showing proposed alterations by Messrs. Shepley, Rutan & Coolidge, Architects." *AABN* 45 (Aug. 11, 1894): 54.

Van Rensselaer, *Works*, pp. 20, 59–66, 143–145.

Weinberg, Helene Barbara. "John La Farge and the Decoration of Trinity Church, Boston." *JSAH* 33 (Dec. 1974): 323–353.

Miscellaneous Resources

Drawings: Houghton Library, Harvard University.

Photographs: Boston Athenaeum; Boston Public Library; Bostonian Society; Library of Congress; Society for the Preservation of New England Antiquities.

Archives: Trinity Church, Boston.

Letters: Archives of American Art Microfilm Roll 643.

45a
Trinity Church,
Boston, Massachu-
setts, 1872–1877,
plan; *AABN* 2
(Feb. 3, 1877).

45b
Trinity Church, un-
der construction
(ca. 1876); Society
for the Preservation
of New England
Antiquities.

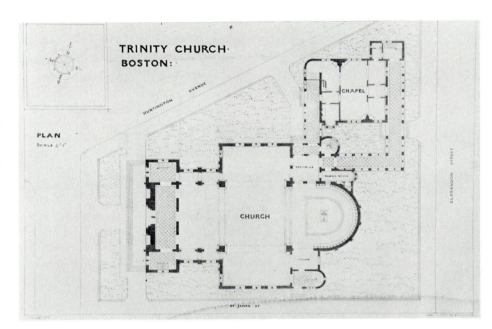

45c
Trinity Church;
AABN 2 (Feb. 3,
1877).

45d
Trinity Church,
parish house (ca.
1883); Society for
the Preservation of
New England An-
tiquities, photo by
John L. Gardner.

45e
Trinity Church,
view of apse,
tower, and cloister;
Society for the Pres-
ervation of New
England Antiqui-
ties, photo by Bald-
win Coolidge.

45f
Trinity Church, detail of cloister (ca. 1890); Society for the Preservation of New England Antiquities.

45g
Trinity Church, detail of cloister (ca. 1890); Society for the Preservation of New England Antiquities.

45h
Trinity Church, interior; Society for the Preservation of New England Antiquities.

45i
Trinity Church, interior; Society for the Preservation of New England Antiquities.

45j
Trinity Church,
"corona," now de-
stroyed; Society for
the Preservation of
New England
Antiquities.

45k
Trinity Church,
with later altera-
tions and rede-
signed Copley
Square (1972).

46

**American Merchants Union
Express Company Building,
1872, 1874–1880   G&R**
21 West Monroe Street
Chicago, Illinois
Demolished 1930

Van Rensselaer dates the commissioning of this project September 1872. Construction began in 1873, but severe settling led to rebuilding between 1874 and 1880. Rebuilt under the supervision of Peter B. Wight, the structure had less fenestration and a heavier cornice than the original. The new structure stood until June 7, 1930, when it was destroyed by fire. It was never photographed in its original form, but Webster has identified drawings and woodcuts.

The American Express building shows further development of Richardson's approach to the commercial building. The plan filled a rectangular lot with street frontage of 90 feet and a depth of 190 feet. Light entered the interior through a court which cut through the building about halfway along its depth. The street facade of the five-story building was to be executed in stone with large windows to allow as much light as possible to penetrate. The building was topped by mansard roof broken by dormers with pointed arches.

Textual References

Two Years After the Fire: Chicago Illustrated. Chicago: J. M. Wing and Company, 1873, p. 3.

Hitchcock, Henry-Russell. "Richardson's American Express Building: A Note." *JSAH* 9 (Mar.-May, 1950): 25–30.

Hitchcock, *Richardson*, 1966, pp. 132–133.

Illustrations of Greater Chicago. Chicago: J. M. Wing and Company 1875, p. 9.

Van Rensselaer, *Works*, p. 55.

Webster, J. Carson. "Richardson's American Express Building." *JSAH* 9 (Mar.-May, 1950): 21–24.

Miscellaneous Resource

Drawing: Houghton Library, Harvard University.

46a
American Merchants Union Express Company Building, Chicago, Illinois, 1872, 1874–1880; Hitchcock, *Richardson*, 1966.

1873

47
George Minot Dexter Memorial
(Project ?), 1873–1877   G&R
Trinity Church, Copley Square
Boston, Massachusetts

George Minot Dexter (1802–1872), the Boston architect, was a senior warden of Trinity Church and a member of the church building committee. The recommendation that a memorial tablet to Dexter be placed in the new Trinity Church (no. 45) was made by the wardens and vestry November 28, 1872, a request probably relayed to Richardson early in 1873.

Based on analysis of the drawings, O'Gorman suggests that the design dates from soon after 1873, although Richardson wrote to Augustus Saint-Gaudens October 21, 1877, for a carving of the portrait.

Apparently the memorial was not executed. Only a plain gray stone memorial tablet was erected on the east wall of the north transept of Trinity Church.

The Dexter tablet design was to be rather flat, with the Saint-Gaudens portrait in the center of the upper portion with text below. Richardson's letter to Saint-Gaudens mentions that he intended a wrought iron and brass frame.

Textual Reference

O'Gorman, *Selected Drawings*, pp. 186–187.

Miscellaneous Resources

Drawings: Houghton Library, Harvard University.

Letter: Saint-Gaudens Papers, Baker Memorial Library, Dartmouth College.

48
Benjamin F. Bowles House,
1873–1874   G&R
School Street at Union Street
Springfield, Massachusetts
Demolished 1926

48a
Benjamin F. Bowles
house, Springfield,
Massachusetts,
1873–1874;
Springfield City
Library.

Member of a leading Springfield family, Benjamin F. Bowles (1833–1876) was overshadowed by his older brother Samuel Bowles III, who was editor of the *Springfield Republican* and by his son, Admiral Francis Tiffany Bowles, a major American naval figure. Benjamin Bowles was educated as a banker, but became a partner in his brother's newspaper. After a short tenure he retired and lived off the income from his one-third ownership of the paper. He commissioned a house from Richardson in 1873, but did not live long after its completion. He died in Paris in 1876.

According to Van Rensselaer the Bowles commission entered the office in May 1873. It was completed by mid-1874. After Bowles's death in 1876, the house passed through a succession of owners until its demolition in 1926 for the Gladmore Apartments. Only one photograph of the Bowles house is known.

The two-story rectangular house occupied a corner site. The red brickwork included black stripes similar to those in the later pavilions of the Buffalo State Hospital (no. 30). The high roof was broken in several places by dormers. Unfortunately all plans have been lost so the interior arrangement is unknown.

Textual References

Hitchcock, *Richardson*, 1966, pp. 154–155.

Tomlinson, Juliette. *Ten Famous Houses of Springfield*. Springfield: Connecticut Valley Historical Museum, 1952.

Van Rensselaer, *Works*, p. 108.

Miscellaneous Resource

Photograph: Springfield Public Library.

1874

**Library of Congress Project
(Competition), 1874 G&R
Washington, D.C.**

Ainsworth Rand Spofford (1825–1908) was appointed first assistant to the Librarian of Congress in 1861 and chief Librarian of Congress in 1865. For the next five years he pressed for a law, passed in 1870, making the Library of Congress the office for records of all American copyrights and the permanent depository of all copyrighted publications—the Library to receive two copies of each item granted a United States copyright. By 1871, the limited space in the Capitol, where the Library was housed, was overflowing. Consequently, Spofford requested a new building in his reports of 1871 and 1872.

Congress appropriated $585,000 for purchase of a four-acre site about 500 yards east of the Capitol and in March, 1873, authorized a competition for the design of a fireproof building to hold 2,000,000 volumes. Sixteen firms entered the competition, which was won by (John L.) Smithmeyer (1852–1908) and (Paul J.) Pelz (1841–1918) of Washington. But in 1874 Congress reopened the competition because the winning design was judged insufficiently impressive. Richardson entered the competition at this time.

Smithmeyer and Pelz were retained as architects even after the 1874 competition, but the project was embroiled in controversy. Not until 1886 did Congress authorize funds for construction, and the building was not occupied until 1897.

Richardson's entry has been completely lost. The fact that he entered is known from Smithmeyer's *History of the Construction of the Library of Congress.*

Textual References

Cole, John Y. "Smithmeyer and Pelz: Embattled Architects of the Library of Congress." *Quarterly Journal of the Library of Congress* 29 (Oct. 1972): 282–307.

Smithmeyer, John L. *History of the Construction of the Library of Congress, Washington, D.C.* Washington: Beresford, 1906.

Francis M. Wild House Alterations, 1874   G&R
58 East Forty-fifth Street
New York, New York
Demolished

The alterations to the Francis Wild house were a minor Gambrill and Richardson project of 1874, costing only $3,800. The project was uncovered by Kramer during research in the New York City Department of Buildings.

Textual Reference

Hitchcock, *Richardson*, 1966, pp. 307–308 (see note iv–1 quoting Kramer).

51

William Watts Sherman House, 1874–1876   G&R
2 Shepard Avenue
Newport, Rhode Island

William Watts Sherman (1842–1912) received his M.D. from the college of physicians and surgeons in New York City but joined the New York banking firm of Duncan, Sherman and Company, of which his father had been a partner from 1851 to 1865. In 1871 he married Annie Derby Rogers Wetmore, the daughter of William Shepard Wetmore, a New York merchant in the East India trade, and sister of George P. Wetmore, governor of Rhode Island (1884–1886), and United States Senator (1895–1913). Soon after the marriage, Sherman purchased the site for his Newport home from his brother-in-law, whose own mansion, Château-sur-Mer, was nearby. Both properties remain today, though now they are separated by Shepard Avenue.

Sketch studies and specifications for the Sherman house and stable fill many pages of Richardson's sketchbook, none dated. Van Rensselaer dates the commission September 1874, but it may have been under study before then. Construction began in 1875 and was completed in 1876.

In 1879–1881 Stanford White (1853–1906), who had worked on the house under Richardson in 1874–1876, redecorated three of the main rooms and extended the house to the east, changing the original, mostly rectangular plan to an *L* shape. About 1920 Dudley Newton added a service wing to the north along the original longitudinal axis of the house. Newton's addition was a close approximation of the original in detail, but altered the initial compact appearance of the house by giving it a more horizontal character. The Baptist Church acquired the house in 1949 for use as a home for the aged and added a dormitory wing to the northeast of incompatible design. The roof has been reshingled, but changes to the interior have been restrained so that many rooms retain their 1875–1881 finish. Some of the glass added by John La Farge (ca. 1877) is now in the Museum of Fine Arts in Boston, though his small transoms remain. In 1980 the Baptist Church decided to sell the house. Its future, at this writing, remains uncertain.

Richardson's Sherman house was a large two-and-one-half story house with a basically rectangular, but somewhat irregular plan. The first floor had the familiar great hall occupying the full depth of the house at the center with the specialized spaces of drawing room, library, and dining room opening to left and right. Kitchen facilities were completely in the basement with only pantries on the first floor. The two upper floors were bedrooms. Asymmetrical in composition, the exterior of the house is stone, half-timbering, and shingles. The main roof ridge runs longitudinally, but the front is marked by a broad subsidiary gable. The first story walls are of pink granite in random ashlar with sandstone trim, the upper stories of frame construction covered in shingles and inset with half–timber and stucco panels. With a porte-cochere centered on it, the front gable is composed of horizontal bands of shingles alternating with bands of casement windows and stucco and half-timbering.

Historians have speculated on the influence of Stanford White, who entered Richardson's office in 1872, on the design for this house. Hitchcock credits the mass conception and overall planning to Richardson, but credits White with much of the detailing. To account for the dramatic change in Richardson's style from the earlier Bowles house (no. 48), historians have suggested that the 1874 publication of Norman Shaw's English country house designs had a direct impact on Richardson. Nonetheless, Richardson's work in no way duplicates Shaw's in overall conception, while it utilizes many of Shaw's elements in a personal design.

51a
William Watts Sherman Stables
Project (?)
2 Shepard Avenue
Newport, Rhode Island

Richardson's sketchbook includes specifications for a stable which might have been built at the same time as the house. But no drawings have survived; and the building, if it was ever built, does not remain.

Textual References

"Cottage for W. Watts Sherman, Esq." *New York Sketchbook of Architecture* 2 (May 1875): pl. 18, 19.

Downing, Antoinette F., and Scully, Vincent J. *The Architectural Heritage of Newport, Rhode Island.* Cambridge, Mass.: Harvard University Press, 1952, pp. 142–144.

Elliott, Maud Howe. *This Was My Newport.* Cambridge, Mass.: The Mythology Company, A. M. Jones, 1944.

Hitchcock, *Richardson*, 1966, pp. 156–161.

"House of W. Watts-Sherman, Esq., Newport, R.I." *AABN* 22 (Oct. 22, 1887): 194.

O'Gorman, *Selected Drawings*, pp. 95–96, 214–215.

"One Hundred Years of Significant Building: Houses before 1907." *ARec* 120 (Oct. 1956): 191–194.

Scully, *Shingle Style*, pp. 14–18.

Van Rensselaer, *Works*, p. 103.

Veeder, P. L., II. "The Outbuildings and Grounds of Chateau-sur-Mer." *JSAH* 29 (Dec. 1970): 307–317.

Miscellaneous Resources

Drawing: Houghton Library, Harvard University.

Photographs: Houghton Library, Harvard University; Library of Congress (Historic American Buildings Survey); Newport Historical Society.

Sketchbook: Houghton Library, Harvard University.

51a
William Watts
Sherman house,
plan; Newport
Historical Society.

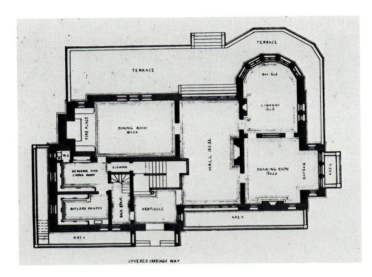

51b
William Watts
Sherman house,
Newport, Rhode Is-
land, 1874–1876,
before additions;
Houghton Library,
Harvard University.

51c
William Watts
Sherman house,
with addition by
Stanford White;
AABN 22 (Oct. 22,
1887).

51d
William Watts
Sherman house, ga-
ble end; Newport
Historical Society.

51e
William Watts
Sherman house,
with service wing
to left by Dudley
Newton; photo by
Wayne Andrews.

51f
William Watts
Sherman house,
staircase; Newport
Historical Society,
photo by W. King
Covell.

51g
William Watts
Sherman house,
central living hall;
Newport Historical
Society, photo by
W. King Covell.

52

**Arthur W. Blake House Project,
ca. 1874   G&R**
Newton Lower Falls,
Massachusetts

52a
Arthur W. Blake
house project,
Newton Lower
Falls, Massachu-
setts, ca. 1874;
*New York Sketch-
book of Architec-
ture* 2 (Feb. 1875).

Arthur Welland Blake (1840–1893) was the son of George Baty Blake (1808–1875) of New York and a partner in Blake Brothers and Company of Boston and New York. He made his home in Brookline, but evidently commissioned this house for Newton Lower Falls about 1874. The project is known only from a drawing which appeared in the *New York Sketchbook of Architecture* in February 1875.

Apparently the Blakes were family friends of Richardson and his wife: George B. Blake was mentioned in letters between Julia and her mother in 1867 and 1868. It appears to be only coincidental that this Blake project was intended for Newton Lower Falls, very near the Weston estate of Francis Blake (1850–1913) where McKim, Mead and White later built a house. Arthur Blake and Francis Blake were distantly related as second cousins.

A somewhat irregular structure of two stories with a partially exposed basement, the house had a strong central mass with a round tower projecting at one corner and a broad porch along two sides. The roof forms appear particularly dramatic in the drawing, the roof at the attic sloping down below the second floor to one side to form the roof over the porch. The materials of this design, stone, shingles, and half-timbering, were very similar to those of the Sherman House (no. 51), which was designed about the same time.

Hitchcock has suggested that the house was largely the work of Stanford White, then in Richardson's office.

Textual References

"Dwelling House for Arthur W. Blake, Esq." *New York Sketchbook of Architecture* 2 (Feb. 1875): pl. 6.

Hitchcock, *Richardson*, 1966, p. 162.

Scully, *Shingle Style*, p. 14.

Miscellaneous Resources

Letters: Archives of American Art Microfilm Roll 1184.

53
Village Church Project
(Competition),
ca. 1874–1875 G&R

The village church project is known
only from a single drawing published
in the *New York Sketchbook of Architecture* in October 1875. No location
was given for the project, but Homolka speculates that this church was
intended for the town of North Easton, Massachusetts. Richardson may
have submitted this design for the
Ames family (see no. 68) commission
for Unity Church, North Easton,
which ultimately went to the Ames
nephew, architect John Ames Mitchell
(1845–1918). Mitchell, a graduate of
Harvard, had studied architecture
with Ware and Van Brunt and then at
the Ecole des Beaux-Arts from 1867
to 1870. He practiced architecture until 1876, then returned to Europe for
four years of study of decorative design, stained glass, and book design
and illustration. In 1883 he founded
Life magazine. As evidence that Richardson's design may have been for the
North Easton Unity Church, Homolka
cites not only the approximately correct date, but also the structure to the
right in the drawing, which may have
been the vestry and parsonage speci-
fied by Oliver Ames II.

The village church design partly follows that of Trinity Church, Boston
(no. 45). The plan is a Latin cross and
a large square tower with a steep roof
rises from the intersection of the nave
and transept. Tall, arched windows
are grouped at the ends of nave and
transept. Two small porches project
from the sides at the front of the nave.
Dormers break the slope of the nave
roof which descends low over the side
walls in a single slope. The exterior is
stone laid up in random ashlar.

Textual References

"Competitive Design for a Village
Church." *New York Sketchbook of Architecture* 2 (Oct. 1875): pl. 40.

Hitchcock, *Richardson*, 1966, p. 141n.

Homolka, Larry J. "Henry Hobson
Richardson and the 'Ames Memorial
Buildings'." Ph.D. dissertation, Harvard
University, 1976.

O'Gorman, *Selected Drawings*, p. 216.

Miscellaneous Resource

Drawing: Houghton Library, Harvard
University.

53a
Village church proj-
ect, ca. 1874–1875;
*New York Sketch-
book of Architec-
ture* 2 (Oct. 1875).

54
Civil War Memorial Project, 1874–1876   G&R
Niagara Square
Buffalo, New York

In July 1874 the Ladies Union Monument Association of Buffalo was incorporated for the purpose of erecting a memorial to soldiers and sailors who had died in the Civil War. F. L. Olmsted was a supporter of the project, since he wished to include the memorial in his redesign of Niagara Square. Moreover, William Dorsheimer (see no. 15) was an honorary member and Mrs. A. P. Nichols (see no. 27) was an officer of the association. Through these connections Richardson was selected as the architect. He mentions the project in a letter to Olmsted dated September 23, 1874. By December Richardson had prepared a design for an arch which Olmsted presented to the park commission. The commission, whose executive committee included Dorsheimer, then approved the design, which was described in the park report of 1875. But the Ladies Monument Associaton took no action at this time. They had raised only $7,500, even though Norcross Brothers estimated Richardson's design would cost over $50,000. Resistance soon developed to the design. Groundbreaking was held July 4, 1876, but according to Kowsky the construction proceeded no further.

A Civil War memorial was erected in Buffalo between 1882 and 1884 from the design of local architect George Keller and sculptor Casper Buberl. It is a column with five sculpted figures located in Lafayette Square. Another monument was later built in Niagara Square, but it was dedicated to President William McKinley, who was assassinated in Buffalo in 1901.

O'Gorman notes that the Richardson design served as the basis for the Shepley, Rutan and Coolidge arch at Stanford University (destroyed by the earthquake of 1906) and for the Washington Square Arch in New York City by Stanford White.

Richardson's design for the Buffalo arch is a development of the earlier scheme for Worcester (no. 12). In both the first scheme in his sketchbook and the developed perspective—O'Gorman suggests the latter may have been drawn by Stanford White—the rectangular block is cut by the large arch in one direction and two much smaller arches on the perpendicular axis. The arch is topped by a horizontal band with the inscription, IN MEMORY OF THOSE CITIZENS OF BUFFALO WHO DIED TO SAVE THE FEDERAL UNION THIS ARCH WAS BUILT, then the sculpted frieze and finally the corbeled cornice. O'Gorman notes that the photograph of a rendering now in the large album at Houghton Library is most likely a later design, showing modifications prepared about August 1876 in response to local criticism of the design.

Textual References

Hitchcock, *Richardson*, 1966, p. 216.

Kowsky, Francis R. *Buffalo Projects: H. H. Richardson.* Buffalo: Buffalo State College Foundation, 1980, pp. 13–14.

———. "The William Dorsheimer House: A Reflection of French Suburban Architecture in the Early Work of H. H. Richardson." *The Art Bulletin* 62 (Mar. 1980): 139n.

O'Gorman, James F. "Richardson, Olmsted and the Rejected Civil War Monuments for Worcester and Buffalo." In *Three Centuries/Two Continents: Essays on the Arts . . . In Honor of Robert C. Smith*, edited by K. L. Ames and N. H. Schless. Watkins Glen, N.Y.: American Life Foundation, in press.

O'Gorman, *Selected Drawing*, pp. 188–190, 214.

Semi-centennial Celebration of the City of Buffalo . . . Celebration of July 4th in Connection with Laying of Corner Stone of Soldiers' and Sailors' Monument. Buffalo: E. H. Hutchinson (under direction of the Buffalo Historical Society), 1882.

Miscellaneous Resources

Drawings: Houghton Library, Harvard University.

Sketchbook: Houghton Library, Harvard University.

Archives: Buffalo and Erie County Historical Society Collection. Minute Book of Ladies Union Monument Association.

Letters: Archives of American Art Microfilm Roll 643.

54a
Civil War memorial
project, Buffalo,
New York, 1874–
1876; Houghton
Library, Harvard
University.

55
William E. Dorsheimer House
Project, ca. 1874–1875   G&R
Albany, New York

William Dorsheimer, Richardson's Buffalo patron (see nos. 15, 30, 40, 54), was elected lieutenant governor of New York in 1874 and served in that capacity for the next four years. He must have turned to Richardson for the design for an Albany residence at that time.

The project was mistakenly identified by Hitchcock in 1936 as drawings for the Buffalo Dorsheimer house which was then unknown. But Hitchcock has since concluded that the design was for Albany. Unfortunately the drawings identified by Hitchcock are not among those now in the Houghton Library collection. Thus, our only knowledge of this project today comes from the plan in the 1936 edition of Hitchcock's *The Architecture of H. H. Richardson and His Times.*

The design adapted for a townhouse the interior planning innovations which had been developed in Richardson's suburban houses (nos. 16, 44, 51). Thus, at the back of the main floor, one level above the entry floor, was a large living hall opening onto a court with a large fireplace at one end and a staircase at the other. Two smaller rooms with an entrance hall between were at the front. A dining room at the rear extended the house plan back to form an *L*, a plan type which Richardson developed in succeeding designs for city houses.

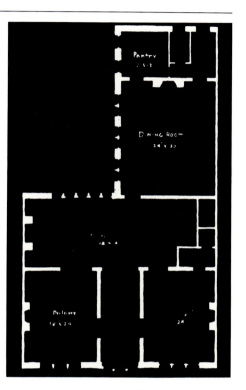

55a
William E. Dorsheimer house project, Albany, New York, ca. 1874–1875; Hitchcock, *Richardson*, 1936.

Textual References

Hitchcock, *Richardson*, 1966, pp. 82–83, 309–310 (see note v–11).

Kowsky, Francis R. "The William Dorsheimer House: A Reflection of French Suburban Architecture in the Early Work of H. H. Richardson." *The Art Bulletin* 62 (Mar. 1980): 134n.

Scully, *Shingle Style*, p. 5n.

1875

56
Hayden Building,
1875–1876   G&R
681 Washington Street
Boston, Massachusetts

Julia Richardson's parents died only two years apart: Dr. John Cole Hayden (1801–1869) of heart disease July 30, 1869, and Susan Ann Buckminster Williams Hayden (1806–1871) August 3, 1871. The Hayden Building was constructed by the Hayden heirs.

The structure was probably under consideration in early 1875. A drawing of the facade is in Richardson's sketchbook, fol. 58r. Construction began July 31, 1875, and the final building department inspection took place April 17, 1876. Unknown to architectural historians, it was identified in 1973 by Zaitzevsky during a survey prior to urban renewal. The project was not mentioned by Van Rensselaer. Since the project was for Richardson's family and no fee was charged, it probably was not entered on the office book from which Van Rensselaer worked in compiling her list.

The Hayden Building is a five-story rectangular commercial structure on a narrow lot at the corner of Washington and LaGrange Streets in downtown Boston. In plan the building fills the narrow lot with windows on the two streets to allow light to reach the interior. The facade of the five-floor structure is divided into zones with the three windows at the second level grouped under a broad arch and those at the third and fourth levels combined vertically under individual arches. At the fifth level, the attic, the windows have flat lintels. The building is constructed of Longmeadow brownstone with granite lintels and arches. It is now expected that, should this area undergo urban renewal, the Hayden Building will be preserved.

Textual References

O'Gorman, *Selected Drawings*, p. 215.

Zaitzevsky, Cynthia. "A New Richardson Building." *JSAH* 32 (May 1973): 164–166.

Miscellaneous Resource

Sketchbook: Houghton Library, Harvard University.

56a
Hayden Building,
Boston, Massachu-
setts, 1875–1876;
photo by Jean Baer
O'Gorman.

Known only from a small sketch in
Richardson's sketchbook (fol. 62r),
this project has some features in common with the village church design
(no. 53). But it is sufficiently different
to have possibly been another project.

Richardson's sketch plan shows a
long church with nave, choir, and
chancel but no transept. Attached to
this were a choir or robing room and
vestry. A large tower with a high roof
rises from four piers along the nave. A
small porch is at one side of the front
of the nave marked by a rose window
over three smaller arched windows.
The design was to be constructed of
stone laid up in random ashlar.

Textual Reference

O'Gorman, *Selected Drawings*, pp. 19,
216.

Miscellaneous Resource

Sketchbook: Houghton Library, Harvard
University.

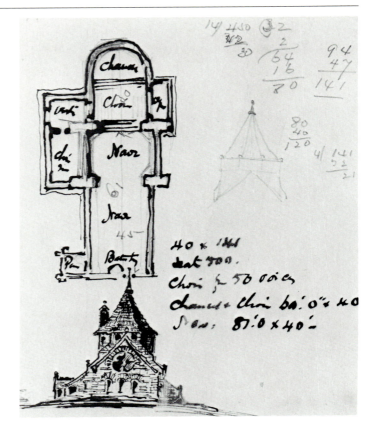

57a
Church project, ca.
1875, Richardson,
sketchbook, fol.
62r, sketch plan;
Houghton Library,
Harvard University.

58
R. and F. Cheney Building, 1875–1876
942 Main Street
Hartford, Connecticut

Members of the Cheney family were leading silk dealers in Hartford and South Manchester. Most likely R. and F. were Rush Cheney (1815–1882) and Frank Cheney (1817–1904), although the R. might have been Ralph Cheney (1806–1897). They commissioned this block of stores and offices in 1875.

Van Rensselaer dates the commission September 1875, but because the elevation was published in the *New York Sketchbook of Architecture* that same month, the design must have been under consideration some months earlier; studies in Richardson's sketchbook, fol. 52r–56r, may date from early summer. Norcross Brothers began construction of the project in November 1875 and completed it in 1876 under the supervision of T. M. Clark.

The interior of the building was reworked several times, first when it became the Brown Thompson Department Store and again when it was absorbed by the G. Fox & Company downtown store. Beginning in 1979 the building was the subject of an $8.5 million renovation which divided it into shops and apartments but left the exterior intact.

Richardson's design here represented an advance over the earlier Hayden Building (no. 56). The two original street-level entrances gave access to a central court from which one gained access to the floors of offices. This court and the fenestration on the two street facades and one alley facade allowed light to penetrate to the interior. The exterior walls are of Berea limestone and Portland brownstone.

The street facades divide into three horizontal zones. At the street level broad arches frame windows for two floors. Above each of these, a pair of arches frame windows for the next three floors. At the sixth floor attic level, four arches supported by colonnettes frame narrow windows. The regularity of the system is broken at the corner by the extension upward of the last bay, creating the effect of a corner tower with the arched openings in a group of three rather than the typical four. Horizontal bands of decoration further emphasize the division into three zones. Alternating brownstone and limestone voussoirs introduce an element of polychromy and emphasize the arches. The two entry portals at street level were each marked by a slightly projecting gable with small round arch.

Textual References

"Extension of the Cheney Block, Hartford, Conn." *AABN* 2 (Oct. 27, 1877): 345.

Hitchcock, *Richardson*, 1966, pp. 164–167.

Lewis, Arnold, and Morgan, Keith. *American Victorian Architecture: A Survey of the 80's and 90's in Contemporary Photographs.* New York: Dover, 1975, p. 45. (Reprint of *L'Architecture américaine*, Paris, 1886.)

O'Gorman, *Selected Drawings*, pp. 110–113, 215.

Stephens, Suzanne. "Richardson on the Half Shell." *PA* 61 (Nov. 1980): 92–95.

"Stores for Messrs. R. and F. Cheney, Hartford, Conn." *New York Sketchbook of Architecture* 2 (Sept. 1875): pl. 35.

Van Rensselaer, *Works*, p. 67.

Miscellaneous Resources

Drawings: Houghton Library, Harvard University.

Photographs: Connecticut Historical Society; Connecticut State Library; Hartford Public Library; Houghton Library, Harvard University; Stowe-Day Foundation.

Sketchbook: Houghton Library, Harvard University.

58a
R. and F. Cheney
Building, Hartford,
Connecticut, 1875–
1876 (ca. 1880);
Houghton Library,
Harvard University.

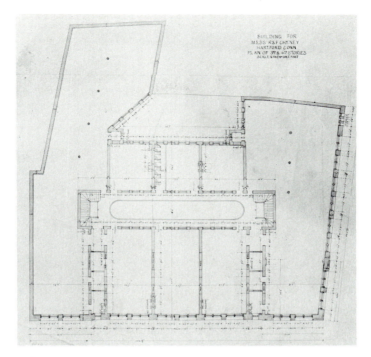

58b
Cheney Building,
plan of third and
fourth floors show-
ing irregular shape
of site and central
light court; Hough-
ton Library, Har-
vard University.

58c
Cheney Building,
corner detail; Ar-
nold Lewis and
Keith Morgan,
*American Victorian
Architecture: A
Survey of the 70's
and 80's in Con-
temporary
Photographs.*

59
Joseph H. Choate House Alterations, 1875   G&R
50 West Forty-seventh Street
New York, New York
Demolished

Joseph Hodges Choate (1832–1917) was a leading New York attorney known for his role in the breakup of the Tweed ring. He was ambassador to Great Britain from 1899 to 1905 and served as a delegate to the International Peace Conference at The Hague in 1907.

Choate commissioned minor remodeling to his New York residence in 1875. The alterations, which cost about $4,000, were discovered by Kramer during research in the New York City Department of Buildings.

Textual Reference

Hitchcock, *Richardson*, 1966, pp. 307–308 (see note iv–1 quoting Kramer).

60
All Souls Church Alterations, 1875   G&R
245 Fourth Avenue
New York, New York
Demolished 1931

All Souls Unitarian Church was erected in 1853 from a design by Jacob Wrey Mould (1825–1886), a New York architect. Of red and white banded brick and stone, the church was done in the Byzantine style and was known locally, because of its appearance, as the "Beefsteak Church." Nothing has been discovered of Richardson's minor renovations, costing only $1,300. The church was destroyed by fire in 1931.

Textual References

The Hotel Guest's Guide for the City of New York. New York: William P. Cleary and Company, 1871, p. 136.

King, Moses, ed. *King's Handbook of New York* 2d ed. Boston: Moses King, 1893, pp. 385–386.

Hitchcock, *Richardson*, 1966, pp. 307–308 (see note iv–1 quoting Kramer).

Miller's Strangers Guide for the City of New York. New York: James B. Miller, 1872, p. 79.

Van Zanten, David T. "Jacob Wrey Mould: Echoes of Owen Jones and the High Victorian Styles in New York, 1853–1865." *JSAH* 28 (Mar. 1969): 41–57.

61
New York State Capitol,
1875–1886 (1867–1899)
G&R
State Street
Albany, New York

The forty-year history of the construction of the New York State Capitol is complex. While the general outlines have been widely known, the specific roles of the various individuals involved were only recently the subject of detailed study for the New York State Capitol Symposium, March 1981.

The New York state government was first located in Albany in 1797. In 1809 it moved into the new state capitol which stood in the Capitol Park just below the crest of State Street hill. Agitation for a larger building began in 1860 and in 1863 a resolution was adopted to procure plans for a new building. Plans were drawn by Thomas Fuller (1822–1898) of Fuller and Jones, who had designed the Canadian government buildings in Ottawa, but no action was taken for two years. The Legislature also solicited invitations from various cities for the Capitol. Offers were received from New York City, Yonkers, Saratoga, Athens and Argyle, as well as Albany. Albany's offer of the land adjoining the existing capitol was accepted by the Legislature in 1865 and in 1866 the parcel was transferred. Construction to Fuller's new plans, chosen over those of several other architects, began in December 1867, with the understanding that the cost of the building would not exceed $4,000,000. Work proceeded slowly. The first stone of the foundation was laid July 7, 1869, and the cornerstone was placed June 24, 1871. In 1874, the project stopped for six months for lack of funds.

In response to complaints about the project, the Senate finance committee launched an investigation and in May 1875 issued a critical report. The existing capitol commission was abolished and a new commission, chaired by Lieutenant Governor William Dorsheimer (see no. 15) was established to manage the construction.

Under Dorsheimer's direction the commission expanded its responsibility. On July 15, 1875, it appointed an advisory board consisting of F. L. Olmsted, Leopold Eidlitz (1823–1906), a prominent New York architect, and H. H. Richardson. The board's mandate included not only advice regarding construction, but also questions of plan and design. The three men visited the site in late July and, in the months that followed, prepared a critique of the project. In September 1875 this group submitted some sketches suggesting revisions to the exterior. A detailed report and large scale drawings appeared in the following months. Meanwhile, the architect Fuller also prepared additional detailed plans and cost estimates. The advisory board's report to Dorsheimer's commission, published March 3, 1876, included the sketches suggesting a change from Renaissance to Romanesque for the capitol exterior. On March 11 *American Architect and Building News* summarized this report, discussed the original design, and showed both Fuller's model and the board's perspective view. The report admitted that Fuller's design was structurally sound, but argued that it was uninspired, showy, and inefficiently planned. Responding to the report, Fuller's letter stated that the legislature had been responsible for many of the faults as a result of its interference in planning and design.

The published design changes brought forth a storm of criticism: the mixing of Romanesque and Renaissance was widely attacked as against all the rules of art. Moreover, the board's professional propriety in criticizing Fuller's design was suspect. The New York chapter of the American Institute of Architects, under the leadership of Richard Morris Hunt, protested, as did architects from Chicago to Boston.

Richardson and the others did not reply, but continued their efforts at the direction of Dorsheimer and the commission. Although the legislature became embroiled in the controversy, a spirit of compromise prevailed. In June 1876 the legislature finally approved the board's revised plans, which had been changed to reduce exterior stylistic incongruities. Fuller's position thus became untenable, and he was dismissed on July 1, 1876. Two months later Olmsted, Eidlitz, and Richardson were officially retained as the architects, and they created the firm Eidlitz, Richardson & Co. to handle the commission.

The stylistic and managerial conflicts continued another year. Dorsheimer's position was weakened when he failed to receive the Democratic nomination for governor in August. Although Dorsheimer was reelected as lieutenant governor, Lucius Robinson of Elmira, an opponent of spending on the new capitol, won election as governor. Moreover, Fuller, who continued to maintain his Albany office, approached the legislature again in hopes of regaining the commission. The style of the capitol remained in dispute, and a succession of prominent architects testified on Fuller's behalf.

The legislature finally passed a spending appropriation requiring that the capitol be finished in the Italian Renaissance of its original design. But the measure was vetoed by Governor Robinson, who believed that all spending on the building was a waste. A smaller appropriation was passed by a veto-proof margin. Nevertheless, subsequent work on the project dragged on for many years after the 1879 completion date originally envisioned by Eidlitz, Richardson, and Olmsted in 1876.

In June 1877, after the legislature's adjournment, the Dorsheimer Commission met and accepted a broad Richardsonian interpretation of Renaissance design. Richardson had written to Olmsted in March that the building might be finished in François Ier or Louis XIV, which qualified as Renaissance. Richardson's revisions of the roof actually followed French Renaissance forms more closely than Italian. Thereafter Dorsheimer's Commission was not significantly challenged, and work proceeded under Richardson, Eidlitz, and Olmsted. Closing his Albany office, Fuller eventually returned to Ottawa.

Richardson and Eidlitz divided between them the redesign of the capitol. The exterior was jointly developed, though Richardson's influence prevailed for the walls and roof and Eidlitz's for the tower which was never executed. In the interior Eidlitz designed the assembly chamber and related spaces, while Richardson proceeded with the senate and executive chambers, second court of appeals, state library, and western stair.

Although work was slowed by a shortage of funds after 1877, parts of the capitol were opened and put to use as they were completed. The assembly was opened in 1879 and the senate in

1881. The governor's chambers were completed in 1880. When Grover Cleveland became governor in 1883, he appointed Isaac Perry commissioner of the capitol. Eidlitz, Richardson, and Olmsted were retained as consultants, but Perry took over direction of the work on a regular basis. Construction continued after Richardson's death for thirteen years. Perry directed the work on the western stair and added sculpture not in Richardson's design. He also directed execution of the state library. The building was finally declared complete January 1, 1899.

The New York Capitol remains in use today, although it has been somewhat altered over the years. While a few Richardson pieces still remain in the halls, most of the original furniture has been replaced. Richardson's state library burned in 1911 and his court of appeals was moved intact to the Court of Appeals Building in 1917. The senate chamber was restored in 1978 and rededicated the next year. The building is open to the public and tours are given daily.

The basic plan of the New York Capitol is a square with central courtyard and a tower at each corner. The building consists of five stories plus basement and attic. The exterior of white granite topped with modified hip roofs of red tile is rugged in character. The Renaissance stories by Fuller are separated from those by Eidlitz and Richardson with a transitional third floor so that the mix is not jarring.

Richardson, with Stanford White, began design of the senate chamber in May 1876. In fall 1876 they were still working on it. Although a final set of drawings had been prepared by December 1876, Stanford White's letter to Augustus Saint-Gaudens in May 1878 indicates that the room was still in design. Funds were appropriated for its construction only in 1880. The plan of the senate reduced the size of the pre-existing space given to Richardson by creating a lobby at each end over which were the arcaded visitors' galleries. The room is over 50 feet in height and has an oak-beamed ceiling. The lower walls are finished in gray Knoxville granite, Mexican onyx, and Siena marble, the arcade columns in red-brown granite, and the arches in Siena marble.

The court of appeals and governor's chambers were also in design in 1876. The executive chamber was completed in 1880 and the appeals courtroom in 1881. Each has a fireplace set in an inglenook under an arched wood beam. The executive chamber is paneled in mahogany and the court of appeals in red oak.

The design of the western staircase was altered by Perry in its execution. Construction began in 1884, only two years before Richardson's death, and continued until 1898. It was structurally complete in 1897, but Perry's sculptural embellishments took another year to finish. The staircase fills a well measuring 70 by 77 feet and rising 119 feet to a skylight. In section it shows use of elliptical arches. Although Richardson had indicated only minimal sculpture, Perry turned it into a portrait museum in stone. As a result it cost nearly $1,500,000 and earned the nickname "Million Dollar Staircase."

Textual References

Albany and the New York State Capitol. Brooklyn: A. Witteman, 1901.

"The Albany Capitol." *AABN* 1 (April 8, 1876): 113, 114–115.

Albany Illustrated. Albany: Argus, [ca. 1900].

The Capitol at Albany, N.Y. New York: Judson and Gordon, 1889.

"The Designs for the Albany Capitol." *AABN* 1 (March 18, 1876): 93–94.

"End of Reading Room: State Library in the New York State Capitol, Albany, N.Y." *AABN* 59 (Jan. 1, 1898): 7.

"The Experts and the New York Capitol." *AABN* 2 (March 17, 1877): 85.

Hitchcock, Henry-Russell, and Seale, William. *Temples of Democracy: The State Capitols of the U.S.A.* New York: Harcourt Brace Jovanovich, 1976, pp. 150–154, 200–203.

Hitchcock, *Richardson*, 1966, pp. 161–171.

Howell, George R., and Tenney, Jonathan. *Bicentennial History of Albany: History of the County of Albany, New York, from 1609 to 1886.* New York: W. W. Munsell, 1886, pp. 449–457.

"Mr. Fuller's Reply." *AABN* 1 (Apr. 1, 1876): 105, 106–107.

Murlin, Edgar L. *An Illustrated Legislative Manual: The New York Red Book.* Albany: J. B. Lyon, 1903, pp. 464–481.

"The New Architecture at Albany." *AABN* 5 (Jan. 18, 1879): 19–21; (Jan. 25, 1879): 28–29.

"The New York State Capitol." *AABN* 1 (Apr. 15, 1876): 125.

"The New York State Capitol at Albany." *AABN* 2 (Jan. 13, 1877): 15.

New York State Capitol Symposium Proceedings. Albany: Temporary State Commission on the Restoration of the Capitol, forthcoming.

New York State Senate Chamber History. Albany: Temporary State Commission on the Restoration of the Capitol, 1974.

O'Gorman, *Selected Drawings*, pp. 122–131.

Olmsted, Frederick L., Eidlitz, Leopold, and Richardson, Henry H. *Report of the Advisory Board Relative to the Plans of the New Capitol.* Albany: Argus, 1877.

"Opening of the New York Senate Chamber." *AABN* 9 (March 12, 1881): 165–166.

"Report on the New York State Capitol." *AABN* 1 (Mar. 11, 1876): 81–85.

The Restored Senate Chamber, State of New York. Albany: Temporary State Commission on the Restoration of the Capitol, 1979.

Reynolds, Cuyler. "The New York Capitol Building." *ARec* 9 (October. 1899): 142–157.

Roseberry, Cecil R. *Capitol Story.* Albany: State of New York, 1964.

"Upper Portions of the State Capitol, Albany, N.Y.: From the Southeast." *AABN* 49 (Feb. 12, 1898): 55.

Van Rensselaer, *Works*, pp. 73–77.

Weise, Arthur J. *History of the City of Albany.* Albany: E. H. Bender, 1884, pp. 483–486.

"Work on the Capitol at Albany." *AABN* 3 (Apr. 20, 1878): 138.

Miscellaneous Resources

Drawings: Houghton Library, Harvard University; Office of the New York State Architect.

Photographs: Albany Institute of History and Art; Albany Public Library; Boston Athenaeum; Houghton Library, Harvard University; Library of Congress; New York State Library.

Archives: New York State Library.

Letters: Olmsted Papers, Library of Congress; Saint-Gaudens Papers, Baker Library, Dartmouth College.

61a
New York State
Capitol, Albany,
New York, 1875–
1886 (1867–1899),
perspective drawing
of original scheme
by Thomas Fuller;
McKinney Library,
Albany Institute of
History and Art.

61b
New York State Capitol, first design alterations proposed by Richardson, Eidlitz, and Olmsted (largely the work of Eidlitz); State of New York (Cecil R. Roseberry, *Capitol Story*, 1964).

61c
New York State Capitol, later design proposal by Richardson, Eidlitz, and Olmsted (advanced terrace was later replaced by a stair); McKinney Library, Albany Institute of History and Art.

61d
New York State
Capitol, east eleva-
tion; State of New
York and Hough-
ton Library, Har-
vard University.

61e
New York State
Capitol, southwest
front; *AABN* 62
(Oct. 15, 1898).

61f
New York State
Capitol, west eleva-
tion; McKinney Li-
brary, Albany
Institute of History
and Art.

61g
New York State
Capitol, senate
chamber; Mc-
Kinney Library, Al-
bany Institute of
History and Art.

61h
New York State
Capitol, governor's
chambers; Mc-
Kinney Library, Al-
bany Institute of
History and Art.

61i
New York State
Capitol, court of
appeals courtroom;
McKinney Library,
Albany Institute of
History and Art.

61j
New York State Capitol, western stair, designed by Richardson but executed by Perry; Houghton Library, Harvard University.

61k
New York State Capitol, western stair, designed by Richardson, but executed by Perry; McKinney Library, Albany Institute of History and Art.

1876

62
Zborowski Project (?), 1876–1879   G&R

The Zborowski project is a completely unknown Richardson design. It is mentioned in letters from Richardson to Olmsted beginning in February 1876, but there are no known descriptions of the project and no drawings with the name Zborowski. Nor is there a listing for Zborowski at the Olmsted Site and Archives in Brookline.

Miscellaneous Resources

Letters: H. H. Richardson Papers, Archives of American Art Microfilm Roll 643.

63
Rev. Henry Eglinton Montgomery Memorial, 1876–1877   G&R
Church of the Incarnation
209 Madison Avenue
New York, New York

Henry Eglinton Montgomery (1820–1874) was rector at the Church of the Incarnation from 1855 until his death October 15, 1874.

Richardson's selection as designer of the memorial may have resulted from his having shared office space in 1866 (see no. 1) with architect Emlin Littel, the designer of the church building. Or it could have come through the efforts of Arthur Brooks, brother of Phillips Brooks (see no. 45) who was appointed rector in 1875 after Montgomery's death. From whichever source, Richardson received the commission early in 1876. The memorial mounted in the church was dedicated November 25, 1877.

Richardson's design, an arched gable in Cleveland light sandstone supported by two polished Lisbon marble columns, stands about twelve feet in height and about one and one-half feet in depth. Under the arch is a bronze medallion portrait of Montgomery in high relief by Augustus Saint-Gaudens. Below the bronze profile is a bronze plate with the record of Montgomery's involvement with the church and an inscription in polished letters on a gold ground.

Textual References

O'Gorman, *Selected Drawings*, p. 186.

Perkins, J. Newton. *History of the Parish of the Incarnation, New York City, 1852–1912.* Poughkeepsie, N.Y.: The Senior Warden, Frank B. Howard Press, 1912, pp. 114–115.

171

63a
Rev. Henry Eglington Montgomery memorial, Church of the Incarnation, New York, New York, 1876–1877; photo by Tom Gates.

64
Rush Cheney House Project,
ca. 1876   G&R
South Manchester, Connecticut

Richardson's success in the design of the Cheney Building in Hartford (no. 58) led to commissions from the Cheney family for their residences in the village of South Manchester.

The Rush Cheney house project is known only from the drawing published in the *New York Sketchbook of Architecture* in September 1876. The design must date from early 1876 or perhaps even 1875, but no plan drawing of the Rush Cheney house is known.

The perspective drawing showed a large house of a somewhat irregular, but basically rectangular plan. It was topped by a steep roof with the main gable running longitudinally and subsidiary gables projecting front and back. Like the Sherman house (no. 51), the first floor was stone, and the walls above were shingled with some areas of stucco and half-timber. The fenestration was ample. A porte cochere projected from the front gable, with a second floor balcony above the first floor carriageway. Many of the detail features, such as the barge boards at the front gable, were similar to the details of the Sherman house.

Hitchcock has suggested that the general massing of the house was by Richardson, but that the details were worked out by his assistant Stanford White.

Textual References

"Dwelling House for Rush Cheney, Esq. South Manchester, Conn." *New York Sketchbook of Architecture* 3 (Sept. 1876): pl. 36.

Hitchcock, *Richardson*, 1966, p. 141.

64a
Rush Cheney house project, South Manchester, Connecticut, ca. 1876; *New York Sketchbook of Architecture* 3 (Sept. 1876).

F. H. Harris Flats Project,
ca. 1876   G&R
Springfield, Massachusetts

65a
F. H. Harris flats project, Springfield, Massachusetts, ca. 1876, Richardson, sketchbook, fol. 60r, with Harris Flats notes and sketches; Houghton Library, Harvard University.

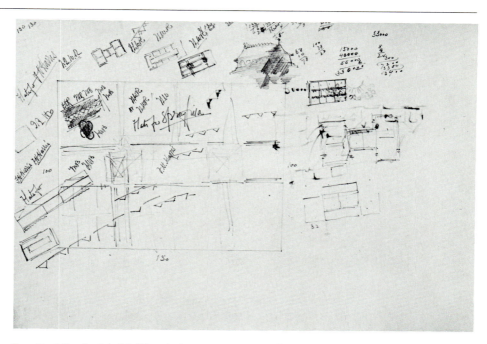

In 1876 Frederick H. Harris (1823–1911) was the cashier of the Third National Bank of Springfield, in 1886 its president. He was also a director of the Springfield Fire and Marine Insurance Company. How he came to consider building "flats" is unknown, but his contact with Richardson probably developed during construction of the Unity Church (no. 1) of which he was a leading supporter.

The Harris Flats project is known only from a brief mention on fol. 60r in Richardson's sketchbook. On the same page are the initials, F. L. W. R., of Richardson's youngest child, Frederick Leopold William Richardson, born July 10, 1876, and named for his collaborators on the New York State Capitol (no. 61): Frederick Law Olmsted, Leopold Eidlitz, and William Dorsheimer. From this it is possible to infer a mid-1876 date for the Harris Flats project. Otherwise, the project remains unknown.

This is the last project found in Richardson's sketchbook. He apparently abandoned sketchbook studies after 1876 in favor of sketches on small sheets of blue or buff personal stationery.

Textual Reference

O'Gorman, *Selected Drawings*, p. 216.

Miscellaneous Resource

Sketchbook: Houghton Library, Harvard University.

Winn Memorial Public Library, 1876–1879   G&R
88 Montvale Street
Woburn, Massachusetts

Charles Bowers Winn (1838–1875), a leather dealer, bequeathed funds for construction of a library building to memorialize his father, Jonathan Bowers Winn (1811–1873); the elder Winn had founded the Woburn Library in 1855 with a donation of $300. Accepted by the town February 17, 1876, the bequest required that the building house "oil paintings" as well as books and that a competition be held to determine the architect.

The competition was held in 1876, including designs submitted in October by Cummings and Sears, Peabody and Stearns, Snell and Gregorson, Ware and Van Brunt, and Gambrill and Richardson. Richardson's design was not selected before December 15, 1876, as his letters to Olmsted indicate, and Van Rensselaer dates the project's entrance into the office March 1877. His design was published in the March 3, 1877, *American Architect and Building News*.

Working drawings, produced in April and May 1877, formed a basis for the construction contract signed by Norcross Brothers May 22, 1877 for $71,625.50. Construction was superintended by T. M. Clark and completed in 1878. Although the library occupied the building in October 1878, it was not officially opened until May 1, 1879.

The Winn Library is the only one of Richardson's library buildings that has not been enlarged. But the building has been somewhat altered by the removal of the wood screens between the entry and stack wing and the introduction of fluorescent lights in the stack wing vault.

The Winn Library is among the most complex of Richardson's library designs. The plan is organized along a longitudinal axis with stack wing, reading room, picture gallery, and museum totaling 163 feet in length. The museum, designed as an octagon, appears almost separate from the rest of the building. Centered on the cross axis of the reading room, the main three-story gable projects forward and backward from the otherwise long rectangular mass of the stack wing and picture gallery. A seventy-seven-foot stair tower topped by a peaked roof is placed at one side of this gable, and the entry porch fills the reentrant angle of the reading room and picture gallery. The exterior random ashlar shows the richest polychromy Richardson ever used. The fenestration of the stack wing is a strip of windows running along its entire length. The stack wing interior has two levels of tiered alcoves and is spanned by a wood barrel vault. Richardson also designed all of the library furnishings.

Richardson was fortunate that his mature career coincided with the rise of the American public library movement. The flowering of public education and the spread of interest in cultural developments led to the creation of many town lending libraries. This was only the first of several library buildings Richardson designed.

While his designs are now often regarded as architectural masterpieces, Richardson's approach was at odds with policies advocated by the American Library Association. The ALA pressed for use of flexible modular shelving for book storage; Richardson designed monumental book rooms with inflexible tiered alcoves.

Textual References

"Accepted Design for the Town Library, Woburn, Mass." *AABN* 2 (Mar. 3, 1877): 68.

Annual Reports of the Library Committee of the Town of Woburn. Woburn: Town of Woburn, 1875–1879.

Cutter, William R. "A Model Village Library." *New England Magazine* n.s. 2 (Feb. 1890): 617–625.

Gilkerson, Ann M. "The Public Libraries of H. H. Richardson." Honors thesis, Smith College, April 1978.

Hitchcock, *Richardson*, 1966, pp. 171–173.

O'Gorman, *Selected Drawings*, pp. 156–159.

"The Public Library, Woburn, Mass." *AABN* 19 (May 1, 1886): 210.

Rudenstein, Roy. "The Libraries of H. H. Richardson." Senior thesis, Harvard University, April 1975.

Van Rensselaer, *Works*, pp. 67–69.

Miscellaneous Resources

Drawings: Houghton Library, Harvard University.

Photographs: Boston Athenaeum; Society for the Preservation of New England Antiquities; Woburn Public Library.

Letters: H. H. Richardson Papers, Archives of American Art Microfilm Roll 643; Olmsted Papers, Library of Congress.

66a
Winn Memorial
Public Library,
Woburn, Massa-
chusetts, 1876–
1879, floor plan;
AABN 2 (Mar. 3,
1877).

66b
Winn Library; Soci-
ety for the Preser-
vation of New
England Antiqui-
ties, photo by Bald-
win Coolidge.

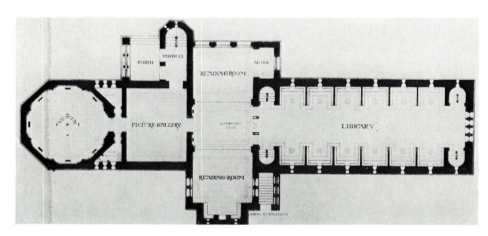

66c
Winn Library, rear
of stack wing and
reading room
(1972).

66d
Winn Library, de-
tail of entry (1972).

66e
Winn Library, interior of stack wing with wood barrel vault; Society for the Preservation of New England Antiquities, photo by Baldwin Coolidge.

66f
Winn Library, interior of reading room; Society for the Preservation of New England Antiquities, photo by Baldwin Coolidge.

1877

67
R. and F. Cheney Building
Addition Project,
ca. 1877   G&R
Main Street
Hartford, Connecticut

Following the success of the large commercial Cheney Building, opened in 1876 (no. 58), the Cheney family evidently asked Richardson to design an addition on the lot immediately across the alley to the north of their structure.

Richardson's design, known only from a published perspective drawing, was for a four-story building topped by a sloped roof broken by a dormer. The first story in stone was marked by a broad arch over a bay shop window. The upper floors were in brick with three arched windows at the second floor and five at the third and fourth. A turret running the height of the upper floors marked the front corner of this addition, which was attached to the existing Cheney Building by a second-floor covered walkway with twisted columns and a sloped roof.

Textual References

Hitchcock, *Richardson*, 1966, p. 161.

"Project for Cheney Block Annex." *AABN* 2 (Oct. 27, 1877): 345.

Van Rensselaer, *Works*, p. 68n.

67a
R. and F. Cheney
Building addition
project, Hartford,
Connecticut, ca.
1877; *AABN* 2
(Oct. 27, 1877).

68
Oliver Ames Free Library,
1877–1879   G&R
53 Main Street
North Easton, Massachusetts.

Oliver Ames I (1779–1863) moved from Bridgewater to North Easton in 1803 to begin the manufacture of shovels. In the period of railroad and canal expansion which followed, Ames prospered by supplying digging and trenching equipment. In 1844 his sons Oakes (1804–1873) and Oliver II (1807–1877) assumed management of the company. They also became involved in railroads beginning in 1855, and were major suppliers of trenching tools to the Union Army in the Civil War. Later they helped finance and construct the Union Pacific Railroad (see no. 73).

On his death Oliver II left $50,000 in trust for a library. The will specified that it was to be a private institution, not owned by the town, but held in trust for the public. The bequest was carried out by the children of Oliver II, Frederick Lothrop (F. L.) Ames (1835–1893) and Helen Angier Ames (1836–1882). F. L. Ames was graduated from Harvard in 1854, in the same class with Charles Gambrill but before Richardson enrolled in 1855. That Trinity Church (no. 45) had been recently completed and Richardson was involved in another memorial library project in Woburn (no. 66) may have influenced the Ames family in selecting Richardson. F. L. Olmsted may have been another point of contact since F. L. Ames was deeply involved in horticulture. Homolka speculates that Richardson may already have tried for another Ames family project, the North Easton Unity Church, built by John Ames Mitchell (no. 53).

The commission, according to Van Rensselaer, entered Richardson's office September 1877. The building was under construction in 1878 and completed in 1879; but it was not opened until 1883, possibly because of cost overruns. The final cost of the building, furnishings, books, and investments in a permanent fund was probably over $80,000.

In 1931 the children's wing in red brick was added to the rear, an addition that eliminated the original lavatory and document room. Additional shelving has been incorporated in the original stack wing to accommodate a greater number of acquisitions.

Richardson's design for the Ames Library is basically rectangular in plan with the major rooms, the stack wing, hall, and reading room, arranged longitudinally. A broad gable projects forward from the north end of the longitudinal mass. This gable is marked by the arched entry to the outside porch on the first floor and by a row of five arched windows separated by pairs of short columns supporting the arches on the second. The stack wing windows form a horizontal band, each group of three separated by four short columns. Construction is of warm light brown Milford granite laid in random ashlar with dark reddish brown Longmeadow brownstone trim. The roof is red-orange tile over a wood barrel-vaulted stack wing ceiling. The fireplace in the reading room is largely the work of Stanford White. The original stone and present bronze medallions of Oliver Ames II were designed by Augustus Saint-Gaudens.

Richardson's success on this project assured him of the continued friendship and patronage of the Ames family. This eventually led to a total of five North Easton buildings, as well as several designs for Boston and an important monument in Wyoming.

Textual References

"The Ames Memorial Building, North Easton, Mass." *Monographs of American Architecture* no. 3. Boston: Ticknor, 1886.

"The Ames Memorial Library, North Easton, Mass." *AABN* 13 (June 30, 1883): 307.

The Architecture of Henry Hobson Richardson in North Easton, Massachusetts. North Easton: Oakes Ames Memorial Hall Association and Easton Historical Society, 1969.

Brown, Robert F. "The Aesthetic Transformation of an Industrial Community." *Winterthur Portfolio* 12 (1977): 35–64.

Gilkerson, Ann M. "The Public Libraries of H. H. Richardson." Honors thesis, Smith College, April 1978.

Hitchcock, *Richardson*, 1966, pp. 185–188.

Homolka, Larry J. "Henry Hobson Richardson and the 'Ames Memorial Buildings.'" Ph.D. dissertation, Harvard University, 1976.

———. "Richardson's North Easton." *AF* 124 (May 1966): 72–77.

"Mr. Richardson's Work at North Easton, Mass." (Book Review). *AABN* 18 (May 8, 1886): 223–224.

Rudenstein, Roy. "The Libraries of H. H. Richardson." Senior thesis, Harvard University, April 1975.

"Sketch for Public Library at Easton, Mass." *AABN* 2 (Nov. 3, 1877): 352.

Van Rensselaer, *Works*, pp. 68–69.

Miscellaneous Resources

Drawings: Houghton Library, Harvard University.

Photographs: F. L. Ames Estate (Langwater); Houghton Library, Harvard University; Society for the Preservation of New England Antiquities.

eot A15

68a
Oliver Ames Free
Library, North Eas-
ton, Massachusetts,
1877–1879, floor
plan; "The Ames
Memorial Building,
North Easton,
Mass.," *Mono-
graphs of American
Architecture*, no. 3.

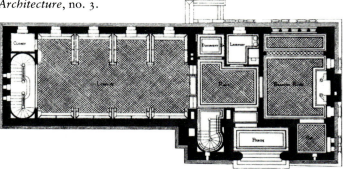

68b
Ames Free Library,
ca. 1880; Hough-
ton Library, Har-
vard University.

68c
Ames Free Library
and Ames Memo-
rial Building (see
no. 72); *Mono-
graphs of American
Architecture*, no. 3;
Society for the
Preservation of
New England
Antiquities.

68d
Ames Free Library,
detail of entry
(1972).

68e
Ames Free Library,
interior of stack
wing; *Monographs
of American Archi-
tecture*, no. 3;
Society for the
Preservation of
New England
Antiquities.

68f
Ames Free Library,
fireplace; *Mono-
graphs of American
Architecture*, no. 3;
Society for the
Preservation of
New England
Antiquities.

1878

69
James Cheney House Project,
ca. 1878 G&R
South Manchester, Connecticut

James Woodbridge Cheney (1838–1919) was the nephew of Rush Cheney, for whom Richardson had designed a house (no. 64) and a commercial block (no. 58).

The design of the James Cheney house is known from the plan and perspective drawing published in *American Architect and Building News*, May 25, 1878, the original of which is at Houghton Library, Harvard University. The drawing shows a large rectangular house with an interior central hall with stair and fireplace, surrounded by subordinate spaces including drawing room, dining room, and downstairs bedroom. Stables were connected to the house by a covered walk. The first floor was to be built of stone laid in random ashlar, with shingles at the second floor and stucco and half-timbered panels on two front gables.

The house follows in the series begun by the Sherman house (no. 51). The drawing was signed by Stanford White, and the design must be considered largely his. This was the last project White designed before leaving Gambrill and Richardson and the last known project before the partnership of Gambrill and Richardson was dissolved. (Another design for the Cheney House, by architect W. E. Cushing, was published in *American Architect and Building News* about two years later. Why Richardson lost the commission to Cushing is unknown.)

Textual References

Hitchcock, *Richardson*, 1966, pp. 162–163.

"House for James Cheney, Esq., South Manchester, Conn." *AABN* 8 (July 17, 1880): 30 (W. E. Cushing design).

"House for James Cheney, Esq., South Manchester, Conn." *AABN* 3 (May 25, 1878): 183.

Scully, *Shingle Style*, p. 81.

Miscellaneous Resources

Drawings: Houghton Library, Harvard University.

69a
James Cheney
house project,
South Manchester,
Connecticut, ca.
1878; *AABN* 3
(May 25, 1878).

70

H. H. Richardson Studios, 1878–1884
25 Cottage Street
Brookline, Massachusetts
Demolished ca. 1890?

When Richardson moved to Brookline in May 1874 to supervise construction of Trinity Church, he rented the Samuel Gardner Perkins House, erected in 1803. His landlord was Edward William (Ned) Hooper (1839–1901), who had graduated along with Richardson from Harvard in 1859 (and from Harvard Law School in 1861). Hooper, Harvard Treasurer from 1876 to 1898, was a connoisseur of fine art and knew Augustus Saint-Gaudens, John La Farge, and Harvard Professors Ephraim W. Gurney and Henry Adams, who were married to his sisters, Ellen and Marian (Clover).

Initially Richardson carried out all of his architectural work in the small room next to the entrance of the Perkins house. For the four years while his partnership with Gambrill continued, preliminary sketches done here were sent to New York to be developed into construction documents. After the partnership dissolved Richardson set his office up in the east parlor of the house, but this soon proved inadequate. A series of additions were therefore extended outward from the southeast corner of the house to serve as drafting rooms and office space. By 1885 they had reached their greatest extent, shown in a plan published in the December 27, 1884 *American Architect and Building News*. The Richardson studios were demolished some time after Richardson's death. By 1892 Richardson's successors, Shepley, Rutan and Coolidge, had moved their offices to the office building of their own design at 1 Court Street, Boston, where their successors still occupy space today.

The design of the Richardson studios was basic, reflecting the serial nature of the additions which were extended further as Richardson's practice grew. Two ranges of drafting alcoves were joined at an obtuse angle with an exhibit and work area at the inside of the angle. These one-story flat-roofed shed spaces were of simple frame construction and earned an appropriate nickname, "the coops." Located at the point farthest to the south, Richardson's study was a fireproof masonry structure measuring twenty-five by thirty feet. It had bookshelves along one wall and a large fireplace at one end.

The nature of Richardson's practice in this home-studio is described in detail by O'Gorman. Its value as a congenial educational setting served to attract to Richardson many of the best new architectural graduates. But more importantly, given Richardson's ill health in his later years, which O'Gorman also discusses, the arrangement allowed him to supervise the progress of work in his office, yet retreat to his bed when necessary. Indeed, without this studio, Richardson might not have been able to design projects in the later years of his life.

Textual References

Hitchcock, *Richardson*, 1966, pp. 145–146.

Little, Nina Fletcher. *Some Old Brookline Houses*. Brookline: Brookline Historical Society, 1949, pp. 63–64.

O'Gorman, *Selected Drawings*, pp. 4–13.

"Sketches of the Studios of Mr. H. H. Richardson, Brookline, Mass." *AABN* 16 (Dec. 27, 1884): 304.

Van Rensselaer, *Works*, pp. 123–131.

Miscellaneous Resources

Photographs: Boston Athenaeum; Houghton Library, Harvard University; Society for the Preservation of New England Antiquities.

70a
H. H. Richardson
studios, Brookline,
Massachusetts,
1878–1884, plan;
AABN 16 (Dec. 27,
1884).

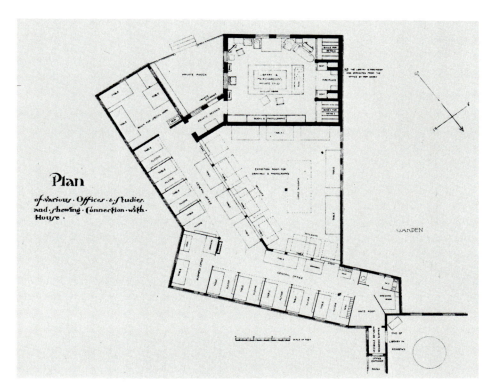

70b
Samuel Gardner
Perkins house;
Richardson studios
were attached at
left rear; Society for
the Preservation of
New England An-
tiquities, photo by
Baldwin Coolidge.

70c
Richardson's work space in Perkins House east parlor, ca. 1878; Houghton Library, Harvard University.

70d
Richardson studios, early view (ca. 1879–1880?); Houghton Library, Harvard University.

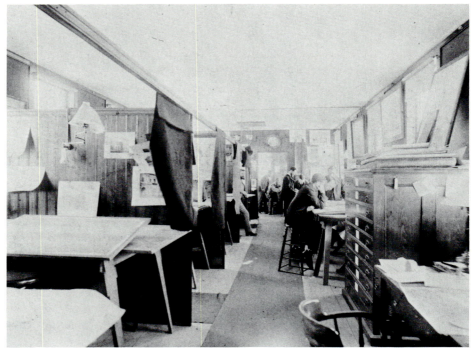

70e
Richardson studios,
drafting rooms;
Society for the
Preservation of
New England
Antiquities.

70f
Richardson studios,
Richardson's study;
Society for the
Preservation of
New England
Antiquities.

71
Sever Hall, 1878–1880
Harvard University
Cambridge, Massachusetts

James Warren Sever (1798–1871) provided a testamentary bequest for a Harvard building if his wife did not survive him. Mrs. Anne E. P. Sever did live six additional years, but in her will she confirmed her husband's bequest of $100,000 to Harvard for a building, $20,000 for a library in the building, and another $20,000 unrestricted.

The president and fellows of Harvard voted to appoint a committee to build Sever Hall and to select Richardson as architect April 29, 1878. Committee members were Edward W. Hooper (see no. 70) and John Quincy Adams, Henry Adams's brother. The first conference was held in May 1878, although the commission entered the office only in October according to Van Rensselaer. This coincides with the October 7 notification by Hooper to the Harvard Corporation that the $140,000 had been received.

Construction of Sever Hall by Norcross began in May 1879 and was completed by the fall of 1880. The structure, little altered, remains in use today as a classroom building.

In this design Richardson responded to the existing Georgian brick buildings of Harvard Yard. Evidently when Richardson was first consulted for the project in May 1878, the site had not been selected; Richardson may have been involved in the final selection. Sever Hall is a three-and-one-half-story rectangular building measuring 176 feet by 75 feet, constructed of red brick from the North Cambridge brickyard of M. W. Sands. The foundations and trim are of Longmeadow stone, and the hipped roof is covered with red-orange tile. The interior has a cross-hall plan on each floor and is divided into classrooms and recitation rooms. An innovative system for heating was developed with boilers in the basement and hot air distributed to the floors by means of four vertical shafts that supplied horizontal ductwork.

The design of the two main facades has been acclaimed by Hitchcock as among Richardson's best work. The west (front) and east (rear) facades are each divided into three sections by two cylindrical towers capped with steep roofs. The windows are arranged in horizontal groups with flat arches and molded brick mullions. Carved brick is used for the belt courses at the second and third floors and for the cornice. The door of the central section of the west facade is beneath an arch of molded brick and above this is a slightly projecting bay. On the east facade the central door is beneath a flat arch and above this is a slightly bulging broad bay supported on corbeled brick. Although the building was larger than many of the existing Harvard Yard structures, it did not overwhelm them. Today, with many more additions to the yard, Sever remains a fine example of Richardson's work, fitting his personal style to the context of a group of buildings of different periods and styles.

71a
Sever Hall, Harvard University, Cambridge, Massachusetts, 1878–1880, study of building placement and proposed quadrangle development; Harvard University Archives.

Textual References

Annual Report of the President and Treasurer of Harvard College, 1878–1879. Cambridge, Mass.: Harvard College, 1880, pp. 40–41.

Hitchcock, *Richardson*, 1966, pp. 188–192.

O'Gorman, *Selected Drawings*, pp. 144–147.

"Sever Hall, Cambridge, Mass." *AABN* 24 (Nov. 3, 1888): 206.

"Sever Hall, Cambridge, Mass." *American Buildings, Selections.* no. 2: pl. 22.

"Sever Hall, Harvard University." *The Brickbuilder* 1 (Mar. 1892): 24.

Twarog, Stanley A. "Notes on Heating and Ventilation of Nineteenth Century Buildings with Particular Reference to H. H. Richardson's Sever Hall." Typescript, Harvard University, January 1975.

Van Rensselaer, *Works*, pp. 69–71.

Miscellaneous Resources

Drawings: Harvard University Archives; Houghton Library, Harvard University.

Photographs: Boston Athenaeum; Library of Congress (Historic American Buildings Survey); Society for the Preservation of New England Antiquities.

Archives: Pusey Library, Harvard University.

71b
Sever Hall, first
floor plan; Hough-
ton Library, Har-
vard University.

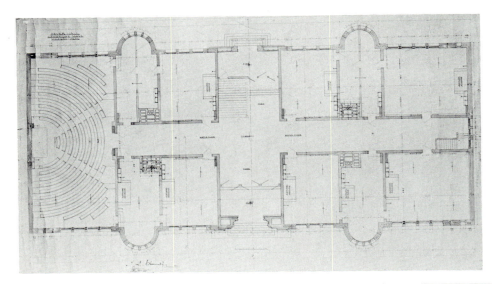

71c
Sever Hall, Har-
vard Yard; Van
Rensselaer, *Works*,
[1888].

71d
Sever Hall, detail of
entry; Boston
Athenaeum.

71e
Sever Hall (1972).

72

(Borland ?) Cottage Project, ca. 1878–1884(?) (Waterford, Connecticut?)

The Richardson drawing collection at Houghton Library includes three plans for an unidentified *L*-shaped house. The first of these is evidently a sketch by Richardson, and the two others are developed plans by a member of Richardson's staff. Richardson's sketch shows two floors superimposed and identifies rooms for "Mr. B.," "Mrs. B.," and "John." The other two drawings are individual plans of the house's two floors. All three drawings were executed in ink, but at the bottom of the two draftsman's plans is the notation in pencil, "Borland Cottage," that must have been added later.

If the pencil notation is correct, the most likely client would have been Dr. John Nelson Borland (1828–1890), who was graduated from Yale in 1848, received his M.D. at Harvard in 1851, and practiced medicine in Boston. Borland was an instructor in clinical medicine at Harvard from 1869 to 1873. Retiring to the New London area in 1878, he purchased a farm on Goshen Point in Waterford and lived there until his death in 1890. Borland had four children, two girls and two boys, one also named John.

The Borland family were Boston relatives of Julia Richardson. The correspondence between Julia Richardson and her mother, including the names of Mrs. Nelson Borland and (Miss) Alida Borland, in the Archives of American Art, begins April 10, 1867. The Borlands may have visited the Richardsons at Staten Island, and their friendship must have developed following the Richardsons' move to Brookline. It is possible that Dr. John Nelson Borland requested a house design from Richardson for his Connecticut property.

The *L*-shaped plan resembled the Andrews house (no. 44). At the interior angle of the *L* was the large central hall, around which were clustered the drawing room, dining room, and stairs. A broad covered porch ran along the outside of one leg of the *L*.

Textual Reference

O'Gorman, *Selected Drawings*, p. 107 (unidentified).

Miscellaneous Resources

Drawings: Houghton Library, Harvard University.

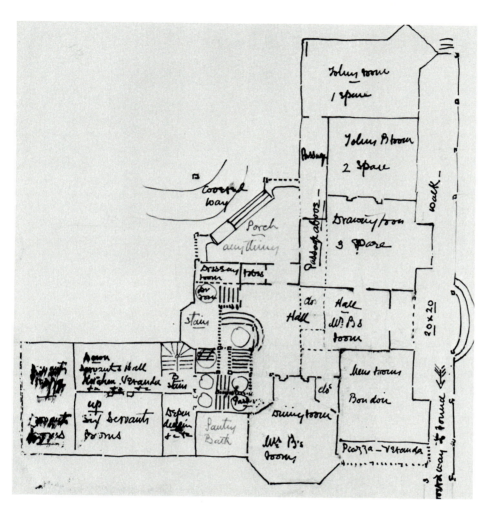

72a
(Borland ?) cottage
project, ca. 1878–
1884, sketch plan;
Houghton Library,
Harvard University.

1879

73
Oakes Ames Memorial Town Hall, 1879–1881
1 Barrows Street
North Easton, Massachusetts

Oakes Ames (see no. 68) was elected to the United States Congress from Massachusetts in 1862 and served until 1873. At President Lincoln's insistence, he became involved in the financing of the Union Pacific Railroad and helped reorganize the Crédit Mobilier construction financing company in 1867. The transcontinental railroad could not have been completed in 1869 without his efforts. In the financial scandal which erupted in 1872 because of the practices of Crédit Mobilier, Ames was censured by Congress, though his guilt was never proved. He retired to North Easton where he continued to protest his innocence and died suddenly in 1873.

After the commissioning of the Oliver Ames Free Library, the children of Oakes Ames, including Oliver Ames III, who would soon embark on a career in state politics (see no. 77), wished a suitable monument to their father and commissioned this project. The site was adjacent to the library in the center of North Easton.

Van Rensselaer lists the commission as entering the office in February 1879. Construction by Norcross began that summer following a bid of $29,910, the extras to cost $1,666. Homolka suggests the final cost may have been over $60,000. The hall was dedicated November 17, 1881, although landscape work by Olmsted continued to 1883 or perhaps 1885.

The building remained largely unused after it was built because town meetings continued to be held in Easton. Moreover, it was eventually closed, because the uppermost floor could only be reached by a single stair and was therefore considered a fire hazard. After 1950 a fire escape was added to the south side and the interior completely remodeled. The building is now used as a meeting hall.

The Ames Hall is basically rectangular in plan, measuring ninety-seven by fifty-one feet. The first floor was planned with a small auditorium and two service rooms, possibly a kitchen and dining room. The second floor was a large auditorium, and the attic was a Masonic Lodge hall. The planning was impractical, as the second floor could be reached only by two small stairs, one in the octagonal projecting tower to the northeast and one in the small projecting tower on the south. The exterior of the building, moreover, shows the results of improvisation during construction. The lower floor is constructed of warm light brown Monson granite trimmed with reddish brown Longmeadow brownstone. The upper floor is brick, but a dormer on the north side is half timber and stucco. The central mass of the building has a tall saddle-back hipped roof covered with red-orange tile. A lower gable roof, also of tile, extends over the southern section of the hall. The windows are all trimmed with brownstone. Roofed in stone, the northeast tower has a frieze with ornamental carvings of the signs of the zodiac in brownstone. A grand stair stretches from the street to the entry arcade through the rocky landscape by Olmsted.

Textual References

"The Ames Memorial Building, North Easton, Mass." *Monographs of American Architecture*, no. 3. Boston: Ticknor, 1886.

The Architecture of Henry Hobson Richardson in North Easton, Massachusetts. North Easton: Oakes Ames Memorial Hall Association and Easton Historical Society, 1969.

Brown, Robert F. "The Aesthetic Transformation of An Industrial Community." *Winterthur Portfolio* 12 (1977): 35–64.

Hitchcock, *Richardson*, 1966, pp. 197–199.

Homolka, Larry J. "Richardson's North Easton." *AF* 124 (May 1966): 72–77.

———. "Henry Hobson Richardson and the 'Ames Memorial Buildings.'" Ph.D. dissertation, Harvard University, 1976.

"Mr. Richardson's Work at North Easton, Mass." (Book Review) *AABN* 19 (May 8, 1886): 223–224.

Oakes Ames: A Memoir with an Account of the Dedication of the Oakes Ames Memorial Hall, at North Easton, Mass., Nov. 17, 1881. Cambridge, Mass.: Riverside Press, 1883.

"Town Hall, North Easton, Mass." *AABN* 13 (May 19, 1885): 235.

Van Rensselaer, *Works*, pp. 71–72.

Miscellaneous Resources

Drawings: Houghton Library, Harvard University.

Photographs: Ames Free Library; Houghton Library, Harvard University; Society for the Preservation of New England Antiquities.

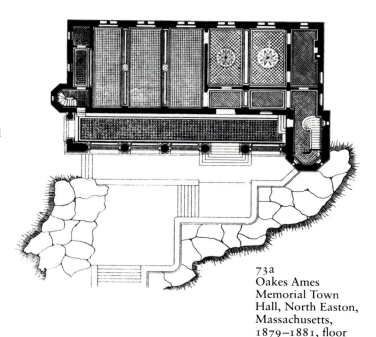

73a
Oakes Ames Memorial Town Hall, North Easton, Massachusetts, 1879–1881, floor plan; "The Ames Memorial Building, North Easton, Mass.," *Monographs of American Architecture*, no. 3.

73b
Ames Memorial
Hall; Houghton Library, Harvard
University.

73c
Ames Memorial
Hall, loggia; *Monographs of American Architecture*, no. 3.

73d
Ames Memorial
Hall (1972).

73e
Ames Memorial
Hall, detail of
tower (1972).

74
Rectory for Trinity Church, 1879–1880
233 Clarendon Street
Boston, Massachusetts

The Trinity Church rectory was built to provide a home for Phillips Brooks, the rector, three years after completion of Trinity Church (see no. 45). Richardson was selected as architect for Brooks's Back Bay residence, the project entering his office in April 1879 according to Van Rensselaer. Construction began later that year and was completed in 1880.

In 1893 the rectory roof was raised and a third floor was added. The design of the existing second story was repeated with the omission of three carved brick panels and the chimney bay. The interior wood trim and ornamental wood carving have been painted, but otherwise remain the same. From June to November 1974 minor remodeling by Shepley, Bulfinch, Richardson and Abbott, Inc. made the house more fit for the incoming rector and his wife, who had long been confined to a wheelchair. This remodeling did not affect the main spaces.

Richardson's design for the rectory fills a lot at the corner of Clarendon and Newbury Streets. The house is built of hard red brick from the North Cambridge brick yard of M. W. Sands. The pitched roof, with a transverse gable at each end, is broken by two dormers of unequal size over the front (west) elevation and twin dormers over the side (south) elevation. The main facade is broken by the deeply recessed entry porch spanned by a broad arch in brownstone. Brownstone is also used in continuous horizontal bands which circle the house. The irregular placement of windows reflects the interior planning. Between the pairs of windows at each end of the second floor are panels of cut brick decoration aligned with the groups of windows on the first floor.

Exterior chimneys are centered on the north and south facades. On the south side a chimney is connected to the wall by curved elements which allow the chimney to become part of a bay window. A small courtyard enclosed by a brick wall fills the space between the house and the alley to the north. The excellent quality of the brick masonry is now largely concealed by the growth of ivy over much of the building.

Textual References

Bunting, Bainbridge. *Houses of Boston's Back Bay: An Architectural History 1840–1917*. Cambridge, Mass.: Belknap Press of Harvard University Press, 1967, pp. 214–221.

Hitchcock, *Richardson*, 1966, pp. 200–202.

"House on Clarendon St., Boston, Mass." *AABN* 15 (May 3, 1884): 210.

[Sheldon, George?] *Artistic Houses: Interior Views of the Most Beautiful and Celebrated Homes in the United States*. New York: D. Appleton and Company, 1884, vol. 2, pt. 2, p. 163.

Miscellaneous Resources

Drawings: Houghton Library, Harvard University.

Photographs: Boston Public Library; Houghton Library, Harvard University; Society for the Preservation of New England Antiquities.

74a
Rectory for Trinity
Church, Boston,
Massachusetts,
1879–1880; Soci-
ety for the Preser-
vation of New
England
Antiquities.

74b
Rectory for Trinity
Church, detail of
entry; Society for
the Preservation of
New England
Antiquities.

74c
Rectory for Trinity
Church, with later
alterations (1978).

74d
Rectory for Trinity
Church, end of li-
brary; [George
Sheldon ?,] *Artistic
Houses*, 1884.

75
Benjamin W. Crowninshield
Apartment House Project,
1879–1880
349–351 Commonwealth
Avenue
Boston, Massachusetts

Richardson's contact with Benjamin W. Crowninshield dates from the Crowninshield House commission of 1868 (no. 9). In 1879 Crowninshield's real estate dealings led him to consider the construction of apartments in Back Bay Boston.

Richardson's design is known from three drawings in the collection at Houghton Library. The plan shows units arranged around a central court which would allow light to reach the interior. The two wide bays at the front were to be topped with gables, and the roof over the rest would have been hipped.

Textual References

Bunting, Bainbridge. *The Houses of Boston's Back Bay*. Cambridge, Mass.: Belknap Press of Harvard University Press, 1967, p. 474.

Hitchcock, *Richardson*, 1966, p. 217.

Miscellaneous Resources

Drawings: Houghton Library, Harvard University.

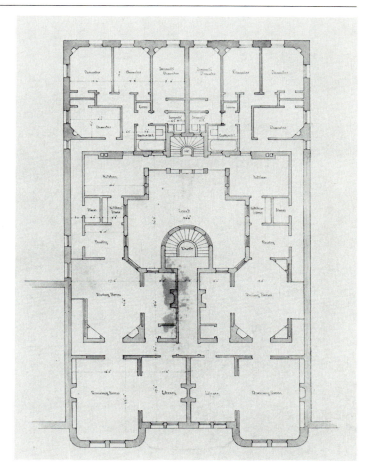

75a
Benjamin W. Crowninshield apartment house project, Boston, Massachusetts, 1879–1880, floor plan; Houghton Library, Harvard University.

76

Ames Monument, 1879–1882
Sherman (Buford), Wyoming

The monument to Oakes and Oliver Ames was another commission which came to Richardson through the patronage of the Ames family (see nos. 68, 73). The idea for the monument may have first been voiced as a rhetorical gesture. In the debate over the censure of Oakes Ames in the Crédit Mobilier scandal, Congressman John B. Alley, who believed in Ames's innocence, suggested that Congress should not censure Ames but build him a monument. On March 10, 1875, stockholders of the Union Pacific meeting in Boston authorized the construction of a monument. No action was taken until 1879, possibly because of continued litigation between the Union Pacific and the Crédit Mobilier. After 1879 F. L. Ames, as a member of the Union Pacific Executive Board, expedited the project and may have been responsible for including Oliver Ames II in the memorial: Oliver Ames II had served as acting president of the Union Pacific from 1866 to 1868 and as president from 1868 to 1871.

Van Rensselaer dates the project as entering Richardson's office November 1879. Construction by Norcross began in 1880 and was completed in 1882. For two years 85 men lived on the site in a dormitory compound, where reportedly no liquor or gambling was allowed. Cut from an outcropping in the area, the granite for the monument was skidded by ox teams a half-mile to the site. The total cost of the monument was $64,773.

Originally the Ames Monument stood 300 feet south of the Union Pacific main line at its highest elevation, 8,247 feet above sea level. But the line was moved south to eliminate unnecessary grades in 1901. Fifteen years later a proposal to move the monument to trackside was considered, but no action was taken. The town of Sherman, just north of the tracks, disappeared after the railroad moved. Today the monument stands alone and can be reached only by little-traveled country roads, although the exit from Interstate 80 is well marked. Unfortunately the portraits have been marred by rifle fire, and the base has been subject to spray-paint vandalism.

The monument was designed as a simple two-stepped pyramid measuring sixty feet square and standing sixty feet high. It is built of rough-hewn local granite, joined with mortar and occasional (concealed) metal clamps. At the base each stone measures about five by eight feet. The lower portion of the monument is laid up in random ashlar, but the upper section is straight courses. Two medallions, each measuring nine feet in height, are located thirty-nine feet above the base: one on the east face is the bust of Oakes Ames, the other on the west face is the bust of Oliver Ames. They were carved by Augustus Saint-Gaudens. On the north face of the monument near the top is the inscription, IN MEMORY OF OAKES AMES AND OLIVER AMES.

Olmsted praised the monument and its environment soon after its completion. Hitchcock, writing in 1934, stated that it was among Richardson's best works and was one of the finest memorials in America.

76a
Ames monument, Sherman, Wyoming, 1879–1882, stone quarrying; Wyoming State Archives, Museums and Historical Department.

76b
Ames monument; Wyoming State Archives, Museums and Historical Department.

Textual References

"The Ames Monument." *Annals of Wyoming* 2 (Jan. 1925): 50–52.

Dieterich, H. R., Jr. "The Architecture of H. H. Richardson in Wyoming: A New Look at the Ames Monument." *Annals of Wyoming* 38 (Apr. 1966): 49–53.

Hitchcock, *Richardson*, 1966, pp. 197–198.

Owen, W. O. "The Great Ames Monument Plot." *The Railroad Man's Magazine* 37 (Sept. 1918): 1–10.

Van Rensselaer, *Works*, p. 72.

Miscellaneous Resources

Photographs: State of Wyoming Archives and Historical Department.

Archives: Hebbard Collection, Western History Archives, University of Wyoming Library.

1880

77
Oliver Ames House Project, 1880
355 Commonwealth Avenue (at Massachusetts Avenue)
Boston, Massachusetts

Oliver Ames III (1831–1895), the son of Oakes Ames of North Easton (no. 73), began his rise in Massachusetts politics in 1880 when he was elected state senator from North Easton. He served as lieutenant governor from 1882 to 1885 and as governor from 1886 to 1889 when he was forced to retire by ill health. For his political career he required a Boston residence.

Plans found in the Houghton collection are dated March 1880 and initialed H. W. for Herbert Langford Warren, one of Richardson's assistants. In 1882 according to Bunting, Boston architect Carl Fehmer replaced Richardson as designer for the house. Fehmer's design was erected and remains standing today.

Richardson's design was to be a rectangular monumental building in masonry. The initial sketches showed a cruciform central space extending to the edges of the lot with subsidiary rooms filling the corners of the cross. In the presentation drawing one cross arm became the porch and vestibule, the second the main stair, the third the music room, and the fourth the library. The main entry would have faced Commonwealth Avenue, and a porte cochere was provided on the Massachusetts Avenue side.

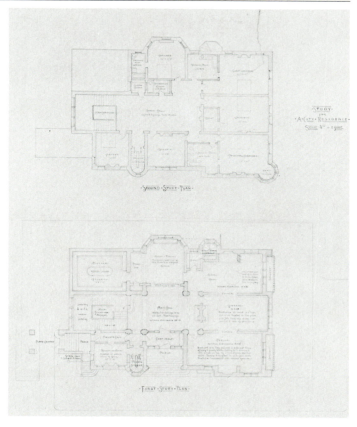

Textual References

Bunting, Bainbridge. *The Houses of Boston's Back Bay*. Cambridge, Mass.: Belknap Press of Harvard University Press, 1967, p. 212.

Hitchcock, *Richardson*, 1966, p. 217.

"House at Corner of Commonwealth Avenue and Chester Park, Boston, Mass." *AABN* 15 (May 3, 1884): 210 (Fehmer design erroneously stated as owned by F. L. Ames).

O'Gorman, *Selected Drawings*, pp. 72–74 ("Hay House," no. 8a on p. 80, is actually the Ames House Project).

Miscellaneous Resources

Drawings: Houghton Library, Harvard University.

Letters: Oliver Ames Papers, Easton Historical Society.

77a
Oliver Ames house project, Boston, Massachusetts, 1880, floor plans; Houghton Library, Harvard University.

78

F. L. Ames Gate Lodge, 1880–1881
135 Elm Street
North Easton, Massachusetts

To the east of the center of North Easton were the large Ames family estates. In 1859 F. L. Ames commissioned Snell and Gregorson of Boston to design his home on Langwater, his estate. John Ames Mitchell (see no. 53) made additions to the house in 1876. Meanwhile, the north part of the estate remained undeveloped, but Richardson, Olmsted, and Ames apparently began planning for it in 1879 and 1880. The ice house project (see no. 79) originally planned for this area was apparently abandoned in the decision to give this part of the estate a more rural character.

The decision to build the gate lodge must have been made in late 1879 or early 1880, since Van Rensselaer dates the project as entering the office March 1880. Construction by Norcross began that summer and was finished the following year. Olmsted later produced landscape designs for the estate which were carried out in 1886–1887. The gate lodge remains today in the private ownership of the Ames family.

Richardson's design was planned to serve several distinct purposes. It was oriented longitudinally and cut by the arched entry to the estate. The large room to the left of the entry was intended to serve as a storeroom for winter flowering plants. The two-story portion to the right of the entry had a caretaker's residence on the lower floor and a "bachelor hall" for masculine socializing and overflow guest bedrooms on the upper floor. Homolka suggests that the character of the building emerged in the design process and that the decision to construct the gate lodge of glacial boulders came rather late. The boulders are arranged with the largest at the bottom and the smallest at the top. The trim of the openings is Longmeadow brownstone. The hipped roof in bright red-orange tile contrasts boldly with the walls. Appearing almost as blisters, eyelid dormers barely break the roof surface. The two-story projection at the rear of the guest quarters offered covered access to a well. Some delicate naturalistic carving by Saint-Gaudens is found inside the upper level porch.

Textual References

"The Ames Memorial Buildings, North Easton, Mass./H. H. Richardson, Architect." *Monographs of American Architecture*, no. 3. Boston: Ticknor, 1886.

The Architecture of Henry Hobson Richardson in North Easton, Massachusetts. North Easton: Oakes Ames Memorial Hall Association and Easton Historical Society, 1969.

Brown, Robert F. "The Aesthetic Transformation of An Industrial Community." *Winterthur Portfolio* 12 (1977): 35–64.

"Gate Lodge to the Estate of F. L. Ames, Esq., North Easton, Mass." *AABN* 18 (Dec. 26, 1885): 304.

Hitchcock, *Richardson*, 1966, pp. 202–205.

Homolka, Larry J. "Richardson's North Easton." *AF* 124 (May 1966): 72–77.

————. "Henry Hobson Richardson and the 'Ames Memorial Buildings.'" Ph.D. dissertation, Harvard University, 1976.

"Mr. Richardson's Work at North Easton, Mass." (Book Review) *AABN* 19 (May 8, 1886): 223–224.

O'Gorman, *Selected Drawings*, pp. 191–192.

Scully, *Shingle Style*, pp. 91–92.

Van Rensselaer, *Works*, pp. 103–104.

Miscellaneous Resources

Drawings: Houghton Library, Harvard University.

Photographs: Houghton Library, Harvard University; Society for the Preservation of New England Antiquities.

78a
F. L. Ames gate
lodge, North Eas-
ton, Massachusetts,
1880–1881, floor
plans; "The Ames
Memorial Building,
North Easton,
Mass.," *Mono-
graphs of American
Architecture*, no. 3.

78b
F. L. Ames gate
lodge; Houghton
Library, Harvard
University.

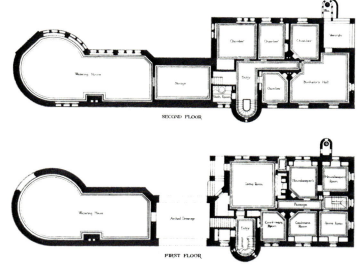

SECOND FLOOR

FIRST FLOOR

78c
F. L. Ames gate
lodge; *Monographs
of American Archi-
tecture*, no. 3.

78d
F. L. Ames gate
lodge; *Monographs
of American Archi-
tecture*, no. 3.

79
F. L. Ames Ice House Project,
ca. 1880–1881
F. L. Ames Estate (Langwater)
North Easton, Massachusetts

79a
F. L. Ames ice house project, North Easton, Massachusetts, ca. 1880–1881; Van Rensselaer, *Works*, [1888].

As F. L. Ames developed his estate, Langwater, he apparently considered constructing an ice house at the north end of the pond near the northern boundary of the estate at Elm Street. Ames, Olmsted, and Richardson discussed the project at an unknown date, and prepared a sketch.

The project was known from a sketch in Van Rensselaer's *Henry Hobson Richardson and His Works*, but remained unidentified until 1976 when Homolka found a reference to it in a letter from F. L. Ames to Olmsted. Written April 29, 1884 to settle accounts, the letter refers to the ice house only in passing and mentions no date for the design. Homolka suggests that it dates from about 1880

and was abandoned when Ames decided to make this area of the estate more picturesque, perhaps at the time that the gate lodge (no. 78) was completed.

Richardson's sketch shows a clear articulation of the elements required for the manufacture of ice. Ice, cut from the pond, would be moved up the ramp to the main storage building, a low, barnlike structure with an attached circular tower. A one-story wing to the rear would dispense ice to horse carts. The foundations and tower would have been masonry and the rest of the structure wood.

Textual References

Homolka, Larry J. "Henry Hobson Richardson and the 'Ames Memorial Buildings.'" Ph.D. dissertation, Harvard University, 1976.

Van Rensselaer, *Works*, p. 117 (illustration only).

Miscellaneous Resource

Letter: Olmsted Papers, Library of Congress.

80
Bridge in Fenway Park,
1880–1883
Charlesgate West
Boston, Massachusetts
Demolished 1965

81
Bridge in Fenway Park,
1880–1884
Boylston Street
Boston, Massachusetts

80a
Bridge in Fenway
Park, Boston, Mas-
sachusetts, 1880–
1883; Hitchcock,
Richardson, 1936.

80b
Bridge in Fenway
Park, detail of
metal work; photo
by Beaumont
Newhall.

F. L. Olmsted made his first presentation of designs for the Boston Fens to the Boston Park Commissioners in 1878. Although the project was developed as a park, its primary purpose was to provide a flood storage basin for Stony Brook and Muddy River. In January 1879 Olmsted presented a revised scheme, similar to that ultimately constructed, which required five bridges near the outflow of the Fens to the Charles River. Three of these bridges, at inconspicuous elevations, were designed by City Engineer Joseph Davis (at Beacon Street, Commonwealth Avenue, and the railroad tracks). For the two other bridges Olmsted sought Richardson's assistance. He wrote to Park Commission Chairman Charles H. Dalton and City Engineer Davis with this request in January 1880, and the commission entered Richardson's office in April 1880, according to Van Rensselaer.

Olmsted dictated the choice of plate girders for the Charlesgate West bridge over the railroad tracks. According to John C. Olmsted's letter of 1898, Richardson merely designed the decorative metalwork including the railings and lamps. Consequently sketches in the Houghton Library collection for a suspension bridge or a truss bridge do not resemble the one erected.

From the evidence uncovered by Zaitzevsky Richardson's role in the design of the stone Boylston Street bridge was also minimal. The Olmsted Site has preserved a sketch for the Boylston Street bridge, dated December 1878, showing a single-arched span. But Richardson's sketches preserved in the Houghton Library collection show his addition of the tourelles and his extension of a stone retaining wall from this bridge to the metal bridge over the railroad tracks. A blind arch was later introduced in the retaining wall.

Richardson's drawings for the Boylston Street bridge were submitted to the Park Commission July 1881, but revisions were required. The question of which stone to use was still unresolved in December 1881. Olmsted's proposal of boulders was replaced by the choice of seam-faced Cape Ann granite. Advertisements for construction of the metal bridge appeared in April 1882. Both bridges were completed by 1884. The metal bridge was demolished in 1965, while the environment of the stone bridge is now much more urban than it was when constructed in the 1880s.

Textual References

Hitchcock, *Richardson*, 1966, pp. 213–215.

O'Gorman, *Selected Drawings*, pp. 193–195.

Van Rensselaer, *Works*, p. 72.

Zaitzevsky, Cynthia. "The Olmsted Firm and the Structures of the Boston Park System." *JSAH* 32 (May 1973): 167–174.

———. "Frederick Law Olmsted and the Boston Park System." Ph.D. dissertation, Harvard University, 1975.

Miscellaneous Resources

Drawings: Houghton Library, Harvard University; F. L. Olmsted National Historic Site.

Photographs: Houghton Library, Harvard University; Olmsted Associates.

Reports: Boston Park Commission Annual Reports, 1879–1884.

81a
Bridge in Fenway
Park, Boston, Mas-
sachusetts, 1880–
1884; Houghton
Library, Harvard
University, photo
by Jean Baer
O'Gorman.

82
Stony Brook Gatehouse,
1880–1882
Fenway Park
Boston, Massachusetts

82a
Stony Brook gate-
house, Fenway
Park, Boston, Mas-
sachusetts, 1880–
1882; photo by Jeff
Sledge (1980).

82b
Stony Brook gate-
house; photo by
Jeff Sledge (1980).

F. L. Olmsted's design for the Back Bay Fens (see nos. 80, 81) required control of the outflow from Stony Brook into the Fens and thence to the Charles River. To achieve this, flood-gates were required at the junction of Stony Brook and the Fenway. In Olmsted's revised scheme of January 1879 a small gatehouse appeared there.

Evidently when Olmsted sought Richardson's assistance with the two bridges, he also consulted Richardson about the gatehouse. Although not listed by Van Rensselaer, John C. Olmsted credited Richardson with the design in his 1898 letter uncovered by Zaitzevsky. The design was submitted to the Boston Park Commissioners in July 1881 along with that for the Boylston Street Bridge and was ap-proved immediately.

In 1910 a second, matching gate-house was built beside Richardson's when Stony Brook was enlarged to a double channel. Both buildings remain in use today.

Richardson's design is a small rec-tangular building of Roxbury pud-dingstone laid up in random ashlar. The hipped roof is slate.

Textual References

Zaitzevsky, Cynthia. "Frederick Law Olmsted and the Boston Park System." Ph.D. dissertation, Harvard University, 1975.

———. "The Olmsted Firm and the Struc-tures of the Boston Park System." *JSAH* 32 (May 1973): 167–174.

Miscellaneous Resources

Photographs: F. L. Olmsted National His-toric Site, Brookline, Mass.

83
Thomas Crane Public Library,
1880–1882
40 Washington Street
Quincy, Massachusetts

In 1810 the family of Thomas Crane (1803–1875) moved to Quincy. There Crane attended school and trained as a stone–cutter before moving to New York in 1829. By 1835 he owned a stone yard and prospered by dealing in Quincy granite. Besides spending his summers in Quincy, Crane visited the town frequently until his death in 1875. On February 20, 1880 Albert Crane (1842–1918) offered the town of Quincy funds to construct a library as a memorial to his father.

In April 1880 Richardson and Crane traveled together to Quincy for their first discussions with the town selectmen, trustees, and their chairman Charles Francis Adams (1835–1915). Charles Francis Adams, Henry Adams's brother, had been graduated from Harvard in 1856 and may have known Richardson from that time. By 1880 he was a director of the Union Pacific Railroad and therefore well aware of Richardson's involvement with F. L. Ames and his previous design of the Ames Library (no. 68). Adams probably recommended Richardson to the Crane family. Although the first meeting was a "free consultation with suggestions," Richardson was awarded the commission soon afterward. Van Rensselaer gives April 1880 as the date the commission entered the office.

Ground was broken for the project in September 1880, construction by Norcross Brothers completed in the spring of 1882, and the building dedicated May 30, 1882. O'Gorman uncovered evidence that Richardson requested a bronze portrait of Thomas Crane by Saint–Gaudens in 1881, but it was never executed.

In 1908 an addition, the gift of the Crane family, was made to the rear by architect William M. Aiken, who had worked in Richardson's office. This wing houses additional stacks in a design matching Richardson's in scale, materials, and detailing. In 1939 the Albert Crane Memorial wing was built to the southeast with funds provided in the estate of Albert Crane and augmented by a Work Projects Administration grant. This wing nearly doubled the size of the library. In design it copies the original, although modifications were required to permit improved lighting. Otherwise, the original Richardson building remains largely unchanged.

Richardson's building is the simplest of his library designs. The overall plan is a rectangle with the three major spaces, stack wing, hall, and reading room arranged along the longitudinal axis. The stack wing is organized with tiered alcoves, but the ceiling is beamed, not a barrel vault as in earlier Richardson libraries. The woodwork is North Carolina pine. The exterior of the building is a rectangular mass with a sloped roof contained between two parapetted gables at the east and west ends. A single gable is placed two thirds of the way along the front from the west. To the right of center of this gable, a low broad arch leads to the entry porch or vestibule; to the left side of the gable is a round circular stair tower with a conical roof. The fenestration of the stack wing is arranged in a horizontal band which extends almost to the end wall. The rear slope of the roof is longer than the front, so the end gables are asymmetrical. The original rear facade with its central gable is now obscured by the 1908 addition. The foundation is of Quincy granite and the building of North Easton granite laid up in random ashlar. Including several horizontal courses which circle the building, the trim is Longmeadow brownstone. Two John La Farge windows are found in the reading room, though not in their original locations. Richardson was also responsible for the design of the library furniture.

The Crane Library is generally regarded by architectural historians as the masterpiece of Richardson's libraries. In this design he achieved the fullest integration of the various elements of the library program.

Textual References

Address of Charles Francis Adams, Jr. and Proceedings of the Dedication of the Crane Memorial Hall at Quincy, Mass., May 30, 1882. Cambridge, Mass.: John Wilson and Son—University Press, 1883.

Annual Reports of the Public Library. Quincy: Quincy Public Library and Thomas Crane Public Library, 1872–1939.

"The Crane Library, Quincy, Mass." *AABN* 13 (June 30, 1883): 306–307.

Edwards, William C. *Historic Quincy*, rev. ed. Quincy: City of Quincy, 1957.

Gilkerson, Ann M. "The Public Libraries of H. H. Richardson." Honors Thesis, Smith College, 1978.

Hill, L. Draper, Jr. *The Crane Library.* Quincy: Trustees of the Thomas Crane Public Library, 1962.

Hitchcock, *Richardson*, 1966, pp. 210–213.

McDevitt, Dorothy McCann. Untitled manuscript, Thomas Crane Library, n.d.

O'Gorman, *Selected Drawings*, pp. 160–161.

Rudenstein, Roy. "The Libraries of H. H. Richardson." Senior thesis, Harvard University, 1975.

Van Rensselaer, *Works*, pp. 78–80.

Miscellaneous Resources

Drawings: Houghton Library, Harvard University.

Photographs: Boston Athenaeum; Crane Library; Houghton Library, Harvard University; Society for the Preservation of New England Antiquities.

Archives: Crane Library.

83a
Thomas Crane
Public Library,
Quincy, Massachu-
setts, 1880–1882,
floor plan; Van
Rensselaer, *Works*,
[1888].

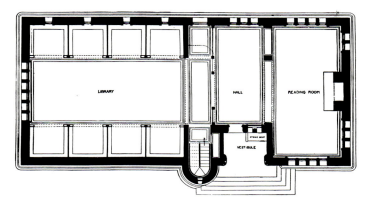

83b
Crane Library;
Society for the
Preservation of
New England
Antiquities.

83c
Crane Library, detail of entry (1972).

83d
Crane Library, end of stack wing and 1908 addition to rear (1972).

83e
Crane Library, interior of stack wing; Society for the Preservation of New England Antiquities.

83f
Crane Library, detail of stacks; *AABN* 13 (June 30, 1883).

83g
Crane Library, fireplace; *AABN* 37 (Aug. 20, 1892).

84
Dr. John Bryant House,
1880–1881
150 Howard Gleason Road
Cohasset, Massachusetts

Dr. John Bryant (1851–1908) was the son of Dr. Henry Bryant of Boston, a Cohasset summer resident. The younger Bryant received his M.D. from Harvard in 1878, and married Charlotte Olmsted, daughter of F. L. Olmsted, on October 15, 1878 in Boston.

The Bryant House commission entered Richardson's office September 1880 by Van Rensselaer's calculation. Plans in the Houghton Library collection, however, are dated November 24, 1880. Construction of the house was completed in 1881.

Bryant was an enthusiastic sailor who enjoyed racing small boats. His house is thus located on a magnificent site overlooking Cohasset harbor, originally on Margin Road, Hominy Point, now called Bryant Point. The building has suffered through fire, reconstruction, and additions by several owners. It now serves as a retreat, called Bellarmine House, for the Jesuit fathers of Boston College.

The Bryant house is a large, shingled building whose plan is basically rectangular, with the service wing at the rear projecting at an angle over a bridge. The main block of the house is two rooms deep, and the stair hall is separated from the living hall by the central fireplace. All of the interior rooms open into each other through large sliding doors. Entry to the house is from the carriageway below the service wing. Originally the profile was varied. The roofs were steeply pitched at a 45° angle, forming a *T* in plan with the east end gable facing the sea and a cross gable at the west. One small covered porch projected to the south and a two-story porch projected to the east. Exterior trim and decorative detail have been minimized.

Immediately following the Ames gate lodge (no. 78) and the Crane Library (no. 83), yet very different from them, the Bryant house demonstrates how broad Richardson's capabilities had become by this time.

84a
Dr. John Bryant Stables Project,
ca. 1880
150 Howard Gleason Road
Cohasset, Massachusetts

Six drawings in the Houghton Library collection show a project for the Bryant stables, which apparently were never constructed. The undated drawings show a small rectangular building of wood and shingles with a low hipped roof.

Textual References

Hitchcock, *Richardson*, 1966, pp. 205–209.

O'Gorman, *Selected Drawings*, pp. 97–98.

Pratt, Burtram J. *The Narrative History of the Town of Cohasset*, vol. 2. Cohasset: Committee on Town History, 1956, pp. 74–76.

Scully, *Shingle Style*, p. 93.

Miscellaneous Resources

Drawings: Houghton Library, Harvard University.

Photographs: Boston Athenaeum; Houghton Library, Harvard University.

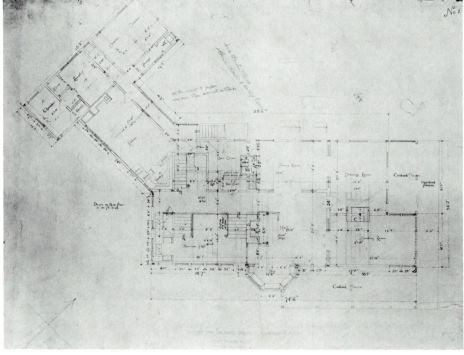

84a
Dr. John Bryant
house, Cohasset,
Massachusetts,
1880–1881;
Houghton Library,
Harvard University.

84b
Bryant house; first
floor plan; Hough-
ton Library, Har-
vard University.

234

84c
Bryant house; Boston Athenaeum.

84d
Bryant house, with later alterations (1972).

85
City Hall, 1880–1883
Eagle Street at Maiden Lane
Albany, New York

The Old City Hall in Albany was begun in 1829 and completed in 1832 on the site of the present city hall. It was a classical building in marble with a Doric temple front and gilded dome. In February 1880 it was destroyed by fire. A commission, created by legislative act, including Mayor Michael N. Nolan, Chairman of the Board of Supervisors Edward A. Maher, Erastus Corning, C. P. Easton, Robert C. Pruyn, Leonard G. Hun, Albertus W. Beeker, and William Gould, was responsible for erection of a new building.

Six architectural firms, four from Albany, one from New York, and H. H. Richardson from Brookline, were invited to submit designs in a limited competition. Richardson was probably invited to participate as a result of his involvement in the New York State Capitol (no. 61). Besides enumerating the required spaces, the competition program required a fireproof building and set a budget of $185,000. Richardson's building, with an estimate of $184,000 by Norcross Brothers, was selected, but following the substitution of granite for brownstone, requested by the committee, Norcross raised the estimate to $204,000. Van Rensselaer dates the project November 1880, which means it must have been designed earlier in the year. Construction by Norcross Brothers began in 1881 and was completed in 1883; the total cost including furnishings and fees was $325,000.

Richardson was not pleased with the interior, but felt that the limited budget required his solution. About 1919 the interior was altered by local architects C. G. Ogden and J. J. Gander. The exterior is considerably darkened with age.

The city hall is a three-and-one-half-story rectangular building with an attached tower, which stands 202 feet high. The building is constructed of pink Milford granite in random ashlar and trimmed with Longmeadow brownstone. The cruciform roof is composed of the major east–west hipped roof, which dominates the front dormer, and the north–south gabled roof. The front entrance is marked by a triple compound arch. The council chamber at the second floor opens to a loggia framed by four arches above the entry. Both the entry and the loggia are carved with intricate decoration. The windows on the south side are treated more simply. Intended for storage of city archives, the engaged square tower is topped by a steep pyramidal roof. A cylindrical stair tower is attached to the southeast corner of the building. A stone "bridge of sighs" and jail shown in an early sketch were never built.

Textual References

Albany and the New York State Capitol. Brooklyn: A Witteman, 1901.

"The Albany City-Hall Competition." *AABN* 9 (Apr. 2, 1881): 165–166.

Albany Illustrated. Albany: Argus, [ca. 1900].

"Alterations to the City Hall at Albany, N.Y." *American Architect* 117 (June 30, 1920): 809–815.

"The City Hall, Albany, N.Y." *AABN* 26 (July 13, 1889): 17.

"City Hall, Albany, N.Y., H. H. Richardson, Architect." *Building* 6 (May 28, 1887).

"Entrance to the City Hall, Albany, N.Y." *AABN* 25 (Mar. 2, 1889): 102.

"Entrance to the City Hall, Albany, N.Y." *American Buildings, Selections.* 2: pl. 23.

Hitchcock, *Richardson*, 1966, pp. 215–216.

Howells, George R., and Tenney, Jonathan. *Bicentennial History of Albany: History of County of Albany, New York, from 1609 to 1886.* New York: W. W. Munsell, 1886, pp. 677–678.

O'Gorman, *Selected Drawings*, pp. 132–134.

Van Rensselaer, *Works*, pp. 82–83.

Miscellaneous Resources

Drawings: Houghton Library, Harvard University.

Photographs: Albany Institute of History and Art; Albany Public Library; Boston Athenaeum; Society for the Preservation of New England Antiquities.

Specifications: Avery Library, Columbia University (gift of Henry-Russell Hitchcock).

85a
City Hall, Albany,
New York, 1880–
1883; Society for
the Preservation of
New England
Antiquities.

85b
City Hall, Albany,
rear corner; Boston
Athenaeum.

85c
City Hall, Albany,
rear elevation;
McKinney Library,
Albany Institute of
History and Art.

85d
City Hall, Albany,
detail of entry and
second floor loggia;
Society for the
Preservation of
New England
Antiquities.

1881

86
Boston & Albany Railroad
Station, Auburndale, 1881
Central Street,
Auburndale Center
Newton, Massachusetts
Demolished 1960s

In the late 1860s Chester W. Chapin (see no. 1) brought about the consolidation of the Western Railroad, of which he was president, and the Boston & Worcester, forming the Boston & Albany Railroad. The consolidated Boston & Albany embarked on a program of expansion in the early 1880s, both through the acquisition of other lines such as the Pittsfield and North Adams and the Ware River Railroads, and through construction of new track. This expansion program created a need for new facilities, including stations, freight houses and similar buildings.

Several of these projects were directed to Richardson through the combined efforts of James A. Rumrill and Charles Sprague Sargent (1841–1927). Rumrill, who was Richardson's classmate and friend, had been secretary and attorney for the Western Railroad and served in that capacity for the Boston & Albany until 1880, when he became vice-president of the line. In 1881 he joined the Board of Directors as well. Sargent, an 1862 graduate of Harvard and Richardson's Brookline neighbor and friend, became a director of the line in 1880.

The Boston & Albany responded to the post–Civil War growth of Newton, a Boston suburb, by the extension of commuter train service and eventually by the construction of a commuter line. Newton at that time consisted of a group of small separate villages, including, among others, Auburndale, Chestnut Hill, Waban, Newton Corner, Newton Highlands, Newton Upper Falls, and Newton Lower Falls.

In 1881, the Boston & Albany began the construction of stations on the main line to serve the commuter traffic generated by these villages. Richardson received several commissions for small commuter stations, of which that at Auburndale was the first. Van Rensselaer lists the commission as entering the office in February 1881. Construction by Norcross Brothers was apparently completed late the same year. The total cost of the station, including furnishings, was $16,290. Landscaping for the station grounds was designed by Olmsted.

Although commuter rail service continues over this stretch of the rail line, the Auburndale Station was destroyed when the Massachusetts Turnpike was constructed in the early 1960s.

The Auburndale station was designed as a simple low rectangle of granite dominated by a hipped roof. Doors and windows were openings cut in this granite box and trimmed with brownstone. The interior was divided into separate waiting rooms for men and women, a ticket office, and a baggage room at one end. The ticket office bay window protruded on the track side. The carriage porch was formed by extension of the roof to the front, and the trackside platform was covered by an extension of the roof as well.

Textual References

Around the Station: The Town and the Train. Framingham: Danforth Museum, 1978.

Hitchcock, *Richardson*, 1966, pp. 224–225.

"Railway Stations at Wellesley Hills, Waban, Woodland, Auburndale, Brighton, South Framingham, Palmer, Holyoke and North Easton, Mass." *AABN* 21 (Feb. 26, 1887): 103.

86a
Boston & Albany
Railroad Station,
Auburndale, New-
ton, Massachusetts,
1881; Boston Pub-
lic Library.

Robinson, Charles Mulford, "A Railroad
Beautiful." *House and Garden* 2 (Nov.
1902): 564–570.

[Sargent, Charles S. ?], "The Railroad Station at Auburndale, Massachusetts." *Garden and Forest* 2 (Mar. 13, 1889):
124–125.

Sweetser, Moses Foster, ed. *King's Handbook of Newton*, Boston: Moses King,
1889, pp. 189–190.

Van Rensselaer, *Works*, p. 100.

Miscellaneous Resources

Photographs: Boston Public Library; Library of Congress (Historic American
Buildings Survey).

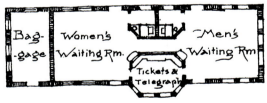

86b
Boston & Albany
Railroad Station,
Auburndale, plan;
AABN 21 (Feb. 26,
1887).

86c
Boston & Albany
Railroad Station,
Auburndale; Bos-
ton Public Library.

86d
Boston & Albany
Railroad Station,
Auburndale; Li-
brary of Congress
(Historic American
Buildings Survey,
photo by Cervin
Robinson, 1959).

86e
Boston & Albany
Railroad Station,
Auburndale, inte-
rior; Library of
Congress (Historic
American Buildings
Survey, photo by
Cervin Robinson,
1959).

87

Austin Hall, 1881–1884
Harvard University
Cambridge, Massachusetts

Edward Austin (1802?–1898) was born into a commercial family. He entered the shipping business at a young age and later turned to the management of railroads, becoming a director of the Boston & Worcester (later Boston & Albany). Although he had never attended Harvard, Austin proposed to University President Charles W. Eliot that he might provide for the greatest immediate need of the university in 1880. Dean Christopher Columbus Langdell (1826–1906), famous for his development of the case method for the study of law, had called for a new law building at Harvard in his 1879 report to Eliot. So Eliot told Austin that the Law School needed larger facilities. Austin replied that he detested lawyers, but then offered $100,000 for the construction of a law building to memorialize his older brother Samuel Austin (?–1858).

Van Rensselaer dates the commission as entering Richardson's office in February 1881. According to O'Gorman, when Norcross Brothers estimated the cost at about $150,000 in spring 1882, Edward W. (Ned) Hooper, Harvard treasurer (see no. 70), negotiated a compromise by which Austin gave additional funds, the law faculty yielded on some of their demands, and Richardson modified his specifications. Based on this compromise, Austin donated $135,000 and construction by Norcross began July 1, 1882. The building opened for students September 27, 1883, although some work remained unfinished. O'Gorman notes letters between Hooper and Austin in July

and October 1884 involving the interior finishes, carving, and the exterior inscription that were finally completed in December. Austin gave additional funds for painting in the spring of 1885. His gifts for Austin Hall totaled $140,500. While Austin, Richardson, and Norcross all had significant roles in the design and construction of this building, Hooper's role as arbiter was crucial according to O'Gorman.

As part of the Harvard Law School, the building remains in use today. The library has been moved to larger quarters, and the upstairs reading room is now a moot courtroom. But Richardson's original three first-floor lecture halls are still in use daily, with many of the original chairs.

Austin Hall is the only stone academic building built by Richardson. Whereas in the design of Sever Hall (no. 71) Richardson had worked in the context of Harvard Yard, for Austin Hall he had few contextual constraints. Perhaps for that reason an exceptional number of drawings for the project are found in the Richardson collection at Houghton Library. Their relationships are not fully clear. Although early sketches for Austin Hall resembled Sever, the design so changed as Richardson progressed that the only overtly similar element is the projecting cylindrical tower. Austin Hall is planned in a *T*-shape: the two-story central mass is flanked by two single-story wings. Behind the central mass extends the two-story reading room wing, the shaft of the *T*. The main facade is dominated by the triple-arched entry porch and the adjacent circular stair tower. Other than this vertical element, the main emphasis of the facade is horizontal with the light bands of the continuous lintel and sill above and below the second-story windows and the wide horizontal band in checkerboard pattern. The polychromy is achieved by the use of light and dark Longmeadow sandstone. Yellow Ohio sandstone is used for the elaborately carved entry arches. The two wings are simpler in design with a single strip of windows high on the facade. The rear of these wings is similar to the front. At the reentrant angle where the reading room wing projects from the main mass of the structure, Richardson introduced a quarter-circle wall which articulates the foyers of the main first floor lecture hall. The central mass is topped with a tall hipped roof to emphasize further its importance relative to the lower wings.

Van Rensselaer regarded the back of this building as one of Richardson's most beautiful architectural compositions. Hitchcock writes that the interior decoration and ornament, particularly of the reading room fireplace, is one of Richardson's finest achievements. Exposed tie beams in the reading room are carved with the heads of dragons and wild boars.

Textual References

Annual Report of President and Treasurer of Harvard College, 1878–1879. Cambridge, Mass.: 1880, pp. 83–86.

"Austin Hall—Harvard College Law School, Cambridge, Mass." *AABN* 17 (Mar. 28, 1885): 151.

"Austin Hall—Harvard Law School, Cambridge, Mass./H. H. Richardson Architect." *Monographs of American Architecture*, no. 1. Boston: 1886.

"The First Monograph of American Architecture." (Book Review). *AABN* 17 (May 16, 1885): 233.

Hitchcock, *Richardson*, 1966, pp. 227–232.

O'Gorman, *Selected Drawings*, pp. 148–154.

Van Rensselaer, *Works*, pp. 83–85.

Miscellaneous Resources

Drawings: Houghton Library, Harvard University

Photographs: Houghton Library, Harvard University; Library of Congress (Historic American Buildings Survey); Society for the Preservation of New England Antiquities.

Archives: Eliot Papers (1885–1886) and College Records, Harvard University.

Letters: Hooper Correspondence, 1880–1883, 1883–1887, Harvard University archives.

87a
Austin Hall, Har-
vard University,
Cambridge, Massa-
chusetts, 1881–
1884, floor plan;
Van Rensselaer,
Works, [1888].

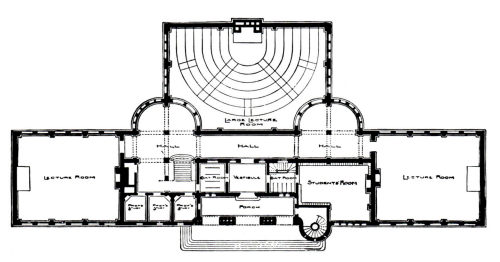

87b
Austin Hall;
Houghton Library,
Harvard University.

87c
Austin Hall, rear
view; Houghton Li-
brary, Harvard
University.

87d
Austin Hall, detail
of arch at entry
porch; Society for
the Preservation of
New England
Antiquities.

87e
Austin Hall, reading room; "Austin Hall, Harvard Law School, Cambridge, Mass.," *Monographs of American Architecture*, no. 1; Houghton Library, Harvard University.

88
F. L. Higginson House,
1881–1883
274 Beacon Street
Boston, Massachusetts
Demolished 1929

Francis Lee Higginson (1841–1923) was the younger brother of Henry Lee Higginson and partner with him and Charles A. Whittier in the Boston investment company Lee, Higginson, and Company from 1869 to 1885. The younger Higginson was a student at Harvard from 1859 to 1863, just after Richardson graduated. The two may have met through mutual Harvard acquaintances.

The commission, Van Rensselaer states, entered the office February 1881. Although Higginson and Whittier purchased adjoining lots in the Back Bay, they employed different architects. Whittier's architects, McKim, Mead and White, and Richardson met and agreed as to roof slope, exterior materials, and horizontal lines so that the two houses, though of independent design, were an exceptional example of architectural coordination.

Since the Whittier house was erected by Norcross Brothers, the Higginson house may have been as well. The two houses were demolished in 1929 to make room for a sixteen–unit apartment building.

Richardson's design for the Higginson house filled the full width of the fifty-five foot lot. The central hall on each floor adjoined the stair and a four-foot-wide light well with gas jets for light at night and air circulation. The primary rooms were placed in front or in back of the central hall with windows either to the street or to the back of the lot. A shallow round bay with conical roof projected from the front of the house, and a similar semicircular bay projected at the rear. The fronts of both the Higginson and the Whittier house were flat stone in horizontal courses at the ground level and brick above. Richardson continued the stone vertically through the entire height of the projecting bay. O'Gorman notes that although carving by Saint-Gaudens was planned for the front of the house, it was never executed.

Textual References

Bunting, Bainbridge. *Houses of Boston's Back Bay: An Architectural History 1840–1917*. Cambridge, Mass.: Belknap Press of Harvard University Press, 1967, pp. 221–222 (incorrectly identifies the house as the Henry Lee Higginson house).

Herndon, Richard. *Boston of Today*. Boston: Post Publishing Company, 1892, pp. 325–326.

Hitchcock, *Richardson*, 1966, pp. 218–221.

"Houses on Beacon Street, Boston, Mass." *AABN* 14 (Nov. 24, 1883): 246.

O'Gorman, *Selected Drawings*, pp. 75–77.

Perry, Bliss. *Life and Letters of Henry Lee Higginson*. Boston: Atlantic Monthly Press, 1921.

Thoron, W., ed. *The Letters of Mrs. Henry Adams*. Boston: Little, Brown, 1936, p. 442.

Van Rensselaer, *Works*, pp. 104–105.

Miscellaneous Resources

Drawings: Houghton Library, Harvard University.

Photographs: Society for the Preservation of New England Antiquities.

Letters: Saint-Gaudens papers, Baker Library, Dartmouth College.

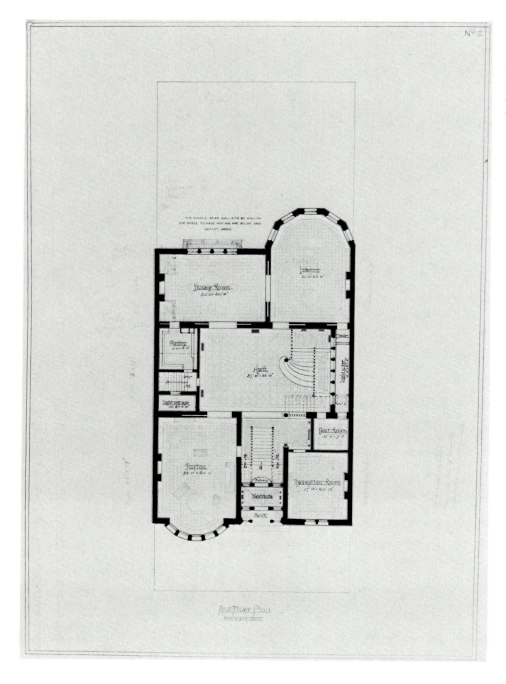

88b
F. L. Higginson and
C. A. Whittier
houses; Society for
the Preservation of
New England
Antiquities.

88c
F. L. Higginson
house; Society for
the Preservation of
New England
Antiquities.

89
**Robert Gould Shaw Monument
Project, 1881–1886 (1897)**
Boston Common opposite
Statehouse
Boston, Massachusetts

89a
Robert Gould Shaw
monument project,
1881–1886 (1897),
elevation; Hough-
ton Library, Har-
vard University.

Colonel Robert Gould Shaw (1837–1863) was the white leader of the Fifty-fourth Massachusetts Regiment, a black regiment formed to fight in the Civil War. Shaw died in the attack on Fort Wagner July 18, 1863.

The idea for the memorial to Shaw developed from the initiative of J. B. Smith, an escaped slave. The original gift grew to $23,000 once a memorial committee was formed. The city of Boston offered to donate $27,000 if the monument was located on the Boston Common.

Edward Atkinson (1827–1905), an economist and Richardson's Brookline neighbor, was chairman of the committee. Through his efforts the commission came to Richardson about February 1881. Richardson arranged for Saint-Gaudens to do the memorial tablet. On February 24, 1881 he wrote to Saint-Gaudens concerning setting a date for a meeting with the committee. Although Saint-Gaudens met with the committee in November 1881, his contract was not executed until February 1884.

Saint-Gaudens worked from plaster casts made from black Bostonians and produced a life-size relief sculpture of Shaw mounted on a horse leading his men. (In battle Shaw never actually rode a horse.) The sculpture was not completed until 1897, long after Richardson's death. The design was completed by McKim, Mead and White, and erected by Norcross Brothers. Henry Lee Higginson and Booker T. Washington spoke at the dedication, May 31, 1897.

The elevation sketch from the Houghton Library collection shows a single figure on a horse inside an architectural frame. A frieze is suggested below the main figure.

Textual References

Atkinson, Edward. "The Shaw Memorial and the Sculptor Saint-Gaudens." *The Century Magazine* 32 (May-Oct. 1897): 176–182.

Benson, Richard and Kirstein, Lincoln. *Lay This Laurel: An Album on the Saint Gaudens Memorial on Boston Common Honoring Black and White Men Together Who Served the Union Cause With Robert Gould Shaw and Died With Him July 18, 1863.* New York: Eakins Press, 1973.

Exercises at the Dedication of the Monument to Col. Robert Gould Shaw and the Fifty Fourth Regiment of Massachusetts Infantry. May 31, 1897. Boston: Municipal Printing Office, 1897.

McKay, Martha Nicholson. *When the Tide Turned in the Civil War.* Indianapolis: Hollenbeck Press, 1929, frontispiece.

O'Gorman, *Selected Drawings*, pp. 196–197.

Riley, Stephen T. "A Monument to Colonel Robert Gould Shaw." *Proceedings of the Massachusetts Historical Society* 75 (1963): 27–38.

Roe, Alfred S. *Monument, Tablets and other Memorials Erected in Massachusetts to Commemorate the Services of Her Sons in the War of the Rebellion 1861–1865.* Boston: Wright and Potter, 1910.

Miscellaneous Resource

Drawing: Houghton Library, Harvard University.

90

N. L. Anderson House,
1881–1883
1530 K Street at Sixteenth
Street N.W.
Washington, D.C.
Demolished 1925

Nicholas Longworth Anderson (1838–1892) came from Cincinnati to Harvard, where he was a classmate of Richardson's. He was a member of a military family and gave up the study of law to enlist as a private in the Sixth Ohio Regiment during the Civil War. At the end of the war he was brevetted a major general, the youngest in the army. Anderson and his wife moved to Washington in 1880 and selected Richardson to design their new house. The correspondence between Anderson and his son Larz (1866–1937), then at Exeter, discussed the project in detail.

Anderson purchased the site on the rapidly developing Sixteenth Street in 1881. The commission entered Richardson's office, according to Van Rensselaer, in April. Construction by Charles and Samuel Edmonston began in 1882. The original estimate of $33,000 proved unrealistic; the total cost was closer to $100,000. Anderson's letters indicated the family had moved into the house by October 15, 1883. Their first visitors were Marian and Henry Adams (see no. 119).

The house remained in the ownership of the Anderson family until 1918. It passed through a succession of owners until 1925 when it was demolished for the Carlton Hotel. Only minimal information about the house was available until the 1978 publication of *Sixteenth Street Architecture* by the Commission of Fine Arts.

The Anderson house was a simply massed two-and-one-half story brick building with a tall roof. In plan the house was organized with a central stair hall around which the entry, drawing room, library, dining room, and study were arranged on the first floor. On the second floor the bedrooms radiated from the stair hall. The interiors were finished with richly beamed ceilings, while oak, mahogany, and pine paneled the walls. John La Farge executed two stained glass windows for the dining room (apparently destroyed in the demolition). The exterior appeared as a simple mass with a round projecting corner bay; a facetted broad bay projected along the side (Sixteenth Street) elevation. The brickwork included some panels of octagonal brick tiles and others of terra cotta.

During construction the house was the subject of considerable discussion in Washington. Its exterior simplicity and massiveness contrasted with contemporary Victorian houses in the city. While several published drawings show a stable adjacent to the house, it does not appear in any photographs and was probably not executed.

Textual References

Anderson, Isabel, ed. *Larz Anderson, Letters and Journals of a Diplomat.* New York: Fleming H. Revell, 1940.

Anderson, Isabel, ed. *Letters and Journals of General Nicholas Longworth Anderson.* New York: Fleming H. Revell, 1942, p. 226.

Friedlander, Marc. "Henry Hobson Richardson, Henry Adams, and John Hay." *JSAH* 29 (Oct. 1970): 236.

Hitchcock, *Richardson,* 1966, pp. 221–222.

Kohler, Sue A., and Jeffrey R. Carson, eds. *Sixteenth Street Architecture.* Washington, D.C.: Commission of Fine Arts, 1978, 1:144–157.

[Sheldon, George?] *Artistic Houses: Interior Views of the Most Beautiful and Celebrated Homes in the United States.* New York: D. Appleton and Company, 1884, vol. 2, pt. 2, pp. 127–128.

Thoron, Ward, ed. *The Letters of Mrs. Henry Adams.* Boston: Little, Brown, 1936, p. 442.

Van Rensselaer, *Works,* p. 105.

Miscellaneous Resources

Drawings: Houghton Library, Harvard University.

Photographs: Boston Athenaeum; the Adams Papers, Massachusetts Historical Society; Society for the Preservation of New England Antiquities; Library of Congress (Frances B. Johnston collection).

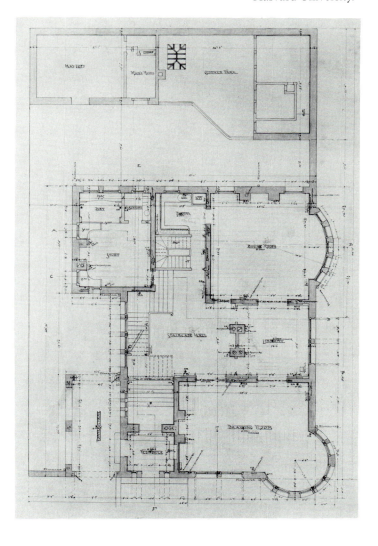

90a
N. L. Anderson house, Washington, D.C., 1881–1883, first floor plan; Houghton Library, Harvard University.

90b
N. L. Anderson
house; Society for
the Preservation of
New England
Antiquities.

90c
N. L. Anderson
house; Library of
Congress (Frances
B. Johnston
collection).

90d
N. L. Anderson
house, detail of ele-
vation; Boston
Athenaeum.

90e
N. L. Anderson
house, hall;
[George Sheldon?,]
Artistic Houses,
1884.

90f
N. L. Anderson
house, dining
room; [George
Sheldon?] *Artistic
Houses*, 1884.

91

Alida Borland House Project, ca. 1881
Back Bay
Boston, Massachusetts

Alida Borland was an unmarried Boston relative of Julia Richardson (see no. 72).

The Miss Borland house project, as it was originally called, is known only from seven drawings in the Houghton Library collection. Hitchcock suggested its date, 1881. The project did not proceed beyond early sketch studies, possibly because Alida Borland purchased a townhouse in Back Bay at 255 Commonwealth Avenue, which Bunting recorded as having been constructed in 1880 by W. Whitney Lewis for H. O. Roberts.

In plan and elevation the Borland project was similar to the Higginson house (no. 88), but modified to fit the narrower forty-foot-wide lot. The house was organized around the central stair hall with rooms at the front and back. A slightly off center round mass projected from the front of the three-story residence.

Textual References

Bunting, Bainbridge. *The Houses of Boston's Back Bay.* Cambridge, Mass.: Belknap Press of Harvard University Press, 1967, p. 474.

Hitchcock, *Richardson*, 1966, p. 217n.

Miscellaneous Resources

Drawings: Houghton Library, Harvard University.

Letters: H. H. Richardson Papers, Archives of American Art Microfilm Roll 1184.

91a
Alida Borland house project, Boston, Massachusetts, ca. 1881, elevation; Houghton Library, Harvard University.

92
Boston & Albany Railroad
Station, Palmer, 1881–1885
Depot Street
Palmer, Massachusetts

The Boston & Albany Railroad Station at Palmer was built to serve the junction of two rail lines, the Boston & Albany and the New London Northern (later Central Vermont). The commission came to Richardson through his friendships with James A. Rumrill and Charles S. Sargent (see no. 86).

Van Rensselaer gives August 1881 as the date the commission was received in the office. Final plans and specifications were sent to Rumrill in April 1882. Construction by Norcross Brothers was apparently not completed until early 1885. The cost was $53,616. F. L. Olmsted designed the landscaping in 1884.

The station remains, though in poor condition. The passenger sheds have been shortened and many of the windows are boarded up. A second floor was introduced across the originally two-story waiting room. The building now houses commercial concerns.

Richardson's design filled a wedge-shaped site between two pairs of crossing tracks. The building is nearly a right triangle with platforms along the two long sides (along the tracks) and the entrances on the end. The interior was planned with a large central double-height waiting room, a dining room and kitchen, and related minor spaces including ticket office, agents' offices, baggage rooms, and restrooms. The building is constructed of Monson granite trimmed with Longmeadow brownstone. It is totally surrounded by porches formed by the extension of the hipped roof, through which high dormers break to provide light for the interior.

Textual References

Annual Report of the Directors of the Boston & Albany Railroad Company to the Stockholders. Nos. 16, 17, 18. Boston: Rand Avery, 1884, 1885, 1886.

Around the Station: The Town and the Train. Framingham: Danforth Museum, 1978.

Eddy, Charles W. *Palmer Illustrated with Pen and Camera.* Ware, Mass.: 1884.

Hitchcock, *Richardson*, 1966, p. 225.

O'Gorman, *Selected Drawings*, pp. 176–177.

"Railway Stations at Wellesley Hills, Waban, Woodland, Auburndale, Brighton, South Framingham, Palmer, Holyoke and North Easton, Mass." *AABN* 21 (Feb. 26, 1887): 103.

Van Rensselaer, *Works*, p. 100.

Miscellaneous Resources

Drawings: Houghton Library, Harvard University.

Photographs: Library of Congress (Historic American Buildings Survey); Palmer Public Library.

Letters: General Correspondence, Olmsted Papers, Library of Congress.

92a
Boston & Albany
Railroad Station,
Palmer, Massachu-
setts, 1881–1885,
floor plan; *AABN*
21 (Feb. 26, 1887).

92b
Boston & Albany
Railroad Station,
Palmer; Charles W.
Eddy, *Palmer Illus-
trated with Pen and
Camera*, 1884; Pal-
mer Public Library.

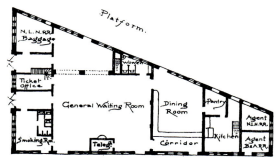

92c
Boston & Albany
Railroad Station,
Palmer (1972).

92d
Boston & Albany
Railroad Station,
Palmer (1972).

92e
Boston & Albany
Railroad Station,
Palmer; Library of
Congress (Historic
American Buildings
Survey, photo by
Cervin Robinson,
1959).

92f
Boston & Albany
Railroad Station,
Palmer, interior
with second floor
added; Library of
Congress (Historic
American Buildings
Survey, photo by
Cervin Robinson,
1959).

93
Pruyn Monument, 1881–1882
Albany Rural Cemetery
Albany, New York

Robert Hewson Pruyn (1815–1882) was a member of one of Albany's leading Dutch families. He was graduated from Rutgers and was successively corporation counsel for the city of Albany, a member of the Board of Aldermen, and speaker of the New York State Assembly. In 1861 Abraham Lincoln appointed him second minister to Japan. After his return from Japan he served as president of the National Commercial Bank and Trust Company of Albany.

The commission, according to Van Rensselaer, entered Richardson's office October 1881, long before Robert Pruyn died in 1882 and his wife, Jane Ann Lansing Pruyn (1811–1886), died in 1886.

The grave marker is a flat slab of polished pink granite, slightly slanted toward the front with lettering in a well-arranged inscription. A small cross and some foliate carving are in one corner.

The monument may be found in the southeast corner of section 30 of the cemetery. It has become dirty with age, and the lettering is slightly clogged.

Textual References

Hitchcock, *Richardson*, 1966, p. 227n.

Phelps, Henry P. *The Albany Rural Cemetery*. Albany and Chicago: Phelps and Kellogg, 1893, pp. 124–125.

93a
Pruyn monument,
Albany Rural
Cemetery, Albany,
New York, 1881–
1882 (1972).

94
Rev. Percy Browne House,
1881–1882
Front Street
Marion, Massachusetts

Percy Browne (1839–1901) was born in Dublin, but came to the United States as a young child. He was graduated from Kenyon College in the same class as a brother of Phillips Brooks (see no. 45). Rector of St. James Episcopal Church, Roxbury, from 1871 to 1901, he succeeded Phillips Brooks as president of the Clericus Club of Boston when Brooks became bishop of Massachusetts.

Van Rensselaer dates the commission in Richardson's office October 1881. It was among the least expensive of Richardson's original designs, costing only a little more than $2,500.

Although constructed as a summer residence, the house is now used all year. A number of alterations have been made, including the addition of a dormer at the north end, the extension of the front porch, and the enclosure of the back porch. Original pointed shingles on the dormers have been replaced by square-cut shingles. The interior has been modernized, but otherwise reflects the original. The house, hidden from the street by a low hedge, remains in private ownership.

The house is sited on a low hill overlooking Marion harbor. Richardson's plan is basically rectangular with rooms arranged along a longitudinal axis so that all would have a view of the harbor. A porch was cut into the center of the front of the house and an *L*-shaped porch wraps around the northwest (rear) corner. The house is two stories in height, but the gambrel roof gives it a deceptively small scale. The house is entirely covered in shingles and wood trim details are minimized with a resulting emphasis on surface continuity. Although the exterior appears small, the many large dormers and windows give the house a feeling of interior spaciousness.

Textual References

Hitchcock, *Richardson*, 1966, pp. 222–223.

Scully, *Shingle Style*, pp. 94–95.

Sommers, Olive Hill. *Three Centuries of Marion Houses*. Marion: Sippican Historical Society, 1972, p. 35.

Van Rensselaer, *Works*, pp. 105–106.

Miscellaneous Resources

Drawings: Houghton Library, Harvard University.

94a
Rev. Percy Browne
house, Marion,
Massachusetts,
1881–1882, floor
plan; Houghton Li-
brary, Harvard
University.

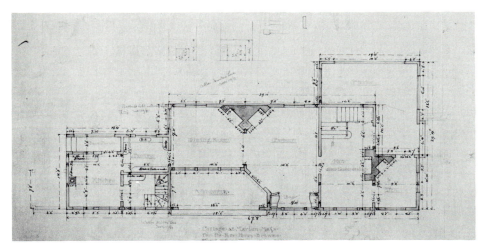

94b
Rev. Percy Browne
house, with later al-
terations; photo by
Berenice Abbott
(ca. 1934).

95
Old Colony Railroad Station, 1881–1884
80 Mechanic Street
North Easton, Massachusetts

F. L. Ames (see no. 68) served as a director of the Old Colony Railroad. In 1881 he personally commissioned this station which he conveyed as a gift to the railroad when it was completed.

Construction began in 1882 on the commission which entered Richardson's office in November of the previous year. F. L. Olmsted landscaped the grounds in 1884.

The Ames family in 1969 bought the station back from the New York Central Railroad for $15,000 and gave it to the Easton Historical Society. The original long passenger sheds are gone; otherwise the station remains. The Society has restored the building for use as a museum.

Richardson's design for the North Easton station is a simple rectangular block oriented parallel to and east of the tracks which run north-south. It was symmetrical with central lobby and ticket office dividing rooms for men and women. The building is covered by a broad hipped roof. On the track side, this roof joined those of the platform sheds. On the opposite side, a hipped projection of the roof carried on an independent pier forms a covered carriageway. The windows are grouped under broad slightly parabolic arches which the pier at the carriageway repeats. The major material of the building is granite, the trim is brownstone, and the roof is covered with slate. The wood framing members of the windows are decorated with carvings of snarling wolves' heads.

Textual References

"The Ames Memorial Building, North Easton, Mass." *Monographs of American Architecture*, no. 3. Boston: Ticknor, 1886.

The Architecture of Henry Hobson Richardson at North Easton, Massachusetts. North Easton: Oakes Ames Memorial Hall Association and Easton Historical Society, 1969.

Around the Station: The Town and the Train. Framingham: Danforth Museum, 1978.

Brown, Robert F. "The Aesthetic Transformation of an Industrial Community." *Winterthur Portfolio* 12 (1977): 35–64.

Gilbert, Bradford Lee. "Picturesque Suburban Railroad Stations." *Engineering Magazine* 2 (Nov. 1891): 336–349.

Hale, Jonathan. "Sic Transit." *AF* 140 (Nov. 1973): 80–81.

Hitchcock, *Richardson*, 1966, p. 226.

Homolka, Larry J. "Richardson's North Easton." *AF* 124 (May 1966): 72–77.

———. "Henry Hobson Richardson and the 'Ames Memorial Buildings.' " Ph.D. dissertation, Harvard University, 1976.

"Mr. Richardson's Work at North Easton, Mass." (Book Review) *AABN* 19 (May 8, 1886): 223–224.

O'Gorman, *Selected Drawings*, pp. 178–181.

"Railway Stations at Wellesley Hills, Waban, Woodland, Auburndale, Brighton, South Framingham, Palmer, Holyoke and North Easton, Mass." *AABN* 21 (Feb. 26, 1887): 103.

Van Rensselaer, *Works*, p. 100.

Miscellaneous Resources

Drawings: Houghton Library, Harvard University.

Photographs: Boston Athenaeum; Houghton Library, Harvard University; Library of Congress (Historic American Buildings Survey); Society for the Preservation of New England Antiquities.

Letters: General Correspondence, Olmsted Papers, Library of Congress.

95a
Old Colony Rail-
road Station, North
Easton, Massachu-
setts, 1881–1884;
Houghton Library,
Harvard University.

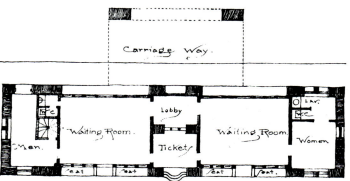

95b
Old Colony Rail-
road Station, North
Easton, floor plan;
AABN 21 (Feb. 26,
1887).

95c
Old Colony Rail-
road Station, North
Easton; Boston
Athenaeum.

95d
Old Colony Rail-
road Station, North
Easton (1972).

96

Old Colony Railroad Freight House Project, ca. 1881
Mechanic Street
North Easton, Massachusetts

96a
Old Colony Railroad Freight House project, North Easton, Massachusetts, ca. 1881, sketch; Houghton Library, Harvard University.

The Old Colony freight house was apparently planned at the time of the station commission (see no. 95) or soon afterward. A similar structure was built about 1890, but it was not of Richardson's design.

Known from drawings in the Houghton Library collection, the project was to have been a one-story structure with an attached two–story cylindrical tower intended as a water tower for servicing steam engines. The freight house would have been built of stone and probably shingles, its site south of Richardson's passenger station.

Textual References

Homolka, Larry J. "Henry Hobson Richardson and the 'Ames Memorial Buildings'." Ph.D. dissertation, Harvard University, 1976.

O'Gorman, *Selected Drawings*, pp. 178–181.

Miscellaneous Resources

Drawings: Houghton Library, Harvard University.

97
Boston & Albany Railroad Dairy Building, 1881–1883
Castle Street (between Tremont Street and Shawmut Avenue)
Boston, Massachusetts
Demolished before 1900

The Boston & Albany Dairy Building remains one of the most elusive of Richardson's commissions. An 1874 Boston city atlas shows a small milk depot on the site of the dairy building. The Boston & Albany apparently decided to replace this depot with much larger facilities. James A. Rumrill and Charles S. Sargent (see no. 86) must have directed this project to Richardson.

Van Rensselaer gives the date November 1881 for the commission's entry into Richardson's office. The construction contract with Norcross Brothers totaled $55,373. The Boston & Albany *Annual Report* for 1883 indicates an expenditure of $6,692 for a "New Milk Depot"—possibly the cost of completing construction in that year. However, no visual evidence of the construction of this project has been uncovered. Photographs taken of Castle Street between 1899 and 1901 during the construction of the elevated railway show the dairy building site to be vacant, leading some to speculate that it was never actually constructed. It was built but had been demolished by 1900.

The dairy building was designed for a long narrow site between Castle Street and the Boston and Albany Railroad tracks. Access from Castle Street was at the first floor, but the tracks, a full story below, were served from the basement. To fill this site, Richardson designed a four-floor building (including basement) measuring 345 feet by only 28 feet. The structure was to be plainly built of brick with a repeating window system of arched windows and dormers to break a sloped roof. A later study shows dormers extending down in the form of rectangular projections from the second story above the street. There was no ornament of any kind on this building.

Textual References
Annual Report of the Directors of the Boston & Albany Railroad Company to the Stockholders. No. 16. Boston: Rand Avery, 1883.

Hitchcock, *Richardson*, 1966, p. 226.

Miscellaneous Resources
Drawings: Houghton Library, Harvard University.

97a
Boston & Albany
Railroad Dairy
Building, Boston,
Massachusetts,
1881, elevation de-
tail; Houghton Li-
brary, Harvard
University.

E. F. Mason House Alterations, 1881–1882
Rhode Island Avenue and
Bath Road
Newport, Rhode Island
Demolished 1902

Robert Means Mason (1810–1879) was a partner in the leading Boston mercantile house Mason and Lawrence. He was also a leading member of the Episcopal Diocese of Massachusetts. At his death his Newport estate passed into the control of his two unmarried daughters, Ellen Francis Mason (1846–1930) and Ida Means Mason (1856–1928). The two Mason sisters, though only summer residents of Newport, were very active in the affairs of the community. Ellen Mason served as president of the Newport Civic League for many years. She also translated selections from Plato's works for publication in the United States. The *Portrait of Ida Mason*, painted in 1878 by William Morris Hunt, hangs in the Boston Museum of Fine Arts. When the two sisters died within two years of each other, they left an estate of over five million dollars almost entirely to charity.

In 1881 the Mason sisters turned to F. L. Olmsted for improvements to their Newport estate. Olmsted, in turn, requested Richardson's assistance in the remodeling of the Mason residence. In 1936 Hitchcock reported examining a plan for the remodeling, incorrectly identifying "Miss *Edith* Mason" as the client, but noted no features of interest. Unfortunately the drawing is now lost; the Houghton Library holds no drawings for the Mason project. While the Olmsted Site holds eight drawings of the Mason estate from 1881 to 1882 and another thirty-four from 1902 to 1920, none gives any indication of Richardson's project.

The house burned in 1902, and a new house was constructed on the property in 1903.

Textual Reference

Hitchcock, *Richardson*, 1966, p. 252n.

Miscellaneous Resources

Drawings: F. L. Olmsted National Historic Site.

Letters: General Correspondence, Olmsted Papers, Library of Congress.

William James House Project, ca. 1881–1884?
Quincy Street
Cambridge, Massachusetts

William James (1842–1910), known as the father of American psychology, was a member of the Harvard faculty from 1872 until his death. His contact with Richardson may have been through Henry Adams (see no. 119) or through any of Richardson's other Harvard faculty friends.

The James house project is known only from a single autograph sketch on Richardson's personal blue stationery. This sketch, now in the Houghton collection, is unfortunately undated. Another drawing of an unidentified house in the Houghton collection includes the notation, "see James House for upper story," but no upper story plan of the James house survives. This unidentified sketch, too, is undated. Richardson only began doing studies on blue stationery in 1876, so the house must be after that date.

The drawing shows only the first floor of a small house against one side of a lot measuring 100 feet by 112 feet. The basically rectangular design includes a large study, central stair hall, dining room, and kitchen.

Textual Reference

O'Gorman, *Selected Drawings*, p. 107.

Miscellaneous Resources

Drawings: Houghton Library, Harvard University.

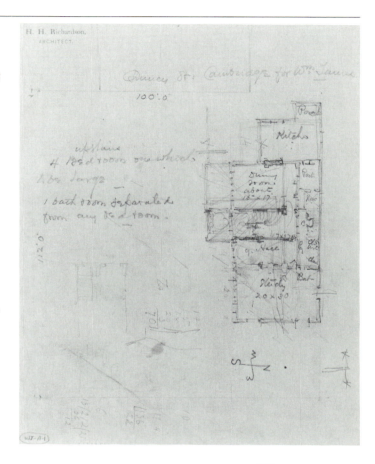

99a
William James house project, Cambridge, Massachusetts, ca. 1881–1884, floor plan; Houghton Library, Harvard University.

1882

100

Grange Sard, Jr., House, 1882–1885
397 State Street
Albany, New York

Grange Sard, Jr. (1845–1924), was a partner and later chairman of Rathbone, Sard and Company, an Albany stove manufacturer. He also served as president of Union Trust Company and Albany Home Building Company, and was on the boards of several Albany banks.

The commission, according to Van Rensselaer, entered Richardson's office January 1882, and construction was completed in 1885.

The house was occupied by Grange Sard until his death in 1924. The next year it was converted to apartments when a high rise apartment building was constructed at the back of the site. The interior has been modified but the facade is unchanged.

On a wide urban site the Sard house was built as a townhouse with a central stair hall and rooms along the front and back to take advantage of natural light. The house stands two-and-one-half stories tall with a third floor partially behind the sloping roof. The two prominent features are a projecting rounded mass which stands three-and-one-half stories in height and the deeply recessed porch with bulging parapet which earned the nickname "Sard's bathtub." The house is built of brownstone in alternating wide and narrow courses.

Textual References

Hitchcock, *Richardson*, 1966, pp. 250–252.

"House of Grange Sard, Esq., Albany, New York." *AABN* 24 (June 1, 1889): 247.

Miscellaneous Resources

Drawings: Houghton Library, Harvard University.

Photographs: Albany Institute of History and Art.

100a
Grange Sard, Jr.,
house, Albany,
New York, 1882–
1885; *AABN* 24
(June 1, 1889).

100b
Grange Sard, Jr.,
house (1972).

101

F. L. Ames Wholesale Store,
1882–1883
Bedford Street at Kingston
Street
Boston, Massachusetts
Demolished 1889

Richardson's North Easton patron, F. L. Ames (see no. 68), was involved in manufacturing, transportation, and real estate. The Bedford Street store was the first of several commercial projects which Richardson designed for Ames.

Van Rensselaer gives March 1882 as the date this commission came to Richardson's office. The building was erected the following year. Destroyed by fire November 28, 1889, it was replaced by a structure by Shepley, Rutan and Coolidge. This was later demolished, and the site is now occupied by a parking lot.

The design for the irregular Bedford and Kingston Streets site recalls that for the Cheney Building in Hartford (no. 58) of seven years earlier. The ground floor was designed as undifferentiated space to be leased as stores and shops, and the upper floors designed for offices. The broad arched windows of the first floor allowed ample natural light to penetrate the commercial space and allowed for display of merchandise. Above each of these first floor windows, a pair of arches framed windows for the next two floors and above each pair four arches framed the windows at the next floor. Behind a sloped roof the attic was lit by windows in high dormers continuing up from the wall surface. The exterior walls of this building were executed in granite.

Textual References

"Details from the Ames Building." *AABN* 16 (Aug. 23, 1884): 92; 16 (Aug. 30, 1884): 103.

Hitchcock, *Richardson*, 1966, pp. 252–253.

O'Gorman, *Selected Drawings*, pp. 113–114.

"Upper Stories of Store, Bedford Street, Boston, Designed for F. L. Ames, Esq." *AABN* 20 (Sept. 11, 1886): 122.

Van Rensselaer, *Works*, pp. 85–86.

Miscellaneous Resources

Drawings: Houghton Library, Harvard University

Photographs: Society for the Preservation of New England Antiquities.

101a
F. L. Ames Whole-
sale Store, Bedford
Street at Kingston
Street, Boston,
Massachusetts,
1882–1883; Soci-
ety for the Preser-
vation of New
England
Antiquities.

101b
F. L. Ames Whole-
sale Store, details at
roof; *AABN* 20
(Sept. 11, 1886).

101c
F. L. Ames Whole-
sale Store, after the
fire, Nov. 28, 1889;
Society for the Pres-
ervation of New
England
Antiquities.

102

F. L. Ames Store, Remodeling, 1882–1885
515–521 Washington Street
Boston, Massachusetts
Demolished before 1930

The Ames Store at 515–521 Washington Street was another of F. L. Ames's speculative ventures in Boston real estate (see nos. 68, 101).

This commission came to Richardson's office, by Van Rensselaer's calculation, April 1882. Confusion has arisen because the project appears totally unlike Richardson's other work of this period. As Ann Adams noted, the drawings in the Houghton Library collection indicate that this was not an original commission, but a major renovation of an existing structure. The Houghton elevations and plans are embossed with Richardson's personal seal and dated 1882. Moreover, photographs show that the building was constructed generally following the drawings. By 1930 it had been demolished.

The Ames Washington Street Store was planned for retail spaces on the first floor and offices on the four upper floors. The sloped roof, oriented longitudinally, was broken by two large gables. Under each gable a broad arch ran the full height of the four upper floors. At the second and third floors the windows under the arches formed slightly projecting bays. The windows at the fourth and fifth floors were recessed. Windows were also placed between the arches so that the wall surface was completely minimized.

Textual References

Damrell, C. S. *A Half Century of Boston's Building*. Boston: L. P. Hager, 1895, p. 54.

Hitchcock, *Richardson*, 1966, p. 325 (see note viii–8).

Miscellaneous Resources

Drawings: Houghton Library, Harvard University.

Photographs: Boston Public Library (Print Department); Society for the Preservation of New England Antiquities.

102a
F. L. Ames Store,
Washington Street,
Boston, Massachu-
setts, remodeling,
1882–1885; Bos-
ton Public Library
Print Department.

103

Mrs. M. F. Stoughton House, 1882–1883
90 Brattle Street
Cambridge, Massachusetts

Mary Fisk Stoughton (?–1901?) was the widow of Edwin Wallace Stoughton (1818–1882), a prominent New York City patent attorney who had been ambassador to Russia from 1877 to 1879. She was also the mother of John Fiske (1842–1901) by her earlier marriage to Edmund Brewster Green, who had been Henry Clay's private secretary. John Fiske, who was born Edmund Fisk Green but had his name legally changed in 1855, was an 1863 graduate of Harvard, later a popular lecturer, historian, and Harvard faculty member. After the death of her husband Mrs. Stoughton moved to Cambridge to be closer to her son.

According to Van Rensselaer the Stoughton house commission entered Richardson's office June 1882. But Richardson left on a European trip June 22, 1882 and returned to Brookline only in late September. Thus the construction documents were probably completed after his return. The house was finished by the end of 1883.

Alterations to the house began soon after its completion. John Fiske converted the second story of the service wing to a library. Later owners extended the house to the rear following designs by Shepley, Rutan, and Coolidge. Glazing of the front porch did much to eliminate the feeling of spatial penetration. The view of the house from the street is now obscured by a high brick wall and open carport. Although much interior woodwork remains, subsequent painting in cheerful colors has destroyed the intended effect.

The Stoughton house occupies a flat lot in Cambridge. Richardson's plan was an *L*-shape, the central hall with stair located at the junction of the base and stem of the *L*. The stair actually follows the inside wall of a curved element introduced at the reentrant angle of the *L*. Around the central hall are clustered the dining room, drawing room, and library. The service wing is at the top of the *L* stem. A porch at the first floor and loggia at the second are cut into the front of the house. The sloped roof runs longitudinally, a perpendicular roof with gable at the base of the *L*. The house was originally sheathed in cypress shingles painted deep olive green. The wood trim was minimized and painted to match the shingles.

Architectural historians have long regarded the Stoughton house as one of the finest works of domestic architecture in America.

Textual References

Hitchcock, *Richardson*, 1966, pp. 232–234.

Scully, *Shingle Style*, pp. 95–96.

Sheldon, George W. *Artistic Country Seats: Types of Recent American Villas and Cottage Architecture with Instances of Country Club-houses.* New York: D. Appleton and Company, 1886–1887, vol. 1: 157.

Sturgis, Russell; Roof, John W.; Price, Bruce; Mitchell, Donald G.; Parsons, Samuel, Jr.; and Linn, W. A. *Homes in City and Country.* New York: Charles Scribner's Sons, 1893, pp. 84–85.

Miscellaneous Resources

Drawings: Houghton Library, Harvard University.

Photographs: Boston Athenaeum.

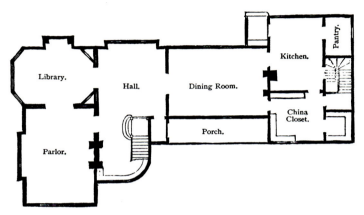

103a
Mrs. M. F.
Stoughton house,
Cambridge, Massa-
chusetts, 1882–
1883, ground floor
plan; George W.
Sheldon, *Artistic
Country Seats*,
1886–1887.

103b
Mrs. M. F. Stough-
ton house, sketch;
Houghton Library,
Harvard University.

103c
Mrs. M. F. Stoughton house, before alterations; Boston Athenaeum.

103d
Mrs. M. F. Stoughton house, with enclosed upper porch; Sheldon, *Artistic Country Seats*.

104

**All Saints Episcopal Cathedral
Project (Competition),
1882–1883**
62 South Swan Street
Albany, New York

The New York State Legislature incorporated the Albany Cathedral of All Saints in 1873 with the stated objective of the "establishment, erection, maintenance and management of a cathedral church and its appurtenances in the City of Albany. . . ." This incorporation had been brought about through the efforts of William Croswell Doane (1832–1913), who had been appointed the first bishop of Albany in 1868. On All Saints Day 1881 Doane announced to the congregation—then meeting in a building that had formerly been an iron foundry—his purpose to begin at once the construction of a cathedral building. The site at the corner of Swan Street and Elk Street was donated by a leading member of the congregation, Erastus Corning, Jr. (see no. 105) who transferred the deed June 30, 1882.

Richardson received a letter from Doane on July 10, 1882 inviting his participation in a competition to design the cathedral. Although Richardson was traveling in Europe at the time, he accepted the terms of the competition in a letter in late August. English–born Albany architect Robert W. Gibson (1854–1927) was the only other competitor. Charles Babcock (1829–1913), the professor of architecture at Cornell who had trained in Richard Upjohn's office, was to serve as Doane's architectural consultant. The terms of the competition are now lost, but from later correspondence a Gothic building was apparently required. Further, it was to be constructed in two stages so that the first might be used until funds were available to construct the second.

Richardson's letter to Julia July 10, 1882 suggested that the drawings were due in January 1883. But another letter on August 27, 1882 put the deadline in November. Richardson actually submitted his drawings in March 1883, accompanied by an estimate by Norcross Brothers and a memorandum explaining the design. Additional correspondence followed, but Gibson's English Gothic design was accepted on April 30, 1883.

In a May 6, 1883 letter to Richardson, Doane explained that the design was too expensive and the temporary structure unsatisfactory. But both Doane and Babcock, O'Gorman notes, may have had a predilection for the English Gothic of Gibson's design. Further, Doane's father, the Bishop of New Jersey, was an American leader of the nineteenth-century ecclesiological movement, which supported Gothic revival architecture as the embodiment of "Christian reality."

The cornerstone for Gibson's building was laid June 3, 1884 after it was modified as required by the committee. It was dedicated in 1888.

Richardson's design is known from the extraordinarily beautiful and elaborately detailed competition drawings. The cathedral was to be a cross in plan with a long nave, transept, choir, and semicircular chancel. Around the choir and chancel Richardson created a triple ambulatory. In the place of the medieval apsidal chapels, Richardson placed vestries for the clergy, choir, and bishop. The dominating feature of the exterior was the tall tower at the crossing. The front elevation was a symmetrical design with three multiple-arched entries, a large central rose window, and two square towers with pyramidal roofs.

Textual References

"Cathedral of All Saints, Albany, New York." *AABN* 17 (May 16, 1885): 235 (Gibson design).

DeMille, George E. *A History of the Diocese of Albany 1704–1923*. Philadelphia: Church Historical Society, 1946, pp. 91–103.

"Design for All Saints Cathedral, Albany, New York." *AABN* 14 (Sept. 1, 1883): 102 (Richardson drawings).

Hitchcock, *Richardson*, 1966, pp. 253–254.

Howell, George R. and Tenney, Jonathan. *Bicentennial History of Albany: History of County of Albany, New York, from 1609 to 1886*. New York: W. W. Munsell, 1886, pp. 539–545.

O'Gorman, James F. "On Vacation with H. H. Richardson: Ten Letters from Europe, 1882." *Archives of American Art Journal* 19 (1979): 2–14.

O'Gorman. *Selected Drawings*, pp. 52–59.

"Proposed Cathedral of All Saints [selected design], Albany, New York." *AABN* 14 (July 14, 1883): 18; (Aug. 11, 1883): 67.

Schuyler, Montgomery. "An American Cathedral." In *American Architecture and Other Writings*, vol. 1, edited by W. H. and R. Coe. Cambridge, Mass.: Harvard University Press, 1961, pp. 229–245.

Van Rensselaer, *Works*, pp. 87–89.

Miscellaneous Resources

Drawings: Houghton Library, Harvard University.

Archives: New York State Library.

Letters: H. H. Richardson Papers, Archives of American Art Microfilm Roll 643; Richard Watson Gilder Papers, Manuscript and Archives Division, The New York Public Library; Astor, Lenox and Tilden Foundations.

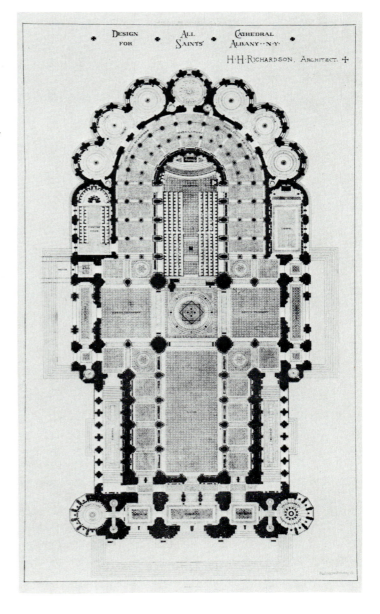

104a
All Saints Episcopal Cathedral project, Albany, New York, 1882–1883, floor plan; *AABN* 14 (Sept. 1, 1883).

104b
All Saints Cathe-
dral project, front
elevation; *AABN*
14 (Sept. 1, 1883).

104c
All Saints Cathe-
dral project, side
elevation; *AABN*
14 (Sept. 1, 1883).

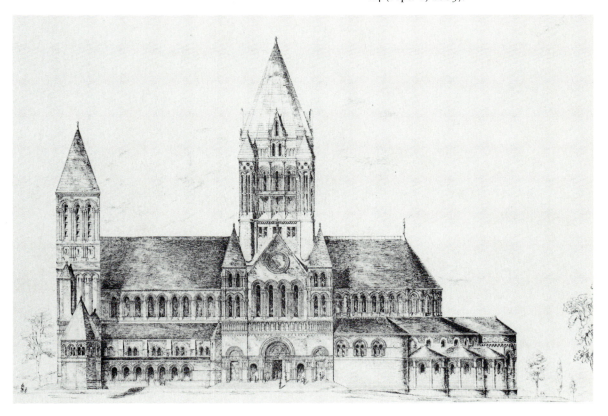

105
Erastus Corning House Project,
ca. 1882–1883
Albany, New York

Erastus Corning, Sr. (1794–1872) was a leading Albany industrialist, the founder and owner of the Albany Iron Works. This company supplied the materials for the first ironclad ships during the Civil War and later pioneered in the Bessemer method of making steel. In 1872 on the death of his father, Erastus Corning, Jr. (1827–1897) succeeded to the ownership of the iron works. The younger Corning was also president of the Albany City National Bank and the Albany City Savings Institution.

Corning, Jr.'s involvement with Richardson probably grew out of Richardson's earlier Albany projects: Corning had served on the commission responsible for erecting the Albany City Hall (no. 85) and was president of the Albany Rural Cemetery Association (see no. 93). A leading member of the Episcopal community of Albany, he served on the site selection committee and then donated the land for the All Saints Cathedral (no. 104).

The Erastus Corning house project is known only from a single elevation drawing in the Houghton Library collection. Hitchcock noted the similarity of this design to the Paine house (no. 117) and suggested a date of 1884, but the connection with the Albany Cathedral indicates more probably an earlier date.

The single surviving drawing for the project shows a house to be constructed of large boulders at the ground floor and sheathed with shingles at the second floor.

Textual Reference

Hitchcock, *Richardson*, 1966, pp. 257–258.

Miscellaneous Resource

Drawing: Houghton Library, Harvard University.

1883

106
Dr. Walter Channing House,
1883–1884
Chestnut Hill Avenue near
corner of Boylston Street
Brookline, Massachusetts
Demolished 1936

106a
Dr. Walter Chan-
ning house, Brook-
line, Massachusetts,
1883–1884, with
later additions;
photo by Berenice
Abbott (ca. 1934).

106b
Channing house,
with later addi-
tions; photo by
Berenice Abbott
(ca. 1934).

Walter Channing (1849–1921) was a leading nineteenth-century alienist. A graduate of the college of physicians and surgeons at Columbia University, he interned at Massachusetts General Hospital and received his M.D. from Harvard in 1872. After postgraduate work in Vienna, he returned to the United States, where he served as an assistant physician at hospitals for the insane in New York and Massachusetts. In 1879 he opened a hospital in Brookline, where he pioneered in the treatment of mental illness as a curable disease, and after 1895 he was professor of mental diseases at Tufts College Medical School.

Dr. Channing commissioned Richardson to design his house on property adjacent to the hospital. Van Rensselaer gives February 1883 as the date that this commission entered Richardson's office. The house was completed in 1884.

Later extended to the rear in keeping with the original design, the house was destroyed when the land was subdivided in 1936.

Richardson sited the house atop a small knoll among some trees. Basically square with an attached porch and a rounded mass projecting from one of the front corners, the two-and-one-half-story house was covered by a hipped roof broken by dormers to light the attic. The exterior was sheathed in shingles, and the wood trim details were minimized.

Textual References

Hitchcock, *Richardson*, 1966, pp. 234–235.

Scully, *Shingle Style*, p. 96.

Miscellaneous Resources

Drawings: Houghton Library, Harvard University.

107

Billings Memorial Library, 1883–1886
University of Vermont
Burlington, Vermont

Frederick Billings (1823–1890), an 1844 graduate of the University of Vermont, was admitted to the Bar in 1849, but joined the rush to California that year and became one of the first attorneys in San Francisco. He served as legal advisor to the state government and worked to keep California in the Union during the Civil War. After retiring to his boyhood Woodstock, Vermont, home in 1866, he was asked to become a director of the Northern Pacific Railroad in 1870. His successful reorganization of the line following its collapse in the Panic of 1873 led to his becoming its president in 1879.

Following his resignation in 1881, Billings purchased a library of 12,000 volumes from the estate of George Perkins Marsh (1801–1882), former congressman and ambassador to Italy from 1861 to 1882. Billings offered to donate a library to the University of Vermont to house these acquisitions and the University's own collection. He initially donated $85,000 and later increased this to $150,000.

Billings selected Richardson after consulting with a number of architects. Van Rensselaer dates the commission in Richardson's office April 1883. O'Gorman notes that Billings, acting through University President Matthew H. Buckham, played an active role in the early design stages by acting as critic. He specifically requested that Richardson's Winn Library (no. 66) serve as a model.

Construction by Norcross began in September 1883. As construction proceeded, some compromises were made for cost reasons, including the substitution of slate for tile on the roof and pine for oak in the interior. The library was dedicated at commencement in June 1885, but construction was not complete until June of the following year. Even with the substitutions, the total cost including heating, gas lighting, and furniture was $103,019.

Alterations to the building began almost immediately. In a letter to George F. Shepley dated March 13, 1886, Richardson noted a commission for an addition to the library, a commission executed by his successors Shepley, Rutan and Coolidge. The stack wing was extended twenty-five feet, a hipped roof substituted for the straight gable, and another wing added at the back. These alterations were completed in 1889. The university eventually outgrew the Billings Library and built entirely new facilities to which library volumes were transferred in 1961. The Billings Library was renovated as a student activities center in 1963.

Richardson's design is similar to that of the Winn Library at Woburn. The three major spaces, the stack wing with tiered alcoves, the central reading room, and the polyagonal room for the Marsh collection, are arranged along a longitudinal axis. Each room rises a full two stories high and each is lit by continuous bands of windows located high in the walls. The main west front is dominated by the arched entrance porch set within a gable and flanked by two corner towers. The taller of the two towers, to the left, is octagonal with tall narrow openings and a pointed roof of stone at the top. The smaller tower to the right is circular, but also topped with a conical stone roof. Extending to the left, the stack wing is balanced by the polygonal Marsh wing to the right. The building is constructed of Longmeadow brownstone laid up in random ashlar, the roof covered with slate.

Textual References

Baker, M. N. "The Queen City of Vermont and its 'Billings Library.'" *Building* 5: 39–43.

The Billings Library, The Gift to the University of Vermont of Frederick Billings, H. H. Richardson, Architect. Boston: Ticknor, [ca. 1888].

Hitchcock, *Richardson*, 1966, pp. 254–255.

Janson, Richard H. "Mr. Billings Richardson Library." *University of Vermont Alumni Magazine* (May 1963): 8–10.

O'Gorman, *Selected Drawings*, pp. 162–165.

Van Rensselaer, *Works*, pp. 80–81.

Miscellaneous Resources

Drawings: Houghton Library, Harvard University.

Photographs: Fleming Museum, University of Vermont; Prothman Associates.

Archives: Buckham Papers, University of Vermont.

Letters: H. H. Richardson Papers, Archives of American Art Microfilm Roll 643.

107a
Billings Memorial
Library, University
of Vermont, Bur-
lington, Vermont,
1883–1886, floor
plan; Van Rensse-
laer, *Works* [1888].

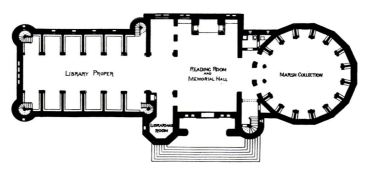

LIBRARY PROPER   READING ROOM AND MEMORIAL HALL   MARSH COLLECTION

LIBRARIANS ROOM

107b
Billings Memorial
Library (ca. 1886);
Prothman Asso-
ciates.

107c
Billings Memorial
Library, with later
additions; *The Bil-
lings Library, The
Gift to the Univer-
sity of Vermont of
Frederick Billings*
[ca. 1888].

107d
Billings Memorial
Library, entrance;
*The Billings Li-
brary* [ca. 1888].

107e
Billings Memorial
Library, interior;
The Billings Library [ca. 1888].

107f
Billings Memorial
Library, interior;
The Billings Library [ca. 1888].

107g
Billings Memorial
Library, interior;
The Billings Library [ca. 1888].

108
Boston & Albany Railroad Station, Chestnut Hill, 1883–1884
Hammond Street
Newton, Massachusetts
Demolished ca. 1960

Richardson's success with the Boston & Albany stations at Auburndale (no. 86) and Palmer (no. 92) assured the continued flow of this kind of work through his office. His next station was at Chestnut Hill, on the Boston & Albany commuter branch line which extended through Brookline into Newton.

Van Rensselaer gives April 1883 as the date this commission entered Richardson's office. It was completed by Norcross Brothers the next year. The Boston & Albany *Annual Report* for 1884 indicates an expenditure of $11,860 for this station, but that may not have been its total cost. F. L. Olmsted was responsible for the design of the station grounds.

Chestnut Hill remains as a commuter rail stop, but the station was demolished about 1960 to make room for a parking lot.

In design the Chestnut Hill station was planned as a simple rectangle with an attached carriage porch and trackside train sheds. The interior included the ticket office, waiting room, and restrooms for men and women. The chief feature of the exterior, the carriage porch, was formed by large arches which continued the planes of the station side walls. The main roof swept down to cover this porch. On the track side the design was less successful, the passenger platform roof supported by a forest of wood posts. The station was built of granite and trimmed with brownstone, the roof covered with slate.

Textual References

Annual Report of the Directors of the Boston & Albany Railroad Company to the Stockholders, No. 17. Boston: Rand Avery, 1884.

Around the Station: The Town and the Train. Framingham: Danforth Museum, 1978.

Hitchcock, *Richardson*, 1966, pp. 226, 255.

Phillips, J. H. "The Evolution of the Suburban Station." *ARec* 36 (Aug. 1914): 122–127.

Robinson, Charles Mulford. "A Railroad Beautiful." *House and Garden* 2 (Nov. 1902): 564–570.

[Sargent, Charles Sprague?]. "The Railroad Station at Chestnut Hill." *Garden and Forest* 2 (Apr. 3, 1889): 159–160.

"Station of the Boston & Albany R.R., Chestnut Hill, Mass." *AABN* 16 (Dec. 13, 1884): 284.

Sweetser, Moses Foster, ed. *King's Handbook of Newton.* Boston: Moses King, 1889, pp. 311–312.

Van Rensselaer, *Works*, pp. 101–102.

Miscellaneous Resources

Photographs: Houghton Library, Harvard University.

108a
Boston & Albany
Railroad Station,
Chestnut Hill,
Newton, Massa-
chusetts, 1883–
1884; Houghton
Library, Harvard
University.

108b
Boston & Albany
Railroad Station,
Chestnut Hill;
Houghton Library,
Harvard University.

109
Dr. Robert W. Hooper House Addition (Project?), 1883
Hale Street
Beverly, Massachusetts

110
Washington Casino Project (Competition), 1883
Connecticut Avenue at L Street
N.W.
Washington, D.C.

Dr. Robert William Hooper (1810–1885) was graduated from Harvard in 1830, studied medicine in Paris, where he received his M.D. in 1836, and practiced as a physician in Boston until his death. He was the father of Edward (Ned) Hooper, Harvard Treasurer and Richardson's landlord (see no. 70), Marian (Clover) Hooper, wife of Henry Adams (see no. 119), and Ellen Hooper, wife of E. W. Gurney (see no. 129).

In 1883 Hooper apparently engaged Richardson for the design of an addition to his summer house in Beverly. The addition is known only from Marian Adams's letter to her father dated May 20, 1883 in which she describes it as including a playroom and study. Whether it was ever executed is unknown, as are the drawings of the design.

Textual References

O'Gorman, *Selected Drawings*, p. 99.

Thoron, Ward, ed. *The Letters of Mrs. Henry Adams*. Boston: Little, Brown, 1936, p. 301.

According to the research of the Commission of Fine Arts, Frederick H. Paine, Charles C. Glover, Theodore B. M. Mason, N. L. Anderson (see no. 90), Henry Adams (see no. 119), and Curtis J. Hillyer drew up acts of incorporation for the Washington Casino Association on June 1, 1883. Their purpose was to create a cultural center, including a casino and opera house, in Washington. Estimated to cost about $200,000, the facilities were to be financed by the sale of stock, with each share, costing $1,000, guaranteeing choice theater seats. Henry Adams attempted, without success, to sell stock in the venture to John Hay.

Architects were invited to submit plans for the new project, the drawings due June 28, 1883. Richardson's letter to F. H. Paine on July 9, 1883, identified by John Coolidge in the papers of the late Joseph P. Richardson, expressed interest in the problem of an opera hall. Richardson wrote that he had studied the construction of the opera in Paris during his years there. He also gave his assurance that his building could be built within the budget of the association. Nonetheless, on July 12, 1883, the scheme by architect J. H. (R.) Thomas of New York was selected, with construction expected to begin soon afterwards. But the project never went beyond the laying of foundations: the association collapsed in 1884.

Richardson's scheme is known from two drawings in the Houghton Library collection. The program required that the opera house seat approximately 1,650 people and measure roughly 80 by 75 feet not including the stage. The casino was to be adjacent to the opera and to include

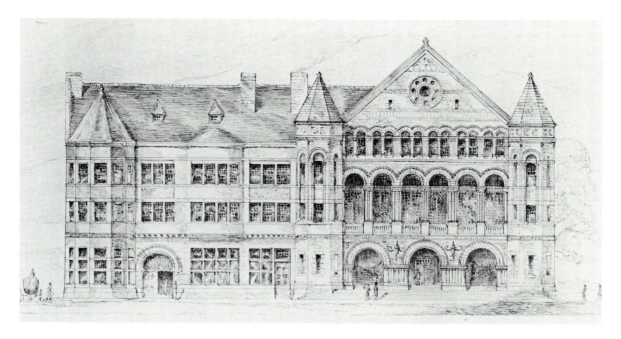

110a
Washington Casino
project, Washing-
ton, D.C., 1883,
elevation; Hough-
ton Library, Har-
vard University.

110b
Washington Casino
project, section;
Houghton Library,
Harvard University.

the required private and public restau-
rants, clubrooms, a ball room, and
garden court. Richardson's section
shows the opera house ceiling as a low
dome on pendentives unlike anything
found in his other work. In Richardson's casino a three-story open space
was roofed by a barrel vault. The elevation shows a building of brick
trimmed with brownstone. Three
arched openings lead to an entry
porch for the opera. Above these at
the second floor are the six arches of a
double height loggia. A great gable
rises above between two octagonal
towers. Marked by rectangular windows, the casino portion of the design
has a roof sloping toward the front
and a rounded mass with conical roof
projecting at one end.

Textual References

Hitchcock, *Richardson*, 1966, p. 257.

Kohler, Sue A., and Carson, Jeffrey R. *Sixteenth Street Architecture.* Washington:
Commission of Fine Arts, 1978, 1: 158–
163.

Miscellaneous Resources

Drawings: Houghton Library, Harvard
University.

Letters: The Adams Papers, Massachusetts
Historical Society.

III
Emmanuel Episcopal Church, 1883–1886
North Avenue at Allegheny Avenue
Pittsburgh, Pennsylvania

The Pittsburgh Emmanuel Episcopal Church purchased the lot at the corner of North Avenue and Allegheny Avenue in 1882. The commission for a new church was awarded to Richardson by the building committee under the direction of Malcolm Hay, a leading Pittsburgh attorney and politician. Van Rensselaer dates the commission in the Richardson office August 1883, but Klukas notes that the Emmanuel vestry minutes do not mention a new structure until January 1884.

Richardson submitted drawings to the church in April 1884. The design with a nave, transept, and tower resembled, on a much smaller scale, Trinity Church in Boston (no. 45). It was also similar to Immanuel Baptist Church in Newton, which was designed one year later (no. 124). The lowest bid on this design, however, was $48,972, about four times greater than the church wished to spend. On July 8, 1884 the building committee returned the original plans to Richardson with a request for a design costing $12,000 to $15,000. In February 1885 Richardson submitted new drawings bid by contractor Henry Shenk in April for only $12,300. Construction began soon after and the new building, which when completed and furnished cost almost $25,000, was dedicated March 7, 1886.

In 1887 Frank Alden of the Pittsburgh architectural firm Alden and Harlow was hired to resolve the problem of the church's leaning west wall. Most likely, Alden and Harlow were also responsible for the design of the parish house built near the southwest corner of the church in the same general style. In 1898 marble reredos were added to the chancel by the Pittsburgh firm of Lake and Green as a

memorial to William Thaw. Although the surrounding neighborhood has since deteriorated, the church remains in use in excellent condition.

The Houghton Library collection includes thirty-five drawings for the Emmanuel Church, but none of these is identical to the church as built. The building is a one-story rectangle with a semicircular chancel at one end. The nave of the church is a single space without side aisles, lit by dormers ending in the round chancel. The roof is supported on trusses of laminated wood. The exterior form, sometimes called the "bake oven," is built of brick with windows in a rhythmic pattern along the walls. The massive roof is broken by three dormers on each side. The brickwork of the front gable and triple arched entry is exceptional, as are the brick archivolts at the various openings and the use of tumbling along the rake of the gable.

Textual References

Hitchcock, *Richardson*, 1966, pp. 255–256.

Klukas, Arnold W. "Henry Hobson Richardson's Designs for the Emmanuel Episcopal Church, Pittsburgh." *American Art Review* 2 (July–Aug. 1975): 64–76.

O'Gorman, *Selected Drawings*, pp. 60–61.

Van Rensselaer, *Works*, p. 85.

Van Trump, James D. "The Church Beyond Fashion." *Charette* 38 (Apr. 1958): 26–29.

Miscellaneous Resources

Drawings: Houghton Library, Harvard University.

Photographs: Carnegie Library of Pittsburgh; Historical Society of Western Pennsylvania; Library of Congress (Historic American Buildings Survey).

111a
Emmanuel Episco-
pal Church,
Pittsburgh, Pennsyl-
vania, 1883–1886,
early floor plan
(does not match
church as con-
structed); Hough-
ton Library,
Harvard University.

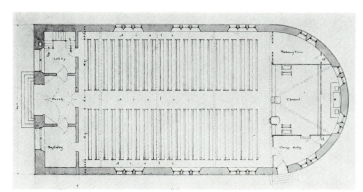

111b
Emmanuel Episco-
pal Church (1972).

111c
Emmanuel Episco-
pal Church; Li-
brary of Congress
(Historic American
Buildings Survey,
photo by Jack E.
Boucher, 1963).

111d
Emmanuel Episco-
pal Church interior
with alterations to
chancel and rere-
dos; Carnegie Li-
brary of Pittsburgh.

Converse Memorial Public Library, 1883–1885
36 Salem Street
Malden, Massachusetts

Although the movement for a public library in Malden had begun as early as 1871, it was not until 1877 that the town voted to establish the Malden Public Library, which opened in a room in the town hall on February 14, 1879. By 1882, the library had outgrown its space, and was seeking new quarters.

Founder of the Boston Rubber Shoe Company, now the Converse Rubber Shoe Company, and organizer and first president of the First National Bank of Malden, Elisha Slade Converse (1820–1904) and his wife Mary Diana Converse (1825–1903) decided to give the city, in trust, a library building as a memorial to their son, Frank Eugene Converse (1846–1863), who had been fatally shot in December 1863 while working as a bank teller in the first bank robbery murder in United States history. The generous donation of the Converses provided not only for a library, but also for a municipal art gallery.

The commission entered Richardson's office in August 1883, according to Van Rensselaer. The design was still under consideration in January 1884 when Richardson and F. L. Olmsted visited Malden together to select the site. Construction by Norcross began the following spring; the building was dedicated October 1, 1885.

The library has had two additions, both to the rear. The first, in 1896, included stacks, a reading room, and a reference room. The second, a children's wing, was built in 1914. Otherwise, the original Richardson building remains largely unchanged today.

The Converse Library differs significantly from the other libraries by Richardson. It was conceived not as a single structure standing alone, but together with a garden, part of a composition with a church to be built on the adjacent lot. One of the perspective drawings in the collection at Houghton Library shows the church and library together. (Richardson was able to design only the library before his death; Shepley, Rutan and Coolidge designed a church for the adjacent site several years later.) In addition, the Converse Library program required much more interior space than Richardson's previous libraries. Therefore, he arranged the functions along two legs of an *L*-shaped plan. Along the longitudinal axis Richardson placed the stack wing, main hall, and reading room; and along the perpendicular axis he arranged the art gallery, anteroom, and trustees room. In the reentrant angle between the two wings he placed a fifty-five-foot-tall octagonal stair tower. The ends of each wing are gabled. The gable facing the street is asymmetrical as the roof of this wing slopes low over the entry porch with its three arches facing the front courtyard and single arch facing the street. Along the stack wing the windows run continuously and end at the corner stair turret. The building is constructed of brownstone with gray slate roof tiles. The ceiling of the stack wing is an oak barrel vault as in Richardson's earlier libraries at Woburn (no. 66) and North Easton (no. 68). The woodwork of the tiers and shelving is also oak. Richardson designed most of the library furniture.

112a
Converse Memorial
Public Library,
Malden, Massachu-
setts, 1883–1885,
perspective drawing
of library and pro-
posed church;
Houghton Library,
Harvard University.

Textual References

"The Converse Memorial Library, Malden, Mass." *AABN* 18 (Oct. 3, 1885):
163.

"The Converse Memorial Library, Malden, Mass." *AABN* 20 (Nov. 6, 1886):
218.

*Dedication of the Converse Memorial Li-
brary Building October 1, 1885.* Boston:
1886.

"Entrance to Converse Memorial Library,
Malden, Mass." *AABN* 24 (Sept. 22,
1888): 135.

Farnham, Anne. "H. H. Richardson's Library Furniture." Typescript, Converse
Memorial Library, n.d.

*Fiftieth Anniversary of the Malden Public
Library 1879–1929. Fifty-first Annual Report of Malden Public Library for Year
Ending December 31, 1928.* Boston:
1929.

Gilkerson, Ann M. "The Public Libraries
of H. H. Richardson." Honors Thesis,
Smith College, 1978.

Hitchcock, *Richardson*, 1966, pp. 256–
257.

O'Gorman, *Selected Drawings*, pp. 166–
168.

*One Hundredth Anniversary of the Mal-
den Public Library 1879–1979.* Malden:
Malden Historical Society, 1979.

Rudenstein, Roy. "The Libraries of H. H.
Richardson." Senior Thesis, Harvard University, 1975.

Van Rensselaer, *Works*, pp. 81–83.

Miscellaneous Resources

Drawings: Houghton Library, Harvard
University.

Photographs: Boston Athenaeum; Con-
verse Memorial Public Library; Library of
Congress (Historic American Buildings
Survey); Society for the Preservation of
New England Antiquities.

Archives: Converse Memorial Library.

112b
Converse Memorial
Library; *AABN* 18
(Nov. 6, 1886).

112c
Converse Memorial
Library, entry log-
gia; Society for the
Preservation of
New England
Antiquities.

112d
Converse Memorial
Library, stair
tower; *AABN* 24
(Sept. 22, 1888).

112e
Converse Memorial
Library, interior;
AABN 20 (Nov. 6,
1886).

112f
Converse Memorial
Library, detail of
stacks; photo by
Jean Baer
O'Gorman.

113

New London Northern Railroad Station Project, 1883
Railroad Street
Willimantic, Connecticut

Willimantic, Connecticut, a major thread manufacturing center, was intersected by four New England railroad routes in the late nineteenth century: the New London Northern (by 1883 leased to the Central Vermont Railroad), the Eastern and Providence Divisions of the New York and New England Railroad (later absorbed by the New York, New Haven, and Hartford), and the Boston and New York Air Line Railroad (then leased as the Air Line Division of the New York, New Haven, and Hartford). By 1883 traffic had expanded so that between fifty and seventy freight and passenger trains passed through the city every day.

According to Gregg M. Turner of the Railway and Locomotive Historical Society, the first Willimantic station, built in the early 1850s, was soon outgrown. In 1855 the Connecticut Railroad Commissioners noted the failings of the depot, but no action was taken. In 1864 the commissioners again noted the many problems of the depot, and the Connecticut General Assembly ordered that they be solved. At that time the railroads stated that they were about to build a new structure, but for the next seventeen years nothing was done. In July 1883 the New York and New England and the New London Northern Railroads were ordered by the commissioners to erect a new station.

Richardson's involvement in the project began at this time. Richardson's patron, James A. Rumrill (see no. 86), a director of the New London Northern, may have asked Richardson to prepare design sketches; or the project may have come to Richardson from the directors of the New York and New England Railroad, many of whom lived in the Boston area. But Richardson's design was not selected; a wood structure of unknown design was constructed instead. It no longer remains.

Richardson's design for the Willimantic station is known from seven drawings in the Houghton Library collection. The general scheme followed closely on the Old Colony Railroad Station at North Easton (no. 95), a rectangle similar to Richardson's earlier station designs. Windows were grouped under arches as at North Easton. The station was to be built of stone with its broad roof sloping down to join the platform roofs. Three eyelid dormers broke the roof on each side, while one wood dormer broke each end roof.

This instance of Richardson's nearly duplicating an earlier design remains unexplained.

Textual Reference

Hitchcock, *Richardson*, 1966, p. 257.

Miscellaneous Resource

Drawings: Houghton Library, Harvard University.

113a
New London
Northern Railroad
Station project,
Willimantic, Con-
necticut, 1883, ele-
vation; Houghton
Library, Harvard
University.

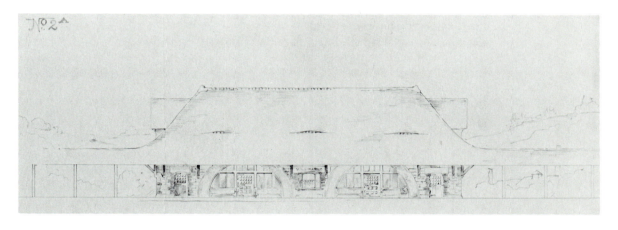

114

Boston & Albany Railroad Station, South Framingham, 1883–1885
Waverly Street at Concord Street
Framingham, Massachusetts

The commission to design the station at South Framingham came to Richardson through the Boston & Albany directors, James A. Rumrill and Charles S. Sargent (see no. 86). Of the nine stations Richardson designed for the line, South Framingham was probably the largest and most active.

Van Rensselaer gives October 1883 as the date this commission entered Richardson's office. Local newspaper accounts indicate that the design was not settled until February 1884. Construction by Norcross Brothers began the following spring and was completed in 1885. The cost of the station, including furnishings, was $62,718.

The station is still used today, but some interior alterations have been made. Part of the roof collapsed in August 1978. It is planned to restore the station for use as a commuter center and restaurant.

The design of the South Framingham station follows the pattern of Richardson's earlier stations. The building is a rectangle 40 feet wide by 120 feet long. At the center is a double height waiting room and adjacent dining room. At each end subsidiary spaces are organized on two floors—the west end with offices above the ladies' room and the east end with the kitchen above the men's room and the serving room. The roof over the central space is supported by a single pipe column with exposed wood trusses running along the diagonals of the space. Built of granite with Longmeadow brownstone trim, the building features an overhanging slate roof that extends at trackside to form the passenger shed. Light is introduced into the interior through three connected high dormers on each side, the window in the central dormer on each side forming the segment of a circle. At the junctions of the dormers on each side are carved stone lion heads.

Textual References

Annual Report of the Directors of the Boston & Albany Railroad Company to the Stockholders. Nos. 17, 18. Boston: Rand Avery, 1884, 1885.

Around the Station: The Town and the Train. Framingham: Danforth Museum, 1978.

Hitchcock, *Richardson*, 1966, p. 255.

"Railway Stations at Wellesley Hills, Waban, Woodland, Auburndale, Brighton, South Framingham, Palmer, Holyoke and North Easton, Mass." *AABN* 21 (Feb. 26, 1887): 103.

Robinson, Charles Mulford. "Suburban Station Grounds." *House and Garden* 5 (Apr. 1904): 182–187.

Miscellaneous Resources

Drawings: Houghton Library, Harvard University.

Photographs: Danforth Museum; Framingham Public Library; Houghton Library, Harvard University; Library of Congress (Historic American Buildings Survey).

114a
Boston & Albany
Railroad Station,
South Framingham,
Massachusetts,
1883–1885, plan;
AABN 21 (Feb. 26,
1887).

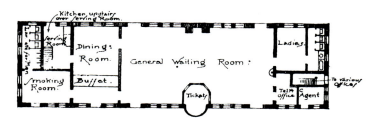

114b
Boston & Albany
Railroad Station,
South Framingham;
Houghton Library,
Harvard University.

114c
Boston & Albany
Railroad Station,
South Framingham
(1972).

114d
Boston & Albany
Railroad Station,
South Framingham,
detail of ticket of-
fice window; Li-
brary of Congress
(Historic American
Buildings Survey,
photo by Cervin
Robinson, 1959).

114e
Boston & Albany
Railroad Station,
South Framingham,
interior; Library of
Congress (Historic
American Buildings
Survey, photo by
Cervin Robinson,
1959).

115

Connecticut River Railroad Station, 1883–1885
Lyman Street at Bowers Street
Holyoke, Massachusetts

James A. Rumrill (see no. 86) served as a director of the Connecticut River Railroad. This, in addition to Richardson's success with the stations for the Boston & Albany, led to the commission for a large station at Holyoke.

Van Rensselaer dates this commission in Richardson's office November 1883. Construction began the next year and was completed in 1885.

The Connecticut River Railroad station is now in poor condition. Many of the windows have been blocked up, and a ceiling has been hung in the two-story waiting room. Fortunately the upstairs created by this ceiling has remained unused, so that the original interior beams and ceiling remain in fair condition. The building is now used by an auto parts dealership.

The Holyoke station for the Connecticut River Railroad is similar to the Boston & Albany Railroad station at South Framingham (no. 114). The plan is a rectangle with a central double-height waiting room lit by high dormers. Adjacent to this were subsidiary spaces including women's room, telegraph, immigrants' room, and baggage room. The building of granite and brownstone has a slate-covered hipped roof with multiple dormers and broad sheltering eaves supported on wood posts.

Textual References

Around the Station: The Town and the Train. Framingham: Danforth Museum, 1978.

Hitchcock, *Richardson*, 1966, p. 255.

"Railway Stations at Wellesley Hills, Waban, Woodlands, Auburndale, Brighton, South Framingham, Palmer, Holyoke and North Easton, Mass." *AABN* 21 (Feb. 26, 1887): 103.

Van Rensselaer, *Works*, p. 100.

Miscellaneous Resources

Drawings: Houghton Library, Harvard University.

Photographs: Holyoke Public Library; Library of Congress.

115a
Connecticut River Railroad Station, Holyoke, Massachusetts, 1883–1885, plan; *AABN* 21 (Feb. 26, 1887).

115b
Connecticut River
Railroad Station:
Van Rensselaer,
Works, [1888].

115c
Connecticut River
Railroad Station
(1972).

116
Allegheny County Buildings,
1883–1888
436 Grant Street
Pittsburgh, Pennsylvania

The first Allegheny County Court-house, a Doric structure, burned in 1882. Consequently the County Commissioners decided to hold a competition for the design of the new county buildings. On April 16, 1883, the commissioners sent out a pamphlet to "leading architects" explaining the requirements of the project; on September 8 the commissioners resolved to accept proposals from only five architects. Nominated September 28, 1883, Richardson competed against John Ord of Philadelphia, E. E. Meyers of Detroit, W. W. Boynington of Chicago, and Andrew Peebles of Pittsburgh, who were also chosen. Drawings were due by January 1, 1884.

The county commissioners chose Richardson's design on January 31, 1884, and the project entered Richardson's office books in February according to Van Rensselaer. Construction documents were delivered on July 1, 1884 to the commissioners, who awarded the construction contract to Norcross Brothers on September 1, 1884. Construction of the jail was completed in 1886. But the courthouse, completed under the direction of Shepley, Rutan and Coolidge, was not dedicated until September 2, 1888. The total cost of the entire complex was $2,268,450.

Alterations to the complex began in 1908 when Pittsburgh architect F. J. Osterling enlarged the jail in keeping with Richardson's original design. In 1912, when streets in the area were lowered as much as twelve feet, the main courthouse entry stair was redesigned by Pittsburgh architects Alden and Harlow. This also meant that basement windows, which had formerly been at sidewalk level, were now high in the walls. In 1928 the Alden and Harlow staircase was removed when Grant Street was

widened, the arched entries extended downwards following a design by local architect Stanley Roush. In 1976 the courthouse courtyard, previously used as a parking lot, was renovated as a small park with a central fountain. It was dedicated to county veterans in 1977. The jail has been threatened several times with destruction, but so far efforts by local preservationists have protected it.

Richardson's scheme for the courthouse and jail is a sophisticated resolution of complex functional requirements. The courthouse is a large hollow rectangle measuring 209 by 301 feet, with a basement and four stories on each side surrounding an open court measuring 70 by 145 feet. The plan of each of the four floors is similar. Courtrooms and offices are grouped around the outside of the building, connected by single-loaded corridors which circle the courtyard. The floor-to-floor height at the first and second floors is twenty-five feet, which allows for impressive spaces in the courtrooms; but the height is cut in half by mezzanine floors in the smaller rooms. The corridors also have lower ceilings, which allows light to enter the courtrooms from the courtyard through mezzanine-level clerestories. Two great staircases lead to large halls at the first and second floors. Other staircases and elevators are found in the corner towers of the courtyard. The exterior walls of the courthouse are constructed of pinkish gray Milford granite laid in alternating wide and narrow courses. The roof is covered with square red terra cotta tiles. The street frontages are marked by round projections which correspond to the locations of the smaller rooms within. The main tower rises an additional five stories above the rest of the building and is topped with a pyramidal roof. The tower was used for document storage and for the fresh air intake required by the advanced heating and ventilating system. (In the basement the air was cleaned, heated, and humidified before being blown through ducts to all parts of the building.) Ornamentation on the building exterior is minimal: moldings, capitals, and stringcourses are very flat with few crevices to accumulate grime.

The jail was planned in the shape of an asymmetrical cross. At the center Richardson placed an octagonal tower housing the guard rooms. Three of the arms were planned with cells and the fourth with a reception area and officers rooms. The jail building and courtyards are enclosed by a stone wall with hexagonal and circular towers. In contrast to the alternating courses of the courthouse, the jail walls are built of Milford granite in single broad courses. The smokestack at the end of one wing is required by the basement boilers for both the courthouse and jail. The jail and courthouse are connected by a stone arch "Bridge of Sighs."

Richardson considered the Allegheny County Buildings one of his finest designs. He believed it would provide part of the foundation for his enduring reputation. Indeed, its impact was immediate and dramatic. Within a few years buildings of similar style were executed for local governments in many parts of the country. Modern architects and historians, beginning with Hitchcock, have tended to regard the jail more highly than the courthouse, probably as a result of its plain outline, functional appropriateness, and lack of almost any historically derived detail.

Textual References

"Allegheny County Courthouse, Pittsburgh, Pa." *Building* 6 (June 18, 1887).

"Allegheny County Courthouse and Jail, Pittsburgh, Pa." *AABN* 28 (May 24, 1890): 123.

"Allegheny County Courthouse and Jail, Pittsburgh, Pa." *American Buildings, Selections*, no. 2, pl. 28. n.d.

"Allegheny County Jail, Pittsburgh, Pa." *AABN* 38 (Nov. 12, 1892): 106.

American Architect 86 (Oct. 22, 1904): 25; 91 (Apr. 27, 1907): 153–154; 91 (May 11, 1907): 190.

A Civic Proposal: Removal of the Present County Jail and Rebuilding of Same in Conjunction with New County Office Building. Pittsburgh: Jail Removal Association, 1924.

Comes, John Theodore. "The Allegheny County Courthouse." *International Studio* 28 (Mar. 1906): 3–7.

"Courthouse, Pittsburgh, Pa." *Inland Architect and News Record* 13 (May–June 1889).

"A Courtroom in the Allegheny County Courthouse, Pittsburgh, Pa." "The Main Staircase of the Allegheny County Courthouse, Pittsburgh, Pa." "Vestibule and Main Staircase of the Allegheny County Courthouse, Pittsburgh, Pa." *AABN* 41 (Aug. 5, 1893): 92.

"Entrance to the Pittsburgh Jail and Courthouse." *American Buildings, Selections*, no. 4, pl. 39, 40.

Fleming, George T. *Pittsburgh: How to See It*. Pittsburgh: William G. Johnston and Company, 1918, pp. 94–95.

Hitchcock, *Richardson*, 1966, pp. 258–262.

Huff, William S. "Richardson's Jail." *Western Pennsylvania Historical Magazine* 41 (1958): 41–59.

Kaufmann, Edgar, Jr. "One Hundred Years of Significant Buildings, Civic Monuments: Allegheny County Buildings." *ARec* 121 (Jan. 1957): 172.

J. M. Kelly's Handbook of Greater Pittsburgh. Pittsburgh: J. M. Kelly Company, 1895, p. 21.

Killikelly, Sarah H. *The History of Pittsburgh*. Pittsburgh: B. C. and Gordon Montgomery Company, 1906, p. 238.

"Looking Backward at the Allegheny County Courthouse, circa 1906." *Charette* 28 (July 1948): 12.

"Main Entrance, Allegheny County Courthouse, Pittsburgh, Pa." *AABN* 38 (Nov. 19, 1892): 123.

Official Report of the Dedicatory Exercises Held at the New Courthouse at the City of Pittsburgh Court of Allegheny County on Monday, September 24, A.D. 1888. Pittsburgh: W. G. Johnston and Company, 1889.

O'Gorman, *Selected Drawings*, pp. 135–142.

"Regarding the Jail Removal Project." *Charette* 5 (Nov. 1925): 8.

Richardson, H. H. *Description of Drawings for the Proposed New County Buildings for Allegheny County, Penn*. Boston: 1884.

Simo, Melanie, ed. *Henry Hobson Richardson: The Allegheny County Courthouse and Jail*. Pittsburgh: Allegheny County, 1977.

"Special Meeting to Discuss Removal of Jail." *Charette* 8 (Feb. 1928): 3.

"Suggested Remodeling of Richardson's Allegheny County Courthouse." *American Architecture* 86 (Oct. 22, 1904): 25.

Toker, Franklin K. B. "Richardson *en concours*: The Pittsburgh Courthouse." *Carnegie Magazine* 51 (Nov. 1977): 13.

Van Rensselaer, *Works*, pp. 89–93.

Van Trump, James D. "Project H. H. Richardson." *Charette* 42 (May 1962): 4–5, 20.

———. "Of Footbridges and Preservation." *Western Pennsylvania Historical Magazine* 43 (June 1960): 135–146.

———. "Revived Romanesque in Pittsburgh." *Carnegie Magazine* 48 (Mar. 1974): 108–113.

———. "The Romanesque Revival in Pittsburgh." *JSAH* 16 (Oct. 1957): 22–29.

Van Trump, James D., and Ziegler, Arthur P. *Landmark Architecture of Allegheny County, Pennsylvania*. Pittsburgh: Pittsburgh History and Landmark Foundation, 1967, pp. 46–48.

Miscellaneous Resources

Drawings: Houghton Library, Harvard University; Pittsburgh History and Landmarks Foundation.

Photoengravings: Avery Library, Columbia University (ca. 1885, gift of Henry-Russell Hitchcock).

Photographs: Carnegie Library of Pittsburgh; Houghton Library, Harvard University; Library of Congress (Historic American Buildings Survey and Seagram County Courthouse Archives); Pittsburgh History and Landmarks Foundation; Western Pennsylvania Historical Society.

116a
Allegheny County
Buildings, Pitts-
burgh, Pennsylva-
nia, 1883–1888,
courthouse third
floor plan; Hough-
ton Library, Har-
vard University.

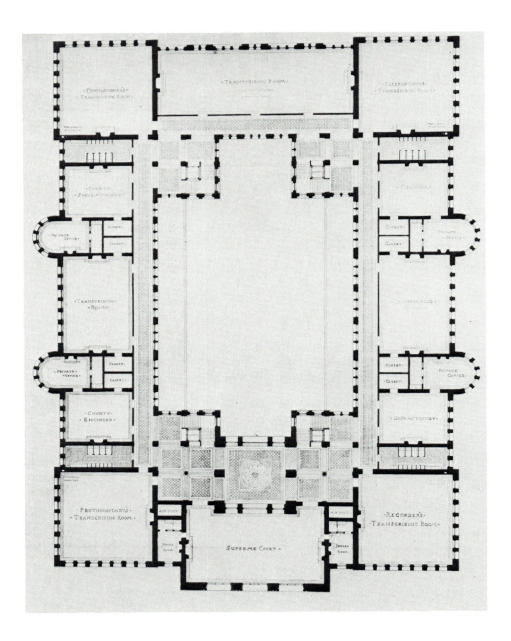

329

116b
Allegheny County
Buildings, court-
house transverse
section; Houghton
Library, Harvard
University.

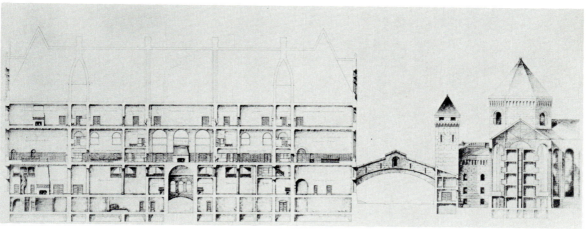

116c
Allegheny County
Buildings, court-
house and jail lon-
gitudinal section;
Houghton Library,
Harvard University.

116d
Allegheny County
Buildings, court-
house; Carnegie Li-
brary of Pittsburgh.

116e
Allegheny County
Buildings, court-
house courtyard;
Carnegie Library of
Pittsburgh.

116f
Allegheny County
Buildings, court-
house entry before
alterations; *AABN*
38 (Nov. 19,
1892).

116g
Allegheny County
Buildings, court-
house main stair;
Carnegie Library of
Pittsburgh.

116h
Allegheny County
Buildings, court-
house main stair;
Carnegie Library of
Pittsburgh.

116i
Allegheny County
Buildings, court-
house, courtroom;
AABN 41 (Aug. 5,
1893).

116j
Allegheny County
Buildings, jail with
courthouse beyond;
AABN 28 (May 24,
1890).

116k
Allegheny County
Buildings, bridge
and jail; *AABN* 38
(Nov. 12, 1892).

116l
Allegheny County
Buildings, jail;
AABN 50 (Oct. 5,
1895).

116m
Allegheny County
Buildings, jail with
alterations and
courthouse in back-
ground; Library of
Congress (Seagram
County Courthouse
Archives, photo by
Richard Pare).

117

Robert Treat Paine House, 1883–1886
577 Beaver Street
Waltham, Massachusetts

In 1793 Theodore Lyman of Boston began assembling parcels of land in Waltham to create his country estate. Lyman built a Palladian country home on the property which he named "The Vale." In 1860 Lydia Williams Lyman, daughter of George Williams Lyman, who then owned The Vale, was engaged to Robert Treat Paine (1835–1910). Paine had been graduated from Harvard in 1855 and admitted to the bar in 1859. Through wise investments in railroads and mining properties, Paine acquired a fortune at an early age and then devoted his life to philanthropic and charitable enterprises. He founded the Workingmen's Building Association, the Workingmen's Loan Association, and the Associated Charities of Boston; and he served as president of the American Peace Society from 1891 to 1910.

In 1862 Paine married Miss Lyman and in 1866 built a modest summer home in Waltham on a site near The Vale, presented by his father-in-law, who upon completion surprised the young couple by paying for the house. According to Floyd's research, the architect of the 1866 house was most likely Henry W. Hartwell. By 1882, however, the original house had become too small for the growing Paine family. When George Williams Paine's death provided funds for expansion, the Paines turned to Richardson and Olmsted for an addition in 1883. Paine had served as a member of the Trinity Church building committee (see no. 45) and therefore had known Richardson for at least twelve years.

Van Rensselaer dates the commission as entering Richardson's office in January 1884, but the project had undoubtedly been under consideration in late 1883. A new location for the house was determined by Richardson and Olmsted in the fall of 1884, and revised plans were accepted about the same time. Begun in spring 1885, construction was substantially complete by April 1886. The cost by contractors Miller and Ladd was just over $36,000.

The Paines called the house "Stonehurst." There Robert Treat Paine lived until his death in 1910. The house remained in the Paine family thereafter and was preserved virtually intact, complete with all the interior furnishings, until the mid-1960s. Paine's son-in-law, architect Charles K. Cummings, enclosed two bays of the garden facade in 1932. In 1974 Theodore Lyman Storer, a grandson of Robert Treat Paine, gave the house and grounds to the town of Waltham, which has worked on restoration of the house and opened it by appointment to special interest groups and events.

Richardson's design for the Paine house was actually an addition to the earlier house of 1866 moved several hundred feet west of its original location. But the addition is over twice the size of the original house, a two-and-one-half-story frame structure with clapboard siding and a mansard roof. Providing a direct contrast with the original, the Richardson addition is lower and much more horizontal in character. Richardson's plan is organized around a central living hall with huge fireplace and beautifully carved grand staircase. Around this were clustered Paine's study, a large summer parlor, a smaller autumn parlor, and a

117a
Robert Treat Paine
house, Waltham,
Massachusetts,
1883–1886; photo
by Berenice Abbott
(ca. 1934).

dining room. The Richardson addition
first story and three round towers are
executed in glacial boulders with
quarry-faced Kibbee brownstone trim.
The second story is sheathed in shingles which flare out to form an offset
course above the stone. The main facade, facing the garden by Olmsted,
was an open porch beneath a loggia
spanning between two round towers.
The end facade to the east is marked
by the large arched opening at the first
floor and a Palladian window at the
second floor.

Textual References

Floyd, Margaret Henderson. *Evaluation
Study and Feasibility Report on the Robert
Treat Paine House "Stonehurst," 577 Bea-
ver Street, Waltham, Massachusetts 02154.*
Boston: Architectural Heritage, 1975.

————. "History and Design of the Robert
Treat Paine House, Waltham, Massachusetts 1884–1886." Unpublished typescript,
? n.d.

Hitchcock, *Richardson*, 1966, pp. 267–
269.

"Plans for the Paine House." *AF* 140
(Nov. 1973): 82.

[Richardson, H. H.]. "Specifications for
Dwelling House for Mrs. Robert Treat
Paine, Jr., Waltham, Massachusetts."
Manuscript and typescript, City of Wal-
tham, n.d.

Scully, *Shingle Style*, pp. 96–97.

Miscellaneous Resources

Drawings: Houghton Library, Harvard
University; F. L. Olmsted National Historic Site; City of Waltham.

Photographs: Library of Congress; City of
Waltham.

Slides: Fogg Museum, Harvard University.

117b
Robert Treat Paine
house, with original
house in back-
ground (1972).

117c
Robert Treat Paine
house (1972).

117d
Robert Treat Paine
house (1972).

117e
Robert Treat Paine
house, stair; photo
by Berenice Abbott
(ca. 1934).

1884

118
John Hay House, 1884–1886
800 Sixteenth Street N.W.
Washington, D.C.
Demolished 1927

119
Henry Adams House,
1884–1886
1603 H Street N.W.
Washington, D.C.
Demolished 1927

118/119a
John Hay house/
Henry Adams
house, Washington,
D.C., 1884–1886;
Society for the Pres-
ervation of New
England
Antiquities.

John Milton Hay (1838–1905) was a leading American statesman. He served as Lincoln's private secretary during the Civil War, as assistant secretary of state from 1878 to 1880, as ambassador to Great Britain from 1897 to 1898, and as secretary of state from 1898 to 1905. His name is associated with the creation of the "Open Door" policy in China between 1898 and 1900.

Henry Brooks Adams (1838–1918) was an American historian, philosopher, and author, best known for his two books, *Mont-Saint-Michel and Chartres* (1904) and *The Education of Henry Adams* (1906). His wife, Marian (Clover) Hooper Adams (1843–1885) was the sister of Ned Hooper (see nos. 70, 109) and the hostess of an unofficial Washington "salon." With her husband she was part of a circle of artists and intellectuals.

In December 1883 Adams convinced Hay to purchase the site at the corner of Sixteenth Street and H Street, part of which Hay then sold to Adams. Adams also introduced Hay to Richardson, his Harvard friend, and both commissioned Richardson-designed houses. In January 1884, according to Van Rennselaer, the commissions entered Richardson's office. Although each house was commissioned separately, they were studied and built as a pair; and historians have always regarded them as such.

Both Adams and Hay supplied plans for Richardson's consideration in designing the houses. Indeed, the Adamses remained involved throughout the design process. Building permits were issued July 23, 1884 to the contractor, Charles Edmonston. In October 1885 Hay and Richardson went shopping in New York for the Hay house furnishings only three months before the two houses were completed. The total cost of the Hay house, with furnishings was $105,356. The cost of the Adams House remains unknown.

Hay in 1890 commissioned two windows by John La Farge, a significant addition to his house when installed in 1892 on either side of the fireplace. In 1918 Alice Hay Wadsworth, daughter of John Hay, then living in the Hay house, purchased the Adams house and leased it to the Brazilian Embassy. Seven years later she leased both properties to developer Harry Wardman, who razed the two houses in January 1927 and built the Hay-Adams Hotel on the site. The mahogany wall paneling from the Hay house, however, was removed and used in the Wadsworth home in Geneseo, New York. The ground floor arches from the Adams house were also modified for a home at 2618 Thirty-first Street N.W., and the door of the Hay house was used without its monumental arch in a home at 3014 Woodland Drive N.W. The two John La Farge windows from the Hay house are now in two different collections: the National Collection of Fine Arts, Washington, D.C. and the Villa Stack Museum, Munich.

Richardson's designs for the houses are quite different. This is due in part to the different functional requirements of the two families, to the different siting of the two houses, and to the deep involvement of Henry and Marian Adams in the design process.

The Hay house was a massive residence measuring 99 feet by 54 feet. The entry off Sixteenth Street led to the grand central hall with an impressive paneled stair. Around this central hall were clustered the parlor, library, dining room, and small reception room. The spaces were large and somewhat formal as required by Hay's diplomatic position. The house stood 38 feet high to the eaves. Although initial design studies show construction of light yellow Ohio stone, brick was ultimately used for all but the exposed portion of the basement. Windows of plate glass were deeply recessed into the walls of brick. The grand arch of the entrance porch was centered under a great gable. To the right of this was an octagonal stair tower. To the left, at the corner of 16th and H Streets was a rounded tower, with a conical roof. Other than the patterns of the brickwork, there was little decoration on the house.

The Adams house was much smaller. It faced only on H Street and was therefore constructed between two solid (party) walls without windows. The house measured 44 feet wide by 48 feet deep. The plan apparently followed Adams's requests closely. The stairs were pushed to the side and back, while the main rooms of the main floor—the study, library, and dining room—formed an *L* around the stair hall. The front elevation was an asymmetrical composition in light Ohio stone at the ground floor. Above this the next three floors presented a symmetrical arrangement of deeply recessed windows in the plain brick wall. The archways at the ground floor of this facade were marked by delicate carving.

Textual References

Cater, Harold Dean, ed. *Henry Adams and His Friends: A Collection of His Unpublished Letters*. Boston: Houghton Mifflin, 1947.

Ford, W. C., ed. *The Letters of Henry Adams*. Vol. 1, 1858–1891. Boston: Houghton Mifflin, 1930.

Friedlander, Marc. "Henry Hobson Richardson, Henry Adams and John Hay." *JSAH* 29 (Oct. 1970): 231–246.

"Gable of Residence of Col. J. C. Hay, Washington, D.C." *The Brickbuilder* 1 (Jan. 1892): 7.

Hitchcock, *Richardson*, 1966, pp. 270–271.

Kohler, Sue, and Carson, Jeffrey R. *Sixteenth Street Architecture*. Washington: Commission of Fine Arts, 1978, 1: 56–88.

O'Gorman, *Selected Drawings*, pp. 78–86 (Ames House Project, 8a p. 80, misidentified).

———. "A Tragic Circle." *Nineteenth Century* 2 (Autumn 1976): 46–49.

"Residence of Col. John Hay, H Street near 16th Street N.W., Washington, D.C." *Building* 6 (Jan. 1, 1887). (Caption incorrect)

Samuels, Ernest. *Henry Adams: The Middle Years*. Cambridge, Mass.: Harvard University Press, 1958.

Scheyer, Ernst. "Henry Adams and Henry Hobson Richardson." *JSAH* 12 (March 1953): 7–12.

Thoron, Ward, ed. *The Letters of Mrs. Henry Adams 1865–1883*. Boston: Little, Brown, 1936.

Van Rensselaer, *Works*, pp. 106–108.

Miscellaneous Resources

Drawings: Houghton Library, Harvard University.

Photographs: Boston Athenaeum; Columbia Historical Society; District of Columbia Public Library; John Hay Library, Brown University; Houghton Library, Harvard University; Massachusetts Historical Society; Society for the Preservation of New England Antiquities.

Letters: John Hay Papers, John Hay Library, Brown University; Adams Family Papers, Massachusetts Historical Society.

118b
John Hay house,
entry; Boston
Athenaeum.

118c
John Hay house,
stair hall; John Hay
Library, Brown
University.

118d
John Hay house,
dining room; John
Hay Library,
Brown University.

119b
Henry Adams
house, under con-
struction; courtesy
Massachusetts His-
torical Society,
photo by Marian
(Clover) Hooper
Adams.

119c
Henry Adams house; courtesy Society for the Preservation of New England Antiquities.

119d
Henry Adams house, detail of ground floor; Boston Athenaeum.

120

F. L. Ames Gardener's Cottage, 1884–1885
149 Elm Street
North Easton, Massachusetts

F. L. Ames (see no. 68) commissioned a gardener's cottage when the space in the Ames gate lodge (no. 78) proved inadequate for the gardener's growing family. The site for this small house was adjacent to the working part of Langwater, the Ames estate, near the stables, conservatory, and planting beds.

Van Rensselaer dates the project as entering Richardson's office in March 1884. Construction of this minor project by local contractors at a cost of only $3,562 was completed by January 1886.

The cottage was later enlarged by Shepley, Rutan and Coolidge, who added a complete second floor in place of Richardson's original asymmetrical gable. The cottage remains in private ownership today. It has been completely reshingled, white shutters of incompatible design have been added to the windows, and the back porch has been enclosed.

Richardson's plan of the cottage was nearly square. The first floor included kitchen, dining, and sitting rooms and the second floor three bedrooms. The roof swept down over the second floor, making an asymmetrical gable toward the front, but this apparently caused too great a reduction in upstairs floor space, so it was modified by Shepley, Rutan and Coolidge. The major unusual feature of the house is the rounded projection at one rear corner topped with a conical roof. Across the back of the house and merging into the round projection was an open porch. The house is sheathed entirely in wood shingles.

Textual References

Brown, Robert F. "The Aesthetic Transformation of an Industrial Community." *Winterthur Portfolio* 12 (1977): 35–64.

Hitchcock, *Richardson*, 1966, p. 272.

Homolka, Larry J. "Richardson's North Easton." *AF* 124 (May 1966): 72–77.

————. "Henry Hobson Richardson and the 'Ames Memorial Buildings.'" Ph.D. dissertation, Harvard University, 1976.

Scully, *Shingle Style*, pp. 97–98.

Miscellaneous Resources

Drawings: Houghton Library, Harvard University.

120a
F. L. Ames gar-
dener's cottage,
North Easton,
Massachusetts,
1884–1885; photo
by Berenice Abbott
(ca. 1934).

120b
F. L. Ames gar-
dener's cottage
(1972).

121

Young Men's Association Library Project (Competition), 1884
Broadway at Washington Street
Buffalo, New York

In 1884 the Young Men's Association (a Buffalo philanthropic organization), the Buffalo Fine Arts Academy (ancestor to the Albright-Knox Art Gallery), the Buffalo Historical Society, and the Society of Natural History joined to construct a new building for their combined use. According to Kowsky, the leading member of the building committee was librarian Josephus Nelson Larned (1836–1913), who visited several eastern cities to consult with architects, possibly including Richardson. On April 16, 1884 official notices of the competition were sent out to every architect in Buffalo and to thirteen others elsewhere. The competition prospectus included suggested plans and the requirement that the stacks conform to a modified version of the metallic book stack system used at Gore Hall, Harvard University (1874–1877) by Ware and Van Brunt.

Richardson's name was probably included at the suggestion of his friend and patron, William Dorsheimer (see no. 15), a major subscriber to the project. By July 1, 1884 when competition entries were due, designs were received from Richardson, C. L. W. Eidlitz (1853–1921) of New York, son of Richardson's New York Capitol collaborator Leopold Eidlitz (see no. 61), W. H. Wilcox of Saint Paul, Minnesota, Van Brunt and Howe of Boston, William Watson of Montreal, Warner and Brockett of Rochester, besides Beebe and Freeman, August Esenwein and F. W. Humble, C. R. Percival, and H. MacDiarmid, all of Buffalo. The building committee made its selection July 11, 1886, but did not announce the winner until July 18, 1886. Eidlitz's design placed first, followed by those of Richardson and Wilcox. Kowsky suggests that one reason for the rejection of Richardson's scheme may have been its probable cost in excess of the $225,000 budgeted for construction.

Eidlitz's design was built and opened in March 1887. In 1963 the building was razed for construction of the new Buffalo and Erie County Public Library.

Richardson's design conformed to the outlines of the triangular downtown Buffalo site. His scheme generally followed the plan suggested in the competition entry, but with modifications designed to achieve a greater degree of compactness. The design was a flattened letter *A* in plan with entrance, offices of the various societies, and reading rooms at the top, while gallery and book stack wings ran along the legs of the *A*. Richardson designed the two wings with a narrow gallery enclosing a small trapezoidal courtyard. At each of the four corners of his building, Richardson placed a round tower topped with a conical roof. The building was to be constructed of red sandstone with a roof of red terra cotta tiles. When Richardson recognized the impossibility of constructing this design for the budgeted $225,000, he added the suggestion that a less expensive building might be executed in brick.

121a
Young Men's Association Library project; *AABN* 21 (Apr. 23, 1887).

Textual References

The Buffalo Library and Its Building. Buffalo: Matthews, Northrup and Company, 1887.

"Design submitted for Young Men's Christian [*sic*] Association Building, Buffalo, N.Y." *AABN* 21 (Apr. 23, 1887): 199.

Hitchcock, *Richardson*, 1966, p. 258.

Kowsky, Francis R. *Buffalo Projects: H. H. Richardson*. Buffalo: Buffalo State College Foundation, 1980, pp. 14–15.

————. "H. H. Richardson's Project for the Young Men's Association Library in Buffalo." *Niagara Frontier* 25 (1978): 29–35.

O'Gorman, *Selected Drawings*, pp. 169–170.

Van Rensselaer, *Works*, p. 83 (plan).

"Young Men's Association Building, Buffalo, N.Y." *Scientific American* 4 (July 1887): 24.

Miscellaneous Resources

Drawings: Houghton Library, Harvard University.

Scrapbook: Buffalo and Erie County Library archives.

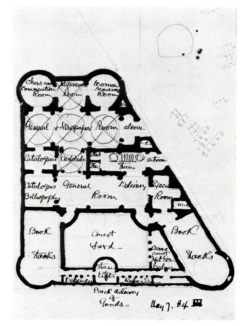

121b
Young Men's Association Library project, Buffalo, New York, 1884, sketch plan; Houghton Library, Harvard University.

122

**Boston & Albany Railroad
Station, Brighton, 1884–1885**
Brighton Center
Boston, Massachusetts
Demolished 1960s

The Brighton station was another of
the commuter stations on the Boston
& Albany main line which came to
Richardson through the efforts of
James A. Rumrill and Charles S. Sargent (see no. 86). Van Rensselaer gives
July 1884 as the date this station was
commissioned. Construction by Norcross Brothers was completed in 1885.
The Boston & Albany *Annual Report*
for 1885 indicates an expenditure of
$13,267 for that year, but the total
cost is unknown. This station was destroyed when the Massachusetts Turnpike was extended through Brighton
Center.

In plan the Brighton station was a
simple rectangle with a central ticket
office and waiting rooms for men and
women to either side. The telegraph
office and baggage room were located
at one end. Of granite laid up in random ashlar and trimmed with brownstone, the station was built on an
embankment above the tracks, a
porch formed by the continuous slope
of the slate roof down to the tracks.
An eyelid dormer allowed light to
reach the underside of the porch.

Textual References

*Annual Report of the Directors of the Bos-
ton & Albany Railroad Company to the
Stockholders.* No. 18. Boston: Rand
Avery, 1885.

*Around the Station: The Town and the
Train.* Framingham: Danforth Museum,
1978.

Hitchcock, *Richardson*, 1966, pp. 225,
263.

"Railway Stations at Wellesley Hills, Waban, Woodland, Auburndale, Brighton,
South Framingham, Palmer, Holyoke and
North Easton, Mass." *AABN* 21 (Feb. 26,
1887): 103.

Robinson, Charles Mulford. "Suburban
Station Grounds." *House and Garden* 5
(Apr. 1904): 182–187.

Miscellaneous Resources

Photographs: Boston Public Library;
Houghton Library, Harvard University.

122a
Boston & Albany
Railroad Station,
Brighton, Boston,
Massachusetts,
1884–1885, plan;
AABN 21 (Feb. 26,
1887).

122b
Boston & Albany
Railroad Station,
Brighton; Hough-
ton Library, Har-
vard University.

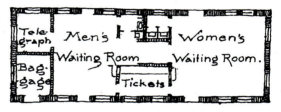

123

Gymnasium Project, 1884
University of Vermont
Burlington, Vermont

The University of Vermont Gymnasium project is known only from four small sketches in the collection at Houghton Library. According to a letter discovered in the university archives by Richard Janson of the university's Fine Arts Department, Richardson submitted sketches of a gymnasium to the University President, Matthew H. Buckham. Although the letter is undated, Gloria Scott determined that it must have been written in 1884 from its discussion of progress on the Billings Library (no. 107). The gymnasium project went no further, probably because of lack of funds. In 1901 a gymnasium was erected from the designs of the Boston firm Andrews, Jacques, and Rantoul. (Andrews and Jacques were both formerly draftsmen in Richardson's office.)

Richardson's drawings show a *T* shaped building. The roof slopes from a ridge along the center of the stem of the *T*. At the end of each arm is an arched opening, one for windows and the other as an entry. Each sketch shows a different distribution of fenestration at the center of the main facade. According to Richardson's letter, he followed the recommendations of Dr. Dudle Sargeant, director of Hemenway Gymnasium at Harvard University, and planned a column-free space measuring 40 by 80 feet with a suspended gallery and lighting from above.

Miscellaneous Resources

Drawings: Houghton Library, Harvard University.

Letter: University of Vermont archives.

123a
Gymnasium project, University of Vermont, Burlington, Vermont, 1884, sketch; Houghton Library, Harvard University.

123b
Gymnasium project, elevation; Houghton Library, Harvard University.

124
Immanuel Baptist Church, 1884–1886
187 Church Street
(at Centre Street)
Newton, Massachusetts

The Newton Baptist Society was organized in 1860 and built its first meeting house three years later. Growth of Newton was paralleled by growth of the society. In 1880 a committee was formed to erect a new building. The purchase of the site at the corner of Centre Street and Church Street, Newton Center, was announced to the congregation in 1884. Plans were then solicited from several architects, but each time the designs were rejected as too expensive. Subsequently, Richardson became involved in the project by agreeing to receive no fee unless he produced an acceptable design.

The commission entered Richardson's office in October 1884, according to Van Rensselaer. Construction by Norcross Brothers began in February 1885, and the cornerstone was laid May 1. The building, which cost about $70,000, was dedicated February 22, 1886.

Several alterations have been made to the church interior since 1886. In 1907 the chancel was completely redone, while stained glass windows were added over the years. In the 1960s the church was hit by lightning and the ensuing fire destroyed much of the interior. The reconstructed tower ceiling was lowered, cutting off light from the tower windows. Of the Richardson interior little remains save for some of the original pews. The society is now smaller and services are not usually held in the main auditorium.

Richardson's design for Immanuel Baptist Church has a cruciform plan with a square tower rising over the crossing. The ground floor was occupied by offices, classrooms, dining room, and kitchen, the upper floor by the main auditorium. The focus of the design was the raised baptistry at the center of the chancel. The dressing rooms for the baptismal candidates were organized in a radial pattern along the curved chancel wall. The pews in the nave and transept were concentrically arranged to focus on the baptistry. The building was simply constructed of brownstone laid in courses, even through early drawings in the Houghton collection show polychromy and carved detailing (these details were rejected by the society). The projecting stone blocks at the main roof were meant to be carved, but this was never done. Now painted over in a cream color, the original interior was dark red with blue stenciling.

Van Trump suggested that this building is a modified version of the rejected scheme for Emmanuel Church (no. 111). The exterior design resembles the earlier project, but the two interiors are completely different.

Textual References

"Baptist Church, Newton, Mass." *AABN* 22 (Oct. 1, 1887): 159.

"Baptist Church, Newton, Mass." *American Buildings, Selections*, no. 3, pl. 19.

Beale, Margaret E. "The Newton Baptist Church: A Late Building by H. H. Richardson." Typescript, Harvard University Fine Arts Department, January 1975.

Feldman, Lynn. "A History of H. H. Richardson's Immanuel Baptist Church, Newton, Massachusetts." Typescript, Harvard University, 1975.

Hitchcock, *Richardson*, 1966, pp. 262, 327 (see note xiii–24).

Sweetser, Moses Foster, ed. *King's Handbook of Newton*. Boston: Moses King, 1889, pp. 76–77.

Van Rensselaer, *Works*, pp. 94–95.

Van Trump, James D. "The Church Beyond Fashion." *Charette* 38 (Apr. 1958): 26–29.

Miscellaneous Resources

Drawings: Houghton Library, Harvard University.

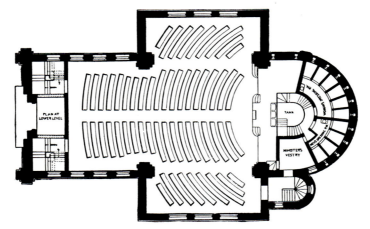

124a
Immanuel Baptist
Church, Newton,
Massachusetts,
1884–1886, plan;
Van Rensselaer,
Works, [1888].

124b
Immanuel Baptist
Church; *AABN* 22
(Oct. 1, 1887).

124c
Immanuel Baptist
Church (1972).

124d
Immanuel Baptist
Church, door detail
(1972).

125

**Boston & Albany Railroad
Station, Eliot, 1884–1888**
Circuit Avenue
Newton, Massachusetts
Demolished

125a
Boston & Albany
Railroad Station,
Eliot, Newton,
Massachusetts,
1884–1888;
Houghton Library,
Harvard University.

In 1883 the Boston & Albany Railroad decided to create a metropolitan commuter rail loop by constructing a three-mile segment of track from the existing commuter branch at Newton Highlands to the existing main line at Riverside. The completed line, called the "Circuit," served commuter traffic from all of the villages of Newton, with as many as thirty-five trains daily.

Construction of the new track was inaugurated in late 1883. In October 1884, according to Van Rensselaer, Richardson was awarded the commissions for the three new stations, at Eliot, Waban, and Woodland, on the new line, probably through the efforts of James A. Rumrill and Charles S. Sargent (see no. 86). The new line was opened May 16, 1886, and the three stations were opened as they were completed.

Although the Eliot Station was commissioned as one of the three "Circuit" stations, it was the last of this group to be completed. Construction by Norcross Brothers began in fall 1887 and was completed in December 1888 at a cost of $6,143.

The "Circuit" line is now operated as part of the network of the Massachusetts Bay Transportation Authority. The stations at Eliot and Waban have both been destroyed for parking lots.

The Boston & Albany Eliot station was the simplest of Richardson's commuter designs. Constructed of granite with brownstone trim, the building was a low rectangle with a general waiting room, small baggage room, restrooms, ticket office and inset porch on the trackside. It was covered by the high slate roof which bulged slightly above the bay window of the ticket office. A carriage porch projected away from the track.

Textual References

Annual Report of the Directors of the Boston & Albany Railroad Company to the Stockholders. Nos. 16, 19. Boston: Rand Avery, 1883, 1886.

Around the Station: The Town and the Train. Framingham: Danforth Museum, 1978.

Hitchcock, *Richardson*, 1966, p. 263.

Miscellaneous Resources

Photographs: Houghton Library, Harvard University.

126

**Boston & Albany Railroad
Station, Waban, 1884–1886**
Woodward Street at Beacon
Street, Waban Square
Newton, Massachusetts
Demolished

The Waban station of the Boston & Albany Railroad was the second of the three commuter stations on the Newton "Circuit" (see no. 125) awarded to Richardson's office in October 1884. Construction by Norcross Brothers began in March, 1886, and was completed in July at a cost of $5,631. According to *King's Handbook of Newton*, the Waban station opened August 16, 1886, the first of the three Circuit stations to be put in operation.

Waban remains a transit stop, but the station has been destroyed, again for a parking lot.

In plan the Waban station was a rectangle with a single round projection at one corner on the track side which served as the ticket office. The plan also included a general waiting room, rest rooms, and a baggage room. The building of granite with brownstone trim had a low roof with projecting eaves and a single dormer on the track side to light the waiting room.

Textual References

Annual Report of the Directors of the Boston & Albany Railroad Company to the Stockholders. Nos. 16, 19. Boston: Rand Avery, 1883, 1886.

Around the Station: The Town and the Train. Framingham: Danforth Museum, 1978.

Hitchcock, *Richardson*, 1966, p. 263.

"Railway Stations at Wellesley Hills, Waban, Woodland, Auburndale, Brighton, South Framingham, Palmer, Holyoke and North Easton, Mass." *AABN* 21 (Feb. 26, 1887): 103.

Robinson, Charles Mulford. "Suburban Station Grounds." *House and Garden* 5 (Apr. 1904): 182–187.

Sweetser, Moses Foster, ed. *King's Handbook of Newton*. Boston: Moses King, 1889, pp. 231–233.

Van Rensselaer, *Works*, p. 100.

Miscellaneous Resources

Drawings: Houghton Library, Harvard University.

Photographs: Boston Public Library; Houghton Library, Harvard University.

126a
Boston & Albany
Railroad Station,
Waban, Newton,
Massachusetts,
1884–1886, plan;
AABN 21 (Feb. 26,
1887).

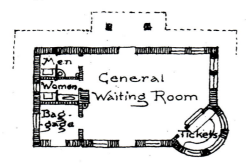

126b
Boston & Albany
Railroad Station,
Waban; Houghton
Library, Harvard
University.

127
Boston & Albany Railroad Station, Woodland, 1884–1886
1897 Washington Street,
Woodland
Newton, Massachusetts

The Woodland Station of the Boston & Albany was the third station of the group which entered Richardson's office in October 1884, according to Van Rensselaer (see no. 125). This station was the last of Richardson's small commuter stations in the villages of Newton, although his successors, Shepley, Rutan and Coolidge, were responsible for several others. Like all his other work for the Boston & Albany, this station came to Richardson through the efforts of James A. Rumrill and Charles S. Sargent (see no. 86).

Construction of the station was completed in 1886, after Richardson's death. The building cost $5,761. It remains today, but is now owned by the Woodland Country Club. It is used as a tool and equipment shed.

The station is a typical rectangle of granite and brownstone topped with a steep slate roof. The waiting room filled most of the interior with two restrooms and a baggage room at one end. Two porches were inset on either side of the ticket office on the track side.

Textual References

Annual Report of the Directors of the Boston & Albany Railroad Company to the Stockholders. Nos. 16, 19. Boston: Rand Avery, 1883, 1886.

Around the Station: The Town and the Train. Framingham: Danforth Museum, 1978.

Hitchcock, *Richardson*, 1966, p. 263.

"Railway Stations at Wellesley Hills, Waban, Woodland, Auburndale, Brighton, South Framingham, Palmer, Holyoke and North Easton, Mass." *AABN* 21 (Feb. 26, 1887): 103.

Robinson, Charles Mulford. "A Railroad Beautiful." *House and Garden* 2 (Nov. 1902): 564–570.

Van Rensselaer, *Works*, p. 102.

Miscellaneous Resources

Photographs: Boston Public Library; Houghton Library, Harvard University; Library of Congress (Historic American Buildings Survey).

127a
Boston & Albany
Railroad Station,
Woodland, New-
ton, Massachusetts,
1884–1886, Hough-
ton Library, Har-
vard University.

127b
Boston & Albany
Railroad Station,
Woodland, plan;
AABN 21 (Feb. 26,
1887).

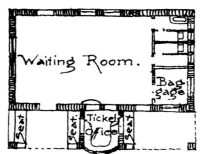

127c
Boston & Albany
Railroad Station,
Woodland; Library
of Congress (His-
toric American
Buildings Survey,
photo by Cervin
Robinson, 1959).

127d
Boston & Albany
Railroad Station
(1972).

128

Private Car (Project ?), ca. 1884
Boston & Albany Railroad

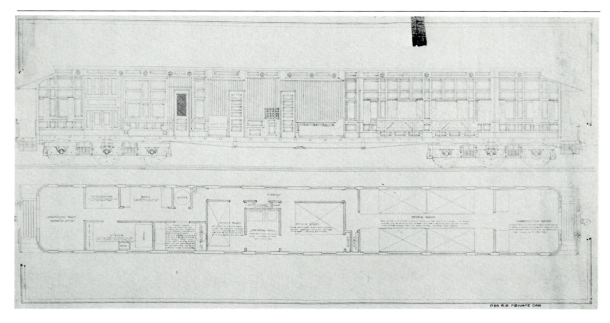

The private car commission undoubtedly came to Richardson through his
friends and patrons, Boston & Albany
directors James A. Rumrill and
Charles S. Sargent (see no. 86). It is
known only from drawings in the
Houghton Library collection, the date
1884 suggested by Hitchcock. It is unknown if the designs were executed.

The car had a wood exterior typical
of the period. The interior plan included staterooms, a dining room, ob-
servation rooms, and related service
and support facilities.

Textual References

Hitchcock, *Richardson*, 1966, p. 258.

O'Gorman, *Selected Drawings*, pp. 182–
183.

Miscellaneous Resources

Drawings: Houghton Library, Harvard
University.

128a
Private car
(project?), Boston
& Albany Rail-
road, ca. 1884,
plan and section;
Houghton Library,
Harvard University.

129
Ephraim W. Gurney House, 1884–1886
6 Greenwood Avenue
Beverly, Massachusetts

Professor Ephraim W. Gurney (1829–1886), who taught history and classics at Harvard University, became the first dean of the college during the presidency of Charles W. Eliot. With his wife Ellen Hooper, sister of Harvard Treasurer Edward (Ned) Hooper (see no. 68) and Marian (Clover) Hooper, wife of Henry Adams (see no. 119), Gurney purchased fifty acres of land in Beverly Farms near the village of Pride's Crossing on Boston's north shore.

Although Van Rensselaer dates the commission in Richardson's office December 1884, local newspaper accounts show that the design was under consideration as early as October, according to O'Gorman. Drawings were sent to Gurney in March 1885. The local contractors were selected in May 1885, and construction began soon after. The cost was $21,502. The family moved into the house August 14, 1886, after Richardson's death.

The house has been much altered by subsequent owners so that the complex massing is now confused. The house remains privately owned, even though it stood empty for twenty years after 1950. Since 1974 the house has been further modified inside to accommodate the new owners.

Richardson's design for the house apparently went through several stages. *The Beverly Citizen* report of October 18, 1884 described it as wood construction and Queen Anne style. Drawings in the Houghton collection show a house with a stone first floor and shingled second floor. Actually constructed of glacial boulders to the full height of the exterior walls, the house is rectangular with a two-story service wing to one side of the

central mass, a porch with a conical roof to the other side. A second porch was formed at the back of the house by the continuation of the steep slope of the slate roof. The interior is organized around a central stair and fireplace with the dining room to one side and living rooms to the other. The original interiors of delicate white painted wood were not typical of Richardson.

Textual References

Hitchcock, *Richardson*, 1966, p. 272.

O'Gorman, *Selected Drawings*, pp. 99–102.

———. "A Tragic Circle." *Nineteenth Century* 2 (Autumn 1976): 46–49.

Miscellaneous Resources

Drawings: Houghton Library, Harvard University.

Photographs: Boston Athenaeum.

129a
Ephraim W. Gurney
house, Beverly,
Massachusetts,
1884–1886; Boston
Athenaeum.

1885

Fountain Project, 1885
Fenway Park
Boston, Massachusetts

**Benjamin H. Warder House,
1885–1888**
1515 K Street N.W.
Washington, D.C.
Partially Rebuilt 1923

Zaitzevsky uncovered a card in the Olmsted National Historic Site files for a tracing paper drawing, "Richardson's Fountain Plan" (Back Bay Fens Plan No. 28). The date given is January 12, 1885. No description is given nor is the exact location known. The drawing has either been lost or misfiled.

Evidently the project came to Richardson as part of Olmsted's development of the Fens (nos. 80, 81). No other evidence or information has surfaced concerning this project.

Textual Reference

Zaitzevsky, Cynthia. "The Olmsted Firm and the Boston Park System." Ph.D. dissertation, Harvard University, 1975.

Benjamin Head Warder (1824–1894) founded a farm implements company in Springfield, Ohio about 1850. In 1864 the company was renamed Warder, Bushnell, and Glessner when J. J. Glessner (see no. 134) and Asa Bushnell (later governor of Ohio) became partners. Warder retired to Washington, D.C., in 1885, though he maintained close ties with his Springfield home—he later gave a public library building designed by Shepley, Rutan and Coolidge in Springfield.

Warder apparently selected Richardson as architect because Richardson was also designing a house for J. J. Glessner, his business partner, in Chicago (see no. 134). The Commission of Fine Arts also noted that as Warder and Nicholas Anderson (see no. 90) were both from Ohio, they may have been acquainted, and Anderson may have recommended Richardson. John Hay (see no. 118) also was from Ohio and might have introduced Richardson to Warder.

Van Rensselaer lists the commission as entering Richardson's office March 1885. Construction, by Norcross Brothers and others, did not begin until March 1886. Estimated at a cost of $80,000, construction proceeded after Richardson's death under the direction of Shepley, Rutan and Coolidge. The final cost of the house, completed in 1888, was $133,265.

The Warder family were socially prominent and used the house for entertaining and socializing. After her husband's death Mrs. Warder lived in the house until 1921. The house was then sold for development and demolition began soon after. The front portal was saved, however, for the Smithsonian where it remains as part of the

National Collection of Fine Arts (though it is now in storage). When the house was being demolished, George Oakley Totten (1866–1939), a Washington architect, bought all the materials except for the entry portal and re–erected the house at 2633 Sixteenth Street N.W. Totten recreated Richardson's facade, but redesigned the interior to accommodate three luxury apartments. Subsequently the house served as a clinic and then as the Lutheran Church Center. Since 1972 it has been owned by the Antioch (College) School of Law.

The Warder house was the largest of Richardson's Washington dwellings. It had an *L*-shaped plan and measured 73 feet wide by 77 feet deep. The plan of the house at the first floor was arranged around the grand entrance hall and stair. These were placed at the intersection of the *L* and were approached from the entry at the end of the wing of the *L* nearest K Street by a vestibule adjacent to the library. The longitudinal wing was filled by the large dining room and behind it a picture gallery. The outside angle of the *L* was the drawing room. Photographs of the interior show that carved stone arches spanned the openings between the entrance hall and stair, the dining room and picture gallery, and the vestibule and entrance hall. The exterior walls were constructed of smooth-faced cream-colored Ohio sandstone with nearly invisible joints. The roof of slate had gable ends and sloped steeply. A round tower with conical roof was located at the reentrant angle of the *L*-shaped plan. The windows were crisply cut into the mass of the house. Stone carving appeared at the entry portal, the second floor loggia, and a few other locations in marked contrast to the otherwise smooth-faced walls.

Textual References

Anderson, Isabel. *Letters and Journals of General Nicholas L. Anderson, 1854–1892*. New York: Fleming H. Revell, 1942.

Hitchcock, *Richardson*, 1966, pp. 278–279.

"House of B. H. Warder, Esq., Washington, D.C." *AABN* 33 (Aug. 1, 1891): 75.

Kohler, Sue A., and Carson, Jeffrey R., eds. *Sixteenth Street Architecture*. Washington: Commission of Fine Arts, 1978, 1: 121–142, 417–434.

"Reconstruction by George Oakley Totten, Jr. of the Original B. H. Warder House, Designed by the Late H. H. Richardson." *American Architect* 129 (May 20, 1926). n.p.

"Residence of B. H. Warder, Esq., Washington, D.C." *American Buildings, Selections*, no. 1: pl. 61, 72.

Van Rensselaer, *Works*, pp. 108–109.

Miscellaneous Resources

Drawings: Houghton Library, Harvard University.

Photographs: Frances B. Johnston collection, Library of Congress; Public Library of the District of Columbia.

131a
Benjamin H. War-
der house, Wash-
ington, D.C.,
1885–1888; Li-
brary of Congress
(Frances B. John-
ston collection).

131b
Benjamin H. Warder house, detail of entry; Library of Congress (Frances B. Johnston collection).

131c
Benjamin H. Warder house, entrance hall and stair; Library of Congress (Frances B. Johnston collection).

131d
Benjamin H. Warder house, dining room with gallery beyond; Library of Congress (Frances B. Johnston collection).

131e
Benjamin H. Warder house, reconstruction (1972).

Bagley Memorial Fountain, 1885–1887
Campus Martius
Detroit, Michigan

John Judson Bagley (1832–1881) was a major figure in the Detroit financial community as organizer of the Michigan Mutual Life Insurance Company, president of the Detroit Safe Company, and director of the American National Bank of Detroit. He also served as police commissioner, alderman, and the sixteenth governor of Michigan from 1873 to 1877.

In his will Bagley provided a bequest for a drinking fountain to provide "water cold and pure as the coldest mountain stream" for thirsty Detroiters. The Bagley family selected Richardson as the architect.

Van Rensselaer dates the commission as entering Richardson's office April 1885. Norcross Brothers executed the project at a cost of $7,339. It was unveiled May 30, 1887 in a location south of the Detroit City Hall.

In September 1925 the Detroit Common Council authorized moving the Bagley fountain to its present site on a traffic island. The water no longer spouts from the four carved lion heads but from a standard metal spigot instead.

Richardson's design for the Bagley fountain, executed entirely of white Worcester granite, includes four columns supporting a pyramidal roof with foliate carving. It stands eighteen feet high and is modeled on a ciborium in St. Mark's Cathedral, Venice. Originally the water in the fountain was cooled by ice deposited in the base over coils through which the

water passed. Four lion heads in the center discharged water, but only two expelled the cold water—the two others expelled normal-temperature water. The fountain was to operate from April to November each year.

Textual References

Ferry, W. Hawkins. *The Building of Detroit*. Detroit: Wayne State University Press, 1968, p. 130.

Hitchcock, *Richardson*, 1966, p. 279.

Van Rensselaer, *Works*, p. 98.

Miscellaneous Resources

Drawings: Houghton Library, Harvard University.

Photographs: Detroit Historical Museum; Detroit Public Library; Society for the Preservation of New England Antiquities.

132a
Bagley Memorial Fountain, Detroit, Michigan, 1885–1887; Society for the Preservation of New England Antiquities.

Marshall Field Wholesale Store,
1885–1887
West Adams Street at South
Franklin Street
Chicago, Illinois
Demolished 1930

Marshall Field (1834–1906) moved to Chicago from Massachusetts in 1856, and rose from a clerkship in a dry goods firm to become a partner in Cooley, Farwell and Company within six years. This company passed through a succession of partnership changes until Marshall Field & Company was established in 1881 with two divisions, retail and wholesale. The retail division was oriented to fashionable Chicago women; the wholesale division catered to the needs of out-of-town travelers on tight schedules. By 1883 the initially more successful wholesale division was five times larger than the retail division. Field also speculated in Chicago real estate, and in 1881, he completed acquisition of the half-block site for the construction of a new wholesale store.

The project entered Richardson's office in April 1885, according to Van Rensselaer. Preliminary studies, O'Gorman noted, must have been completed in spring and summer 1885, because Richardson required a site survey in August. Richardson visited Chicago in October and must have brought the working drawings at that time. The construction contract was awarded to Norcross Brothers when the construction documents were issued in the last week of October 1885, the cost estimated at $800,000.

Construction began in November and proceeded under the supervision of Shepley, Rutan and Coolidge after Richardson's death. Delayed by labor troubles in Chicago, including the Haymarket Riot, the building finally opened June 20, 1887. The final cost of the building was $888,007.

But the building stood only 43 years. By the 1920s the retail division of Marshall Field & Company had totally superseded the wholesale division. The wholesale trade was transferred in 1930 to a portion of the newly opened Merchandise Mart, and the Richardson store was demolished, without protest, for a parking lot during the months of May and June. Only two fragments of the building survive, as bench supports for the Horace Oakley Memorial Bench on the second fairway of the Lake Zurich (Illinois) Golf Club, west of Chicago.

Richardson's design passed through several stages traced in detail by O'Gorman. The initial scheme was a complete rectangle with a central light court. This was changed to a broad *U*-shaped plan with a loading dock in the center of the *U* off Quincy Street. A glass roof over the dock would have been supported by an iron suspension system, if built according to the drawings. The building rose seven stories above a basement with a total area of roughly 500,000 square feet. Each floor was divided into three rectangular sections by fire walls running north and south, separating the base of the *U*-shaped plan from the two sides. The otherwise open floors were supported by a regular grid of columns. Those from the basement to the third floor were iron with terra cotta fireproofing. Those of the fourth through seventh floors were heavy timber. The exterior walls of the store were constructed of a rock-faced Missouri red granite at the lower floor and cut East

Longmeadow red sandstone above. Richardson, O'Gorman states, had also studied brick for the walls, but Field insisted on stone. The windows above the first floor were grouped under arches in a rhythm which doubled and then quadrupled at the higher floors. The entry from Adams Street simply took the place which would have been occupied by the central window opening at the first floor. The masonry was laid up in even horizontal courses at the ground floor except for a narrow band at the window sills. A smooth-faced belt course formed the second floor window sills and above that the masonry alternated in wide and narrow courses. A band of squared stones was introduced at the fourth floor arch spandrels, the whole topped by a cornice with a foliate motif and a parapet cap.

The Field Store is probably the most famous of Richardson's buildings, one that Richardson himself saw as among his most significant. It inspired immediate comment by eastern writers who brought it to the attention of a broad audience. Louis Sullivan used it as a model for his early works and then praised it in *Kindergarten Chats*. Since its destruction it has become widely known from a few photographs which appear in virtually every history of modern architecture. But not until O'Gorman's efforts in 1978 had the building ever been the subject of scholarly research.

Textual References

Ditchett, Samuel H. *Marshall Field and Company: The Life Story of a Great Concern.* New York: Dry Goods Economist, 1922.

Flinn, John J. *Chicago: Marvelous City of the West.* Chicago: The Standard Guide Company, 1891, pp. 511–512.

Granger, Alfred H. *Chicago Welcomes You.* Chicago: A. Kroch, 1933, pp. 119–120.

Hitchcock, *Richardson*, 1966, pp. 273–277.

McLintock, S. "History of Marshall Field & Company." Unpublished typescript, Marshall Field & Company archives, n.d.

O'Gorman, James F. "The Marshall Field Wholesale Store: Materials Toward a Monograph." *JSAH* 37 (Oct. 1978): 175–194.

O'Gorman, *Selected Drawings*, pp. 115–120.

Tallmadge, Thomas E. *Architecture in Old Chicago.* Chicago: University of Chicago Press, 1941, pp. 137–142.

Twyman, Robert W. *History of Marshall Field & Co.* Philadelphia: University of Pennsylvania Press, 1954, pp. 96–97.

Van Rensselaer, *Works*, pp. 95–97.

Wendt, Lloyd and Kogan, Herman. *Give the Lady What She Wants.* New York: Rand McNally, 1952, p. 194.

"Wholesale Store of Marshall Field & Co., Chicago." *American Buildings, Selections*, no. 4, pl. 36.

Miscellaneous Resources

Drawings: Houghton Library, Harvard University.

Photographs: Art Institute of Chicago; Chicago Architectural Photographic Company; Chicago Historical Society.

Letters: H. H. Richardson Papers, Archives of American Art Microfilm Roll 643.

133a
Marshall Field
Wholesale Store,
Chicago, Illinois,
1885–1887, second
floor plan showing
regular column grid
and framing, cen-
tral staircase, fire-
walls, and roof
suspended over
loading dock;
Houghton Library,
Harvard University.

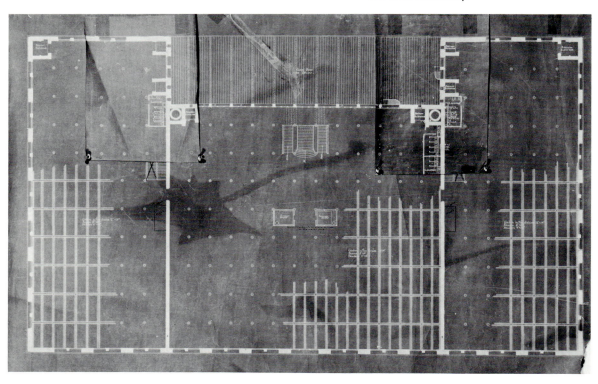

133b
Marshall Field
Wholesale Store;
Chicago Architec-
tural Photograph-
ing Company.

133c
Marshall Field
Wholesale Store;
Chicago Historical
Society.

133d
Marshall Field
Wholesale Store,
loading dock on
Quincy Street;
S. H. Ditchett,
*Marshall Field and
Company*, 1922.

133e
Marshall Field
Wholesale Store,
interior, drapery
and upholstery de-
partment; Ditchett,
*Marshall Field and
Company.*

133f
Marshall Field
Wholesale Store,
interior, eighth
floor packing de-
partment; Ditchett,
*Marshall Field and
Company.*

134

J. J. Glessner House, 1885–1887
1800 South Prairie Avenue
Chicago, Illinois

John Jacob Glessner (1843–1936) was vice-president of Warder, Bushnell and Glessner, a farm implements manufacturer in Springfield, Ohio. In 1885 Glessner moved to Chicago in connection with the business of his firm, the same year his partner Warder retired to Washington, D.C., and commissioned a residence from Richardson (see no. 131). Seventeen years later Warder, Bushnell and Glessner was one of five companies merged to form International Harvester, of which Glessner became a vice president.

Glessner purchased lots at the corner of South Prairie Avenue and Eighteenth Street, a fashionable area where both Marshall Field and George Pullman also lived. The Glessners enumerated the rooms they required and insisted that Richardson design as he thought best. According to Glessner's own account, Richardson sketched the plan of the house the day after he visited the site. Sprague dated this sketch May 16, 1885. (Van Rensselaer also dates the commission in May.) The basic construction documents were completed in February 1886 and sent in early March, although details were drawn as late as 1887. Norcross was selected as builder and signed a contract for construction May 20, 1886. The cost of the project was $98,830. The Glessners occupied the house after December 1, 1887.

Glessner wrote for his children an unpublished book describing life in the house, which was frequented by literary and cultured Chicagoans. But the neighborhood changed rapidly; by Glessner's death in 1936, it had become an area of light industry. Glessner willed the house to the Chicago chapter of the American Institute of Architects, but they were unable to maintain it and therefore returned the house to the Glessner estate. The heirs then gave it to the Armour Institute, now the Illinois Institute of Technology. The house passed to the Graphic Arts Technical Foundation in 1958. In 1966 the Chicago School of Architecture Foundation was formed to save and renovate the Glessner house. From 1966 to 1972 the group worked on its restoration. The stables were converted to an auditorium, and the Chicago AIA chapter now occupies space in the house, where tours for the public are given daily.

Richardson's plan for the Glessner house was a marked departure from previous construction along Prairie Avenue, which had been detached houses facing the street. Richardson designed the house in an *L*-shaped plan with the outside walls of the *L* pushed right up to the two street property lines. Almost all of the major rooms on the first floor faced the interior court. The central hall with stair was located at the center of the *L* plan with the library and parlor adjoining and the dining room beyond the parlor. The service wing occupied the top of the *L*, beyond which was the stable. The exterior walls on the two streets were built of rock-faced granite laid in horizontal courses of varying width. The lintels over the windows were flat but a large arch was used over the front door and a second arch was over the side entrance porch. The walls facing the court, executed in brick with granite lintels and sills, were marked by three round projections of varying function and design.

Textual References

"The Architects Club of Chicago." *American Architect* 127 (Jan. 14, 1925): 11–12.

"Chicago School of Architecture Foundation." *Inland Architect* 10 (May 1967): 12–13.

Glessner, John J. "The Story of a House." Unpublished, 1923. Excerpts in Lee, Percy Maxim and Lee, John Glessner. *Family Reunion.* ?: privately printed, 1971.

Hitchcock, *Richardson*, 1966, 277–278.

"Hope for Glessner House?" *PA* 47 (June 1966): 60, 63.

Miller, Nory. "A New Life for Glessner House, that 'Granite Hut' on Prairie Avenue." *Inland Architect* 15 (Sept. 1971): 30–33.

Newman, M. W. "Granite Hut: H. H. Richardson's Glessner House is Sowing New Oats on Chicago's South Prairie Avenue." *AF* 137 (Nov. 1972): 34, 41.

O'Gorman, *Selected Drawings*, pp. 87–91.

Price, Charles. "H. H. Richardson: Some Unpublished Drawings." *Perspecta* 9–10 (1965): 200–210.

"Residence of J. J. Glessner, Chicago." *American Buildings, Selections*, no. 1; pl. 67.

"Residence of J. J. Glessner, Chicago, Illinois." *ARec* 6 (July–Sept. 1886): 83.

"A Solid Base for the Chicago School." *AIAJ* 49 (Feb. 1968): 76.

Sprague, Paul. "Glessner House." *Outdoor Illinois* (May 1973): 8–23.

Van Rensselaer, *Works*, pp. 109–110.

Van Zanten, David T. "H. H. Richardson's Glessner House, Chicago, 1886–1887." *JSAH* 23 (May 1964): 106–111.

Miscellaneous Resources

Drawings: Houghton Library, Harvard University.

Photographs: Art Institute of Chicago; Chicago Architectural Photograph Company; Chicago Historical Society; Library of Congress (Historic American Buildings Survey).

Archives: Chicago School of Architecture Foundation.

Letters: H. H. Richardson Papers, Archives of American Art Microfilm Roll 643.

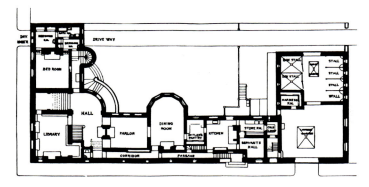

134a
J. J. Glessner house, Chicago, Illinois, 1885–1887, floor plan; Van Rensselaer, *Works*, [1888].

134b
J. J. Glessner house, front elevation; Library of Congress (Historic American Buildings Survey, photo by J. J. Glessner, 1923).

134c
J. J. Glessner house, side elevation; Library of Congress (Historic American Buildings Survey, photo by Cervin Robinson, 1963).

134d
J. J. Glessner house,
courtyard; Library
of Congress (His-
toric American
Buildings Survey,
photo by J. J.
Glessner, 1923).

134e
J. J. Glessner house,
detail of gable and
chimney; Library of
Congress (Historic
American Buildings
Survey, photo by
J. J. Glessner,
1923).

134f
J. J. Glessner house,
stair hall; Library
of Congress (His-
toric American
Buildings Survey,
photo by J. J.
Glessner, 1923).

134g
J. J. Glessner house,
stair hall; Library
of Congress (His-
toric American
Buildings Survey,
photo by J. J.
Glessner, 1923).

134h
J. J. Glessner house,
library; Library of
Congress (Historic
American Buildings
Survey, J. J. Gless-
ner, 1923).

135
Franklin MacVeagh House, 1885–1887
103 North Lake Shore Drive
(at Schiller Court)
Chicago, Illinois
Demolished 1922

Franklin MacVeagh (1837–1934) was a Chicago attorney and owner of Franklin MacVeagh and Company, wholesale grocers. He was nominated for the United States Senate in 1894 and served as U.S. secretary of the treasury from 1909 to 1913.

According to Van Rensselaer, the MacVeagh commission entered Richardson's office in July 1885. Richardson probably met MacVeagh through one of his other Chicago clients: Glessner (see no. 134) or Field (see no. 133). Construction of the house by local contractors began in 1886 and was completed the following year at a cost of $81,492.

The MacVeagh house was demolished in 1922. This area of the lakefront is now occupied by high rise apartment buildings (1400 Lake Shore Drive).

The MacVeagh house was a three-story building organized on an *L*-shaped plan. From the street the house appeared as a solid mass. The main entry, on Schiller Court, led to a vestibule and then to the central hall at the corner of the *L*. Around this were arranged the interior living spaces. At the front of the house a broad loggia faced Lake Michigan. A service wing with laundry and stables was at the top of the *L*. The three-story building was constructed of granite in alternating wide and narrow courses. The front of the house was marked by the contrasting treatment of the corners, one rounded and one faceted, each with a pointed roof separate from the main mass of the high roof. On the courtyard side a round projection with conical roof was located at the reentrant angle of the *L*.

Textual References

"Entrance to the Residence of Franklin MacVeagh, Chicago." *American Buildings, Selections*, no. 1, pl. 78.

Hamlin, A. D. F. "The Genesis of the American Country House." *ARec* 42 (Oct. 1917): 291–299.

Hitchcock, *Richardson*, 1966, pp. 279–280.

"Residence of Franklin MacVeagh, Esq., Chicago." *AABN* 36 (Apr. 15, 1893).

Van Rensselaer, *Works*, p. 108.

Miscellaneous Resources

Drawings: Houghton Library, Harvard University.

Photographs: Art Institute of Chicago; Chicago Historical Society.

135a
Franklin MacVeagh
house, Chicago, Il-
linois, 1885–1887;
Chicago Historical
Society.

135b
Franklin MacVeagh
house; Art Institute
of Chicago.

135c
Franklin MacVeagh
house, detail of en-
try; Art Institute of
Chicago.

136
Chamber of Commerce
Building, 1885–1888
Fourth Street at Vine Street
Cincinnati, Ohio
Demolished 1911

The Cincinnati Chamber of Commerce was founded in October 1839. After occupying six different locations over the next thirty-eight years, the Chamber in 1876 began to plan for a permanent meeting place. On March 13, 1883, the Chamber bylaws were amended to create a board of real estate managers for the purpose of constructing a new building, and the first board was elected in September 1883. Fund raising proceeded thereafter and was so successful that on December 17, 1884, the Board sent out a circular inviting architects to submit plans for the new structure. Six architects and firms were selected to compete and were each paid $500 for their drawings: H. H. Richardson of Boston; George B. Post of New York; Burnham and Root of Chicago; and James W. McLaughlin, Samuel Hannaford, and A. C. Nash, all of Cincinnati. In addition, Samuel Thayer and F. M. Clark, both of Boston, Bruce Price of New York, M. E. Beebe and Son of Buffalo, and Charles Crapsey of Cincinnati also submitted entries. Joint designs were received from A. G. Everett and E. M. Wheelwright of Boston, and Edwin Anderson and H. E. Siter of Cincinnati.

Richardson's design was accepted June 8, 1885, the project entering his office books in August. According to Rudd, Richardson modified his scheme slightly and then began to prepare construction documents. The chamber purchased the site for the building on December 16, 1885, as they had arranged in 1880. Richardson's plans and specifications were approved and then sent to bidders in January 1886. Received May 17, 1886 (after Richardson's death), the bids so exceeded the original estimate that they were all rejected. Thereafter a separate contract was awarded to Patrick Murray, a local contractor, for excavations and foundations. Further bids were received December 21, 1886, and on January 1, 1887 a contract was awarded to Norcross Brothers. The building was dedicated January 29–30, 1889. The total cost of the building and foundations was $596,414—with the land, furnishings, and fees, $772,674.

The Chamber of Commerce Buildin stood only twenty-three years. On January 10, 1911, a grease fire in a flue from the kitchen spread to the eighth floor and was soon out of control. The building was completely destroyed by fire.

According to documents uncovered by O'Gorman in the archives of Oberlin College, Cass Gilbert suggested in August 1911 that the stone details from the chamber of commerce might be used in new buildings designed for the college, but apparently nothing came of this proposal. In 1927 the Cincinnati Astronomical Society proposed to reuse the stone from the building in the construction of an observatory, with the same results as the Oberlin proposal. Finally, architectural students at the University of Cincinnati held a design competition in 1968 to erect a monument using some of the remaining granite fragments. The winning design was constructed in 1972 on a knoll in Burnet Woods on the outskirts of Cincinnati.

According to O'Gorman, the Cincinnati Chamber of Commerce design recalls Richardson's training at the Ecole des Beaux-Arts in its planning for "served" and "servant" zones. A rectangular area at the rear of the building contained all the vertical circulation and utilities; the rest of each floor was usable space. Vertically the building was organized as a series of layers of different types of space. The ground floor was leased and served different commercial establishments over the life of the building. At the second level was the exchange hall, with forty-eight-foot ceiling height. Above the hall were three stories of offices and clubrooms rented to different organizations. These offices were hung from fourteen iron trusses at the roof level, allowing the exchange hall to be completely column-free. Richardson originally proposed that the building be constructed of either brick or brownstone, but this was changed to Milford granite similar to that used for the Allegheny County Buildings in Pittsburgh (no. 116). The chief features of the exterior were the round corner towers with tall conical roofs. The street facades were marked by the tall arched windows of the exchange hall. Above these the windows of two office floors were grouped under arches and the hipped roof broken by multiple high dormers.

Textual References

"Capitals from the Chamber of Commerce, Cincinnati, Ohio." *AABN* 27 (Mar. 1, 1890): 141.

"Chamber of Commerce, Cincinnati, Ohio." *American Buildings, Selections*, no. 2: pl. 70–72; 4: pl. 16.

Cincinnati Astronomical Society. *Richardson the Architect and the Cincinnati Chamber of Commerce*. Cincinnati: [Cincinnati Astronomical Society?], 1914.

Cincinnati Chamber of Commerce and Merchant's Exchange. *Annual Reports*. Nos. 25–78, 1850–1928. Cincinnati: Chamber of Commerce, 1850–1928.

"Cincinnati Chamber of Commerce Building." *Cincinnati Enquirer Almanac* (1896–1899). Cincinnati: Cincinnati Enquirer, 1899, p. 20.

"Design for Chamber of Commerce and Merchants Exchange, Cincinnati, Ohio." *Building* 3 (Aug. 1885): pl. 171.

"From Chamber of Commerce, Cincinnati, Ohio." *Inland Architect and News Record* 12 (Jan. 1889).

"H. H. Richardson Lives Again." *ARec* 143 (May 1968): 36.

Hitchcock, *Richardson*, 1966, p. 281.

"Interior of the Chamber of Commerce, Cincinnati, Ohio." *AABN* 29 (July 12, 1890): 29.

"Our Cincinnati Letter." *Building, An Architectural Monthly* 3 (July 1885): 110; 3 (Aug. 1885): 126.

"Resurrecting Richardson." *Architecture Plus* 1 (Feb. 1973): 20.

[H. H. Richardson]. *Cincinnati Chamber of Commerce*. Boston: [1885].

Roe, George Mortimer, ed. *Cincinnati: The Queen City of the West*. Cincinnati: Cincinnati Times-Star Company, 1895, pp. 99–101.

Rudd, J. William. "The Cincinnati Chamber of Commerce Building." *JSAH* 27 (May 1968): 115–123.

Schuyler, Montgomery. "The Building of Cincinnati." *ARec* 23 (May 1908): 337–366.

"A Theory Accounting for Structural Weakness." *AABN* 99 (Jan. 25, 1911): 41.

Van Rensselaer, *Works*, pp. 97–99.

Miscellaneous Resources

Drawings: Houghton Library, Harvard University.

Photographs: Boston Athenaeum; Cincinnati Historical Society; Cincinnati Public Library.

Archives: Oberlin College.

136a
Chamber of Com-
merce Building,
Cincinnati, Ohio,
1885–1888, trans-
verse section;
Houghton Library,
Harvard University.

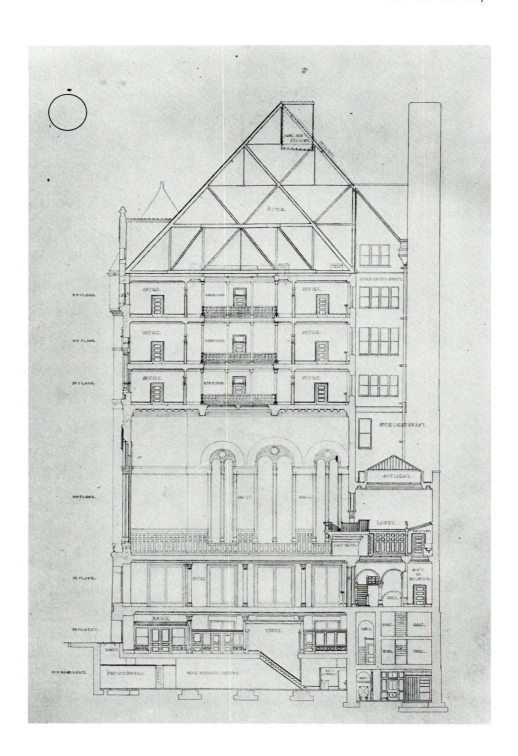

136b
Chamber of Com-
merce Building;
Boston Athenaeum.

136c
Chamber of Commerce Building; Cincinnati Astronomical Society, *Richardson the Architect and the Chamber of Commerce Building*, 1914; Public Library of Cincinnati and Hamilton County.

136d
Chamber of Commerce Building, detail of windows; *Richardson, The Architect and the Chamber of Commerce Building*; Public Library of Cincinnati and Hamilton County.

136e
Chamber of Commerce Building, trading room; Boston Athenaeum.

137
Boston & Albany Railroad Station, Wellesley Hills, 1885–1886
339 Washington Street
Wellesley Hills, Massachusetts

The Wellesley Hills station on the Boston & Albany main line was the last of the commuter station commissions which Richardson executed for the Boston & Albany Railroad. Like Richardson's earlier Boston & Albany projects, this must have come to him through the efforts of James A. Rumrill and Charles S. Sargent (see no. 86).

Van Rensselaer lists the commission as entering Richardson's office in July 1885. Construction by Norcross Brothers began in September 1885 and was completed in January 1886, at a cost of $10,054.

In 1958 the station was remodeled for use as a dry cleaners. The roof and front were altered, and white asphalt shingles were substituted for slate. In 1978 the building was again remodeled for use by a bank.

The station at Wellesley Hills was a rectangle with two round projections at the two trackside corners. The interior was designed with a large square central waiting room with men's and women's restrooms to either side at the front and the ticket office and baggage room to either side at the back. The building was constructed of granite with brownstone trim. The slate hipped roof extended to create wide, sheltering eaves and on the track side swept down to cover the station platform.

Textual References

Annual Report of the Directors of the Boston & Albany Railroad Company to the Stockholders. No. 18. Boston: Rand Avery, 1885.

Around the Station: The Town and the Train. Framingham: Danforth Museum, 1978.

Blair, Eleanor. *Wellesley: College and Community.* Wellesley: 1974, pp. 124–125.

Hitchcock, *Richardson*, 1966, p. 263.

Phillips, J. H. "The Evolution of the Suburban Station." *ARec* 36 (Aug. 1914): 122–127.

"Railway Stations at Wellesley Hills, Waban, Woodland, Auburndale, Brighton, South Framingham, Palmer, Holyoke and North Easton, Mass." *AABN* 21 (Feb. 26, 1887): 103.

Robinson, Charles Mulford. "A Railroad Beautiful." *House and Garden* 2 (Nov. 1902): 564–570.

Miscellaneous Resources

Photographs: Boston Public Library; Houghton Library, Harvard University; Library of Congress (Historic American Buildings Survey).

137a
Boston & Albany
Railroad Station,
Wellesley Hills,
Massachusetts,
1885–1886, plan;
AABN 21 (Feb. 26,
1887).

137b
Boston & Albany
Railroad Station,
Wellesley Hills;
Houghton Library,
Harvard University.

137c
Boston & Albany
Railroad Station,
Wellesley Hills, as
altered for dry
cleaners (1972).

139a
Union Passenger
Station, New Lon-
don, Connecticut,
1885–1887; Ander-
son, Notter, Fine-
gold, Inc. (ca.
1890).

139b
Union Passenger
Station; photo by
Berenice Abbott
(ca. 1934).

Textual References

Anderson, Notter, Finegold, Inc. *Recycling Historic Railroad Stations: A Citizen's Manual.* Washington, D.C.: U.S. Department of Transportation, 1978, pp. 19–23.

"Erasing an Era." *AF* 134 (June 1971): 21.

Fleming, Malcolm M. "The Saving of Henry Hobson Richardson's Union Station." *American Art Review* 2 (July-Aug. 1975): 29–40.

Hale, Jonathan. "Sic Transit." *AF* 140 (Nov. 1973): 76.

Hemphill, Clara. "Saving a Station." *Planning: The ASPO Magazine* 41 (June 1975): 5.

Hitchcock, *Richardson,* 1966, p. 278.

Van Rensselaer, *Works,* p. 100.

Miscellaneous Resources

Drawings: Houghton Library, Harvard University.

Film: "The Rescue of Mr. Richardson's Last Station," New London Landmarks–Union Railroad Station Trust, New London, or Hill Films, Seattle.

139c
Union Passenger
Station (1978).

139d
Union Passenger
Station, detail of
entry before reno-
vation (1972).

J. R. Lionberger House, 1885–1888
Vandeventer Avenue
St. Louis, Missouri
Demolished

140a
J. R. Lionberger
house, St. Louis,
Missouri, 1885–
1888; John A.
Bryan, *Missouri's
Contribution to
American Architec-
ture*, 1928; Mis-
souri Historical
Society.

John Robert Lionberger (1829–1894) was a leading citizen of St. Louis. After acquiring an early fortune through his boot and shoe business, he became active in finance as a founder of the Third National Bank of St. Louis in 1857 and its president after 1867. He was also a director of the North Missouri Railroad and helped finance construction of the Eads Bridge across the Mississippi. His son, I. H. Lionberger (see no. 147), formed the law firm of Lionberger and Shepley with John F. Shepley, the brother of Richardson's assistant and successor, George F. Shepley.

According to Van Rensselaer, the J. R. Lionberger commission entered Richardson's office in November 1885. Richardson's letter of March 6, 1886 to George F. Shepley states that the plans and specifications for the house had been sent to St. Louis, so it is certain they were completed before Richardson's death. Construction of the house took place in 1886 and 1887.

The J. R. Lionberger house was demolished when the Cochrane Hospital was extended.

The design of the Lionberger house appeared to be a scaled down version of the MacVeagh house in Chicago (no. 135). With a high hipped roof, it was a two-story building of granite laid in alternating courses. The front was a symmetrical arrangement with a central arched entry at the ground floor and an inset balcony at the second floor. The two front corners were rounded with individual conical roofs.

140a
J. R. Lionberger Stables,
1885–1888
Vandeventer Avenue
St. Louis, Missouri
Demolished

The drawing collection at Houghton Library includes four drawings for the Lionberger stables which were apparently commissioned at the same time as the house.

Textual References

Bryan, John A. *Missouri's Contribution to American Architecture.* St. Louis: St. Louis Architectural Club, 1928.

Hitchcock, *Richardson,* 1966, p. 280.

LaBeaume, Louis. "Early Architecture of St. Louis—1764–1900." *American Architect* 133 (June 5, 1928): 717 (incorrectly captioned I. H. Lionberger House).

"Residence for John R. Lionberger, St. Louis, Mo." *American Buildings, Selections,* no. 1; pl. 82.

St. Louis Architectural Club. *Catalogue of the Annual Exhibition, 1899.* St. Louis: St. Louis Architectural Club, 1899.

Miscellaneous Resources

Drawings: Houghton Library, Harvard University.

Photographs: Missouri Historical Society.

Letters: H. H. Richardson Papers, Archives of American Art Microfilm Roll 643.

Crystal City, Missouri, which became a major glass manufacturing center in the mid-1870s, was built by the Crystal Plate Glass Company of St. Louis. The president of the company was Ethan Allen Hitchcock (1835–1909), later secretary of the interior (1898–1907) and father-in-law of John Foster Shepley (see no. 140).

This project was evidently one of several from St. Louis that came into Richardson's office in 1885 and 1886 from the friends and relations of his assistant and heir George F. Shepley. O'Gorman has also noted other possible connections, including the glass for the New York State Capitol (no. 61) provided by the Crystal Plate Glass Company.

Richardson's scheme for the Crystal City Church is known from nineteen undated drawings in the Houghton Library collection. O'Gorman discovered drawings by G. F. (or G. H.) Eliot dated May 1886, which served as the basis for construction of this structure, showing a modification of the scheme developed by Richardson. The church, as built, was not of Richardson's design, but his work was a major source.

The building was originally planned as a nondenominational chapel, but was completed as an Episcopal church. Today it is Grace Presbyterian church.

Richardson's drawings showed a stone building with a short nave and round apse. A square tower with pointed roof and attached shed porch was located at the front corner of the nave. A transverse gable was introduced in the nave to allow light to penetrate the roof, which sloped down to the low walls.

141a
Church project,
Crystal City, Mis-
souri, 1885–1886;
Houghton Library,
Harvard University.

Textual References

Douglass, Robert Sidney. *History of Southeast Missouri*. Rept. ed. Cape Girardeau, Mo.: Ramfre Press, 1961 [1912], p. 482.

History of Franklin, Jefferson, Washington, Crawford and Gasconade Counties, Missouri. Rept. ed. Cape Girardeau, Mo.: Ramfre Press, 1958 [1888], p. 439.

Litton, Howard C. "A Brief History of Festus, Missouri and Jefferson County, Missouri." Typescript, Crystal City Library, 1976, pp. 19–20.

O'Gorman, *Selected Drawings*, pp. 62–65.

Rutledge, Zoe Booth. *Our Jefferson County Heritage*. Cape Girardeau, Mo.: Ramfre Press, 1970, p. 114.

Van Rensselaer, *Works*, p. 86 (sketch).

Miscellaneous Resources

Drawings: Houghton Library, Harvard University.

142
Bagley Memorial Armory,
1885–1887
42–44 Congress Street
Detroit, Michigan
Demolished 1946

The Bagley Armory was commissioned by the heirs of the Bagley estate as a memorial to J. J. Bagley (see no. 132).

Richardson, who had already designed the Bagley Memorial Fountain, was selected as the architect by the Bagley family. According to Van Rensselaer, the commission entered Richardson's office December 1885. The completed building cost $34,000.

The street numbering of Detroit was later changed, so that subsequent Detroit city directories give the address as 132 Congress Street. In 1946 the building burned; the site has been occupied by a bus terminal since 1955.

Richardson's design for the Bagley Armory was a simple utilitarian building of brick which filled the 75 by 130 foot mid–block site. Three stores occupied space on the first floor, social rooms on the second floor, and the drill room roofed by a wood barrel vault on the third floor. The brick front with brownstone trim was marked by windows grouped under three broad arches. The large amount of fenestration was required because the party walls on the two long sides of the building were windowless.

Textual References

Ferry, W. Hawkins. *The Buildings of Detroit*. Detroit: Wayne State University Press, 1968, pp. 134–135.

Hitchcock, *Richardson*, 1966, pp. 282–283.

142a
Bagley Memorial Armory, Detroit, Michigan, 1885–1887; W. Hawkins Ferry, *The Buildings of Detroit*, 1968.

143
Castle Hill Lighthouse Project, ca. 1885–1886
Newport, Rhode Island

In 1874 Harvard Professor Alexander Agassiz (1835–1910), who founded the science of oceanography, purchased the Castle Hill peninsula at the eastern side of the entrance to Narragansett Bay, where he built a summer house. The United States Congress, O'Gorman found, initially appropriated money for a lighthouse in this location in 1875 and again on August 4, 1886. Agassiz deeded the site to the government June 10, 1887, on the condition that the lighthouse conform to plans and specifications which he supplied. These drawings are now lost, although they may be in the National Archives.

Richardson's scheme for the Castle Hill lighthouse is known from five drawings in the Houghton Library collection and from a small sketch included by Van Rensselaer. Unfortunately none of the drawings is dated. Although the project might date from any year after 1875, O'Gorman has suggested the years 1885 and 1886.

The existing Castle Hill lighthouse, erected in 1889–1890, is similar to the Richardson design studies, which generally indicated a rectangular two-story building with the round light tower attached to one corner. The tower was constructed of stone laid in horizontal courses. A small roof above the second floor level of the tower covered a bell used to warn ships in foggy weather.

Textual References

"History of Castle Hill Light Station." *Rhode Island History* 10 (Oct. 1951): 103–108.

Hitchcock, *Richardson*, 1966, p. 286.

O'Gorman, *Selected Drawings*, pp. 198–199.

Van Rensselaer, *Works*, p. 111 (sketch).

Miscellaneous Resources

Drawings: Houghton Library, Harvard University.

143a
Castle Hill Lighthouse project, Newport, Rhode Island, ca. 1885–1886; Houghton Library, Harvard University.

1886

144
Sir Hubert Herkomer House, 1886–1894
43 Melbourne Road
Bushey (Hertfordshire), England
Partially Demolished 1939

Sir Hubert Herkomer (1849–1914) was one of the nineteenth century's great eccentrics. Herkomer (originally von Herkomer) was born in Bavaria, but by the 1880s he had become one of England's most fashionable portraitists.

Herkomer visited Richardson in Boston in December 1885. Herkomer's portraits of Robert Treat Paine and Lydia Lyman Paine still hang in the Paine House, which Richardson designed (no. 117). It may have been through Paine that Herkomer and Richardson met.

By the time Herkomer and Richardson were acquainted, Herkomer had already developed plans for a house on his country estate. He proposed that Richardson do elevations for the house in exchange for a portrait. The commission entered the office January 1886, by Van Rensselaer's calculation. In a March 13, 1886 letter to George F. Shepley, Richardson mentions trying to get the project "out of the way."

Herkomer built the house between 1886 and 1894, but modified Richardson's elevations, following only their outline. The interiors, entirely by Herkomer, were rich, handcrafted Victorian. Herkomer named his house "Lululand" after his wife. The house was partially demolished about 1939; only a fragment of the main elevation survives. It is now located in a suburban subdivision and serves as the front of a servicemen's club.

Richardson's main elevation had a high gable flanked by two-story round towers with conical roofs and a broad arch below. To the right of the right-hand tower was the main entrance under a small arch with some carved stone just above the door.

Textual References

Ferriday, Peter. "Sir Hubert von Herkomer." *Country Life*. 153 (Jan. 25, 1973): 222–224; (Feb. 1, 1973): 280–281.

Herkomer, Hubert. *The Herkomers*. London: MacMillan and Company, 1910–1911, 2: 187–188.

Hitchcock, *Richardson*, 1966, p. 284.

"'Lululand' The House of Professor Hubert Herkomer, Bushey, England." *AABN* 38 (Nov. 26, 1892): 138 (reprinted from *Art Journal*).

"Mr. Hubert Herkomer's House and the Way in Which It Was Designed." *AABN* 22 (July 9, 1887): 13.

O'Gorman, *Selected Drawings*, pp. 105–106.

Pevsner, Nikolaus. *Hertfordshire: The Buildings of England*. London: Penguin, 1953, p. 77.

Shepherd, Walter. "Von Herkomer's Folly." *Country Life* 86 (Dec. 16, 1939): 636.

"A Suggestion to Place Herkomer's Portrait of Richardson in the Memorial Hall at Cambridge." *AABN* 20 (July 17, 1886): 26.

Van Rensselaer, *Works*, p. 110.

Miscellaneous Resources

Drawings: Houghton Library, Harvard University.

Photographs: National Monuments Register, London.

Letter: H. H. Richardson Papers, Archives of American Art Microfilm Roll 643.

144a
Sir Hubert Herkomer house, Bushey, England, 1886–1894; National Monuments Record, London.

145b
F. L. Ames Store;
photo by Berenice
Abbott (ca. 1934).

146

Dr. H. J. Bigelow House, 1886–1887
474a Brookline Avenue
Newton, Massachusetts

Dr. Henry Jacob Bigelow (1818–1890) received his M.D. from Harvard in 1841 and thereafter studied in Paris. On returning to the United States, he pioneered the use of anesthesia in surgical techniques. In 1846, with Dr. W. T. G. Morton, Bigelow administered sulfuric ether before operating on Gilbert Abbott at Massahusetts General Hospital. The first to publish an account of the surgical use of ether, he held the chair of surgery at the Harvard Medical School for many years.

Bigelow commissioned this house in January 1886, according to Van Rensselaer, but it must have been under study earlier. Richardson's letter of March 6, 1886 to George F. Shepley noted that Bigelow had signed a contract (presumably for construction) for $15,000. The working drawings and specifications must have been completed by that date. The contractor Miller and Ladd, the same company which had built the Paine House (no. 117), completed the house in 1887 at a cost of $25,167.

Bigelow lived there only three years until his death October 30, 1890. His son, William Sturgis Bigelow, inherited the house, but apparently never lived in it. Instead, he rented the property as a summer residence. After 1907 the house passed through a number of owners and served at various times as an art school, a hospital for crippled children, and a nurses' residence. The house stood empty and was subject to vandalism from 1973 to 1975 when John Howard of Newton organized the Newton Historic Preservation Association to save the Bigelow house.

Through his efforts WGBH-TV, the Boston educational television station, became interested in the house and in 1980 made it the subject of its program series, "This Old House." A regular feature of WGBH, this series carries out the renovation of existing properties in order to show viewers how they can preserve and renovate their own older homes. Consequently the Bigelow house was remodeled into five residential condominiums which were sold to private owners.

The Bigelow house stands atop Oak Hill, one of Newton's highest, and commands views of the surrounding villages. Richardson's early site studies showed his concern for orientation on the property.

The shingle style house is a two-story building with an attached service wing constructed around a courtyard. The main block of the house to the south rises to a height of four stories under the steep ridge roof running perpendicular to the east side. The first floor included the living room, stair, entry hall, and dining room. A small solarium projected from the south side. The second floor included a study, with the projecting turret of the southwest corner, and bedrooms. The third floor included additional bedrooms, and above these was an attic. The peak of the high roof was broken by a belvedere. The two story section just north of the main house included the kitchen and servants' hall on the first floor, and housekeeper rooms on the second floor. The wood shed, ice house, barn, carriage house, and stable areas surrounded the courtyard. The main elevation to the east includes the entrances to the courtyard and the house. A second-story gabled section projects over the main entrance, interrupting the plane of the elevation. Fenestration is varied and irregularly spaced, including some triple-hung full-height openings which once opened from the interior to the verandas that have since disappeared. Five small square windows at the north end of the east elevation mark the five horse stalls. The high roof over the carriage house and stable, whose ridge paralleled that of the main house, provided space for a hay loft. The total area of the complex of house and support spaces was over 10,000 square feet.

The shingle-covered house was marked by a minimum of decorative detail. The window frames were originally painted to match the shingles. Except at the carriage house and barn the second floor slightly overhangs the first. This effect is emphasized by a flared band of shingles and continuous dragon's tooth (shingle) detail. In the conversion of the house for condominiums in 1980, the south and east facades were preserved as Richardson had designed them, the others modified as necessary for the conversion.

Textual References

Hitchcock, *Richardson*, 1966, p. 284.

Sweetser, Moses Foster, ed. *King's Handbook of Newton*. Boston: Moses King, 1889, p. 324.

Vila, Bob. *Bob Vila's This Old House*. New York: E.P. Dutton, 1981.

The Villages of Newton. Newton: Newton Times, 1977, p. 242.

Miscellaneous Resources

Drawings: Houghton Library, Harvard University.

Letter: H. H. Richardson Papers, Archives of American Art Microfilm Roll 643.

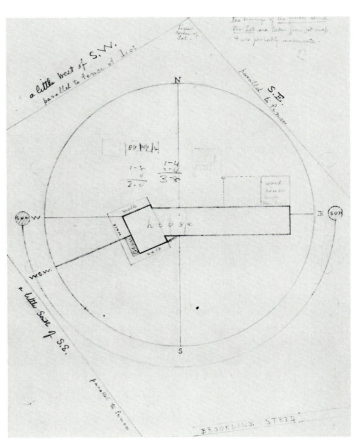

146a
Dr. H. J. Bigelow house, Newton, Massachusetts, 1886–1887, early site plan showing concern for orientation (plan of house as built does not conform to outline shown here); Houghton Library, Harvard University.

146b
Dr. H. J. Bigelow
house, overall view
(trim originally
matched shingles);
photo by Steve Ro-
senthal (1980).

146c
Dr. H. J. Bigelow
house; photo by
Steve Rosenthal
(1980).

146d
Dr. H. J. Bigelow
house (1972).

147

I. H. Lionberger House, 1886–1888

3630 Grandel Square
St. Louis, Missouri

Isaac H. Lionberger (1854–1948), son of John R. Lionberger (see no. 140), was a leading St. Louis attorney who served as assistant attorney general for the United States from 1895 to 1896 under President Grover Cleveland. He married Louise Shepley, sister to his law partner from 1886 to 1900, John F. Shepley, and to Richardson's assistant George F. Shepley.

Although Van Rensselaer did not include this project on her list of Richardson's works, it is clear from the correspondence that the drawings were completed before Richardson's death. In Richardson's March 6, 1886 letter to George F. Shepley, he wrote that plans and specifications for both Lionberger houses had been sent to St. Louis.

The I. H. Lionberger house remains, although it has been substantially altered: the front lengthened, three dormers introduced in the sloping roof, the windows enlarged, and the front entry redesigned. The building now functions as a union hall.

Richardson's scheme for the I. H. Lionberger House was a simple two-story structure of brick. The front roof with gable ends sloped toward the street and was broken by a single small dormer, the roof over the back portion of the house hipped. The windows were incised into the flat brick walls. The only decorative detail was the corbeled brick band supporting the slightly projecting upper floor and a similar brick band at the eaves.

Textual References

Hitchcock, *Richardson*, 1966, pp. 280–281.

Landmarks of St. Louis 1 (Jan. 25, 1961): 7–8.

Miscellaneous Resources

Drawings: Houghton Library, Harvard University.

Photographs: Boston Athenaeum; Library of Congress (Historic American Buildings Survey).

Letters: H. H. Richardson Papers, Archives of American Art Microfilm Roll 643.

147a
I. H. Lionberger
house, St. Louis,
Missouri, 1886–
1888; Boston
Athenaeum.

147b
I. H. Lionberger
house, with later al-
terations and addi-
tions; Library of
Congress (Historic
American Buildings
Survey, photo by
Paul Piaget, 1960).

148
Henry S. Potter House, 1886–1887
5814 Cabanne Avenue (at Goodfellow Boulevard)
St. Louis, Missouri
Demolished 1958

Henry S. Potter (1851–1918), president of the St. Louis Steel Barge Company, was married to Margaret Clarkson Lionberger, daughter of John R. Lionberger (see no. 140).

Van Rensselaer did not include this house in her list of Richardson's works, but the drawings were completed before Richardson's death. In his letter to George F. Shepley March 6, 1886, Richardson states his intention to send the plans and specifications for the Potter house to St. Louis on Monday, March 8. Construction of the house was completed in 1887.

The Potter house was later the residence of architect Ernest J. Russell, a member of the St. Louis office of Shepley, Rutan and Coolidge and a partner in its successor firm, Mauran, Russell, Crowell, and Mullgardt. Russell added some rooms to the rear of the house, but left the front unchanged. In 1950 as a testamentary bequest the house passed to the city, which demolished it to construct a park.

Richardson's plan for the Potter house was in the form of a long narrow *L*. The long leg of the *L* was the two-story living area and the base was the one-story service wing and stables. The orientation of the house was planned so that the main rooms faced south for climatic reasons. A rounded mass projected from each side of the living area. The building was sheathed entirely in shingles, but had a slate roof.

Textual References

Bryan, John. *Missouri's Contribution to American Architecture*. St. Louis. St. Louis: Architectural Club, 1928, p. 73.

Hitchcock, *Richardson*, 1966, p. 284.

O'Gorman, *Selected Drawings*, pp. 103–104.

Russell, Ernest J. "The Potter House." Mimeograph, St. Louis, Nov. 1, 1945 (Missouri Historical Society).

St. Louis Architectural Club. *Catalogue of the Annual Exhibition, 1899*. St. Louis: St. Louis Architectural Club, 1899.

"St. Louis: Progress Report (1840–1908)." *PA* 29 (May 1948): 20.

Miscellaneous Resources

Drawings: Houghton Library, Harvard University.

Photographs: Art Institute of Chicago; St. Louis Historical Society; St. Louis Public Library.

Letters: H. H. Richardson Papers, Archives of American Art Microfilm Roll 643.

148a
Henry S. Potter
house, St. Louis,
Missouri, 1886–
1887; John A.
Bryan, *Missouri's
Contribution to
American Architec-
ture*, 1928; Mis-
souri Historical
Society.

148b
Henry S. Potter
house, with later al-
terations; Art Insti-
tute of Chicago,
photo by Richard
Nickel.

148c
Henry S. Potter
house, with later al-
terations; Art Insti-
tute of Chicago,
photo by Richard
Nickel.

149
Hoyt Library Project (Competition), 1886
905 James Street
(East) Saginaw, Michigan

Jesse Hoyt (1815–1882) was the son of James M. Hoyt of New York, who invested heavily in land in northern Michigan. On the death of his father, Jesse Hoyt took over direction of the family's interests in the Saginaw Valley. Although Hoyt continued to live in New York, he was deeply involved in the development of Saginaw where he constructed buildings, shipyards, and rail lines and where he owned some pine timber tracts. At the time of his death, Hoyt's Michigan estate was valued at over $2 million. He left a bequest of $100,000 for the establishment of a free reference library.

In 1883 a design was prepared by E. D. Meyers of Detroit, but it was not constructed. In late 1885 or early 1886 a competition was announced for the design of the Hoyt Library. The published program was prepared by the Hoyt trustees in consultation with William Frederick Poole (1821–1894), who was then head of the Chicago Public Library, soon to become head of the American Library Association and the American Historical Association. O'Gorman pointed out that Poole was a leading advocate of flexible, functional library space. His approach was strictly utilitarian.

The competition entries were due in February 1886. Apparently Richardson's office made an error in the specifications, about which Richardson showed annoyance in his letter to George F. Shepley March 6, 1886. He also advised Shepley to speak with Poole in Saginaw and added that he had thought "all their recommendations were suggestions."

Other entrants in the competition included Van Brunt and Howe of Boston and McKim, Mead and White of New York. The competition was won by Van Brunt and Howe, whose design closely followed the program recommendations. Erected in 1887–1888, the library opened about November 1, 1890. O'Gorman notes that the design of the Hoyt Library was apparently adapted by Richardson's successors, Shepley, Rutan and Coolidge, for the Howard Memorial Library in New Orleans.

The Richardson scheme was organized on the longitudinal axis with the bookroom to the right, central entry hall and circular reading room to the left. The reading room was to be two stories in height with an open timber ceiling. The bookroom with Richardson's typical tier-ringed stack space terminated in a great fireplace. The building was to be built of local limestone with red sandstone trim; the roof covering was to be red Akron tiles.

Textual References

"The Architect the Natural Enemy of the Librarian." *AABN* 26 (Oct. 13, 1888): 165.

Fletcher, William I. "Architects and Librarians: An Eirenicon." *AABN* 24 (Oct. 27, 1888): 198.

Hitchcock, *Richardson*, 1966, p. 285.

Mills, James Cooke. *History of Saginaw County, Michigan*. Saginaw, Mich.: Seemann & Peters, 1918, 1: 304–307; 2: 244–247.

O'Gorman, *Selected Drawings*, pp. 171–174.

[H. H. Richardson.] *The Hoyt Public Library, East Saginaw, Michigan*. Boston: [1886].

Miscellaneous Resources

Drawings: Houghton Library, Harvard University.

149a
Hoyt Library proj-
ect, Saginaw,
Michigan, 1886;
Houghton Library,
Harvard University.

150
William H. Gratwick House, 1886–1889
776 Delaware Avenue
Buffalo, New York
Demolished 1920s

William Henry Gratwick (1839–1899) organized William H. Gratwick and Company in 1861 and soon became the leading lumber dealer in Albany, New York. In 1877, he moved to Buffalo and formed Gratwick, Smith and Fryer, which became one of the largest lumber companies in America with timber tracts in Michigan, Wisconsin and Louisiana. After 1880, Gratwick began the construction of barges on the Great Lakes to move lumber and other raw materials and was soon president of both the Aetna and Cleveland Steamship Lines.

The Gratwick house is the last commission listed by Van Rensselaer. According to her list, the project entered the office in February 1886. Richardson wrote George F. Shepley on March 13, 1886 that revised studies for the Gratwick house had been sent to Buffalo on March 12. Evidently the design was worked out before Richardson's death. Working drawings, O'Gorman notes, were produced between July and September 1886, but some details were produced as late as 1888. The house was completed by local contractors early in 1889 at a cost of $104,342.

The house was demolished in the late 1920s to make way ultimately for a synagogue now occupying the site.

The design was initially sketched by Richardson, but O'Gorman notes that Charles A. Coolidge worked out many of the features. The plan is *L*-shaped with the carriage porch and main entry at the end of the *L*'s base. The central hall and stair are at the bend of the *L* with subsidiary living spaces clustered around them. The top of the *L* was the service wing. A large round tower with conical roof was set at the outside corner of the *L*, a smaller fac-eted tower at the front corner near the carriage porch, and another rounded mass projected from the center of the leg of the *L*. The high steep roof was broken by three full third-floor dormers on each of the outside faces of the *L*. The windows were set deep into walls of granite set in random ashlar.

Textual References

Hitchcock, *Richardson*, 1966, p. 286.

Kowsky, Francis R. *Buffalo Projects: H. H. Richardson*. Buffalo: Buffalo State College Foundation, 1980, p. 16.

O'Gorman, *Selected Drawings*, pp. 92–94.

"Residence of William H. Gratwick, Buffalo, N.Y." *American Buildings, Selections*, no. 1: pl. 117.

"Residence of William H. Gratwick, Buffalo, N.Y." *Inland Architect and News Record* 14 (Dec. 1889): 84.

Van Rensselaer, *Works*, p. 110.

Miscellaneous Resources

Drawings: Houghton Library, Harvard University.

Photographs: Boston Athenaeum; Buffalo and Erie County Historical Society; Houghton Library, Harvard University.

Letters: H. H. Richardson Papers, Archives of American Art Microfilm Roll 643.

150a
William H. Gratwick house, Buffalo, New York, 1886–1889; Boston Athenaeum.

150b
William H. Gratwick house; Buffalo and Erie County Historical Society.

Appendixes

Summary of Collections
Relating to H. H. Richardson

The following summary is a partial listing of resources for the study of Richardson's works. The holdings noted here are unique to each collection, not periodicals in national circulation or widely held books.

The summary is divided into two sections. The first lists collections which include material relating to Richardson generally or to a wide variety of his projects. The second lists collections which refer to Richardson's work in a single locale.

This summary should not be regarded as complete. Some libraries did not volunteer information on their collections, and others with material may have been missed entirely.

General Collections

Archives of American Art
41 East Sixty-fifth Street
New York, New York 10021

or

FA-PG Building
Eighth and F Streets N.W.
Washington, D.C. 20560

The Archives of American Art collection documents the history of the visual arts in this country. Five million items of original source material are available on microfilm through the offices in New York and Washington, and regional offices in Detroit, Boston, San Francisco, and Houston. Since 1970 the Archives has been affiliated with the Smithsonian Institution.

Materials on H. H. Richardson include his correspondence and papers (roll 643), the correspondence of his wife Julia with her family (roll 1184), and various office books (roll 676).

Avery Library
Columbia University
New York, New York 10027

The Avery Library has several unique holdings relating to Richardson's buildings. The collection includes seventeen photoengravings of the Allegheny County Courthouse and Jail dating from the time of their design and construction, and the original specifications for the Albany City Hall. Both of these items were gifts from Henry-Russell Hitchcock. The library also holds a scrapbook of Ecole des Beaux-Arts projects dedicated to H. H. Richardson.

The Avery Library has been responsible for compiling the *Avery Guide to Architectural Periodical Literature* which provides a thorough if not always complete index to major architectural periodicals.

Baker Library
Dartmouth College
Hanover, New Hampshire 03755

The Dartmouth College Baker Library holds the papers of the sculptor, Augustus Saint-Gaudens, including correspondence and similar material relating to his collaboration with Richardson. The papers are available on microfilm for those who are unable to visit the library.

Boston Athenaeum
10½ Beacon Street
Boston, Massachusetts 02108

The Boston Athenaeum has a collection of about one hundred photographs of many Richardson buildings and a large collection of street photographs of Boston indexed by street, which may include some Richardson photographs. Several drawings for Mr. Tudor's barn (1888) are also in the collection, although these are more likely the work of Shepley, Rutan and Coolidge.

A source for biographical information about leading Boston figures, including many Richardson clients, the Athenaeum is a private organization whose library is open only to members and visiting researchers who may wish to consult its unique holdings. Scholars should contact the Athenaeum in writing before visiting.

Bostonian Society
Old State House
206 Washington Street
Boston, Massachusetts 02109

The Bostonian Society holds an extensive collection of photographs of the city of Boston and its contiguous suburbs. This collection, organized alphabetically by street or area, includes photographs of some of Richardson's buildings. The society also has some clippings and similar material relating to Trinity Church in scrapbooks.

The facilities of the society are available to visiting scholars and researchers, but because the staff has limited time, it requests that visitors contact the society in writing before they come to use the materials.

Films for the Humanities
P. O. Box 2053
Princeton, New Jersey 08540

Films for the Humanities, a distributor of educational films, offers a half-hour color film on Richardson's life and work, titled "Architect of the New American Suburb: H. H. Richardson (1838–1886)." The film was produced by Harvard University, Fogg Fine Arts Films, and was written and narrated by John Coolidge.

Houghton Library
Harvard University
Cambridge, Massachusetts 02138

The Houghton Library collection includes drawings from Richardson's office donated to the library in 1942 by Henry Richardson Shepley, a complete index to which was developed by Charles Price about 1964. The library also holds photographs of many of Richardson's buildings. Recently more material has been donated to the collection by Shepley, Bulfinch, Richardson and Abbott.

Because its collections are fragile, access is restricted at the Houghton Library. Scholars wishing to consult the collection should contact the library in writing prior to their visits.

Library of Congress
Manuscript Division
Washington, D.C. 20540

The very extensive papers of landscape architect Frederick Law Olmsted are held by the Manuscript Division. These include Olmsted's own notes and writings as well as correspondence with the many architects with whom Olmsted dealt in the second half of the nineteenth century.

Library of Congress
Prints and Photographs Division
Washington, D.C. 20540

The Library of Congress holds extensive collections of architectural materials. The most important of these is the Historic American Buildings Survey, a large collection of measured drawings, professional photographs, and miscellaneous documents relating to buildings throughout the United States and its territories. The library has also acquired other collections, which have been indexed separately from the Historic American Buildings Survey. In addition, some Historic American Buildings Survey materials are held at the Survey Office, Office of Archeology and Historic Preservation, Heritage Conservation and Recreation Service, Department of the Interior, Washington, D.C. Many of Richardson's buildings are partially documented in these collections.

The Library of Congress collections are open to the public. Generally they are indexed by location. Because of the complexity of the collections, a number of freelance picture searchers offer their services to aid in locating particular items. A list is available from the library.

Loeb Library
Graduate School of Design
Harvard University
Cambridge, Massachusetts 02138

The Loeb Library holds the collection of Richardson's own books and photographs donated to the Graduate School of Design by Richardson's successors.

Scholars may consult materials in the library collections, but they should contact the library in writing prior to visiting.

Massachusetts Historical Society
1154 Boylston Street
Boston, Massachusetts 02215

The Massachusetts Historical Society collection includes about twenty-five original letters by Richardson, as well as photographs of several of his buildings.

The society also holds the Henry Adams papers, which contain some items relating to Richardson's career.

Frederick Law Olmsted National Historic Site
99 Warren Street
Brookline, Massachusetts 02146

The property comprising Olmsted's former home and office was acquired by the U.S. Park Service in 1979.

The site holds the drawings, photographs, and records of the Olmsted office, including many items relating to the various projects on which Richardson and Olmsted were collaborators.

Pusey Library
Harvard University
Cambridge, Massachusetts 02138

The Pusey Library is the repository for the Harvard University Archives, which hold information on the many Richardson clients who were graduates of Harvard.

The Pusey Library also holds copies of Harvard Ph.D. dissertations. Those by Cynthia Zaitzevsky on F. L. Olmsted and Larry Homolka on Richardson's work in North Easton contain significant information on the architect's career.

Scholars may consult the materials in the Pusey Library, but it is best to contact the library in writing prior to visiting.

Society for the Preservation of New England Antiquities
Harrison Gray Otis House
141 Cambridge Street
Boston, Massachusetts 02114

The Society for the Preservation of New England Antiquities has a collection of nearly one million photographs of New England architecture dating from the colonial period to the present. The collection is organized generally by location, but for Boston it is indexed by street. In each location the materials are divided by date: pre- and post-1840. Photographs of many of Richardson's buildings are included.

The society operates on a limited budget. Its facilities are available to visiting scholars, but contact in writing before visiting is recommended.

Local Collections

The following collections have been listed alphabetically by their city locations.

Albany Institute of History and Art, McKinney Library, 125 Washington Avenue, Albany, New York 12210

State Archives, State Education Department, State University of New York, Albany, New York 12230

Albany Public Library, 161 Washington Avenue, Albany, New York 12210

Boston Public Library, Copley Square, Boston, Massachusetts 02117

Buffalo and Erie County Historical Society, 25 Nottingham Court, Buffalo, New York 14216

Buffalo and Erie County Public Library, Lafayette Square, Buffalo, New York 14230

Buffalo Psychiatric Center Library, 400 Forest Avenue, Buffalo, New York 14213

Robert Hull Fleming Museum, University of Vermont, Burlington, Vermont 05401

Wyoming State Archives and Historical Department, Barrett Building, Cheyenne, Wyoming 82002

Art Institute of Chicago, Michigan Avenue at Adams Street, Chicago, Illinois 60603

Chicago Historical Society, Clark Street at North Avenue, Chicago, Illinois 60614

Cincinnati Historical Society, Eden Park, Cincinnati, Ohio 45202

Public Library of Cincinnati and Hamilton County, Eighth and Vine Streets, Cincinnati, Ohio 45202

City of Detroit Historical Department, Detroit Historical Museum, 5401 Woodward Avenue, Detroit, Michigan 48202

Detroit Public Library, 5201 Woodward Avenue, Detroit, Michigan 48202

Danforth Museum, 123 Union Avenue, Framingham, Massachusetts 01701

Framingham Historical and Natural History Society, Framingham, Massachusetts 01701

Framingham Public Library, Framingham, Massachusetts 01701

Corporate Library, Connecticut General Life Insurance Company, Hartford, Connecticut 06152

Connecticut Historical Society, 1 Elizabeth Street, Hartford, Connecticut 06105

Connecticut State Library, 231 Capitol Avenue, Hartford, Connecticut 06115

Hartford Public Library, 500 Main Street, Hartford, Connecticut 06103

Stowe-Day Foundation, 77 Forest Street, Hartford, Connecticut 06105

Holyoke Public Library, 335 Maple Street, Holyoke, Massachusetts 01040

Malden Public Library, Malden, Massachusetts 02148

Elizabeth Taber Library, P.O. 116, Marion, Massachusetts 02738

Medford Historical Commission, Medford Public Library, 111 High Street, Medford, Massachusetts 02155

Century Association, 7 West Forty-third Street, New York, New York 10036

New York Public Library, Fifth Avenue at Forty-second Street, New York, New York 10018

Ames Free Library, North Easton, Massachusetts 02356

Easton Historical Society, P.O. Box 3, North Easton, Massachusetts 02356

Newport Historical Society, 82 Touro Street, Newport, Rhode Island 02840

Palmer Public Library, 29 Central Street, Palmer, Massachusetts 01069

Carnegie Library of Pittsburgh, 4400 Fobes Avenue, Pittsburgh, Pennsylvania 15213

Historical Society of Western Pennsylvania, 4338 Bigelow Boulevard, Pittsburgh, Pennsylvania 15213

Pittsburgh History and Landmarks Foundation, The Old Post Office, One Landmarks Square, Pittsburgh, Pennsylvania 15212

John Hay Library, Brown University, Providence, Rhode Island 02912

Thomas Crane Public Library, Quincy, Massachusetts 02169

Missouri Historical Society, Jefferson Memorial Building, St. Louis, Missouri 63112

St. Louis Public Library, 1301 Olive Street, St. Louis, Missouri 63101

Springfield Library, 220 State Street, Springfield, Massachusetts 01103

Waltham Public Library, 735 Main Street, Waltham, Massachusetts 02154

Columbia Historical Society, 1307 New Hampshire Avenue N.W., Washington, D.C. 20036

Martin Luther King Memorial Library, 901 G Street N.W., Washington, D.C. 20001

Society of Cincinnati, Anderson House 2118 Massachusetts Avenue N.W., Washington, D.C. 20008

Wellesley Free Library, P.O. Box 308, Wellesley, Massachusetts 02181

Woburn Public Library, P.O. Box 268, Woburn, Massachusetts 01801

Worcester Historical Museum, 39 Salisbury Street, Worcester, Massachusetts 01608

Worcester Public Library, Salem Square, Worcester, Massachusetts 01608

Maps

The maps presented here are in two groups:

The first three maps show the geographical distribution of Richardson's work in the United States, in New England, and in the Boston area. Because of the large number of projects in Boston and in New England, two maps focus on southern New England and the Boston area. No distinction has been made between the buildings by Gambrill and Richardson and those by Richardson alone. Dots signify those buildings which remain, and *x*'s signify those which have been demolished.

The last four maps show the approximate locations of Richardson's extant projects in Boston, Springfield, Albany, and North Easton. These maps are meant only to help orient visitors to the approximate locations of projects within these cities and towns.

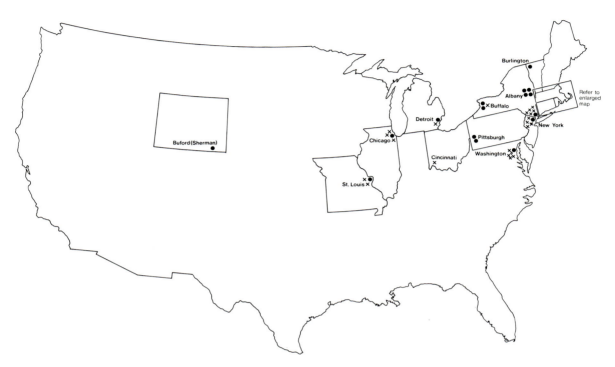

Geographical distribution of Richardson's work in the United States, New England, and the Boston area.

Worcester ×
Framingham ●

Refer to
Boston area
map

● Holyoke
● Palmer
× ×
● × Springfield
● ×

● North Easton

× Hartford

Marion ●

Newport

New London ●

Beverly ●

● Woburn

● Malden
● Medford

● Waltham
● Cambridge
●
Boston (Brighton) ×
× Newton (Auburndale)
●
● Newton (Woodland)
Newton (Waban) × × × Newton (Chestnut Hill)
× ● Newton
Newton (Waban) × × Newton (Eliot) × Brookline
● Wellesley
Hills
● Newton (Oak Hill)

Quincy ●

Cohasset ●

Boston, Massachusetts

1 Benjamin W. Crowninshield House
2 Brattle Square Church
3 Trinity Church
4 Hayden Building
5 Rectory for Trinity Church
6 Bridge in Fenway Park
7 Stony Brook Gatehouse

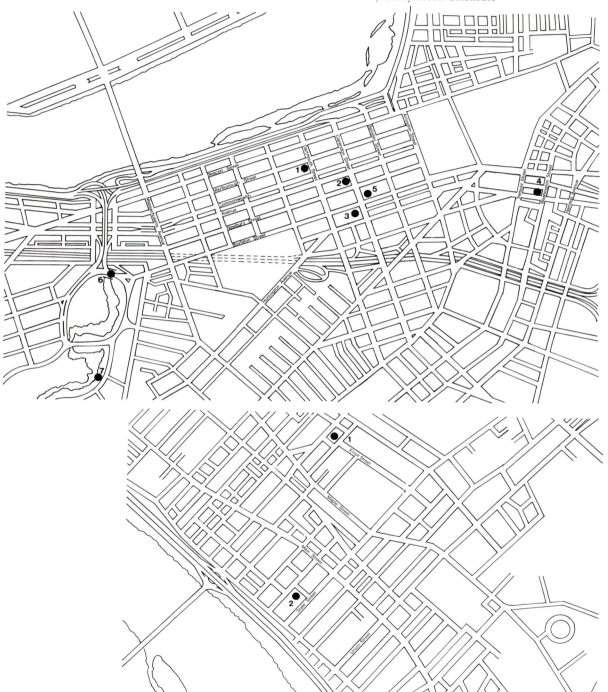

Springfield, Massachusetts

1 North Congregational Church
2 Hampden County Courthouse

1 New York State Capitol
2 Albany City Hall
3 Grange Sard, Jr., House

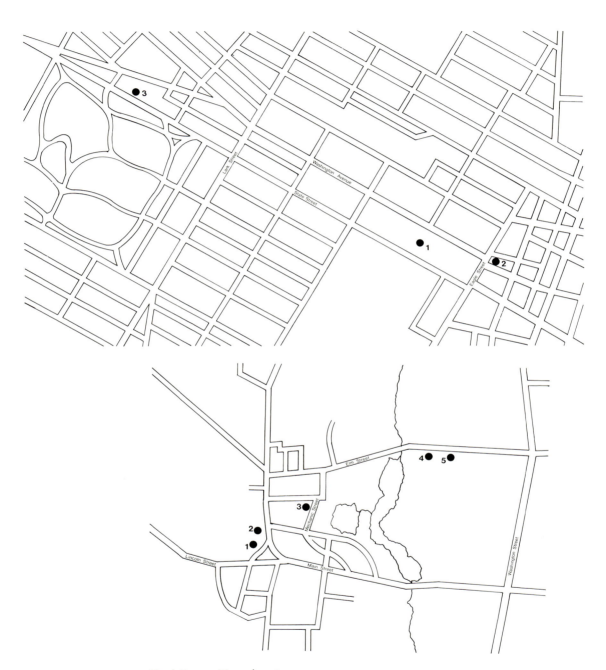

North Easton, Massachusetts

1 Oakes Ames Memorial Town Hall
2 Oliver Ames Free Library
3 Old Colony Railroad Station
4 F. L. Ames Gate Lodge
5 F. L. Ames Gardener's Cottage

Allegheny County Buildings, Pittsburgh

J. J. Glessner house, Chicago

The following Richardson buildings are listed in the National Register of Historic Places:

Hampden County Courthouse, Springfield

North Congregational Church, Springfield (in Quadrangle-Matoon Street Historic District)

Boston & Albany Railroad Station, South Framingham

Benjamin W. Crowninshield house, Boston

Brattle Square Church, Boston

Trinity Church, Boston

Rectory for Trinity Church, Boston

Fenway Park Bridge, Boston (part of Olmsted Park System, Norfolk County)

Sever Hall, Harvard University, Cambridge

Austin Hall, Harvard University, Cambridge

Robert Treat Paine house, Waltham

Grace Episcopal Church, Medford

Boston and Albany Railroad Station, Woodland

Thomas Crane Public Library, Quincy

Oliver Ames Free Library, North Easton

Oakes Ames Memorial Town Hall, North Easton

Old Colony Railroad Station, North Easton

F. L. Ames gate lodge, North Easton

F. L. Ames gardener's cottage, North Easton (all North Easton buildings by Richardson are part of the North Easton Historic District)

William Watts Sherman house, Newport

Billings Library, University of Vermont, Burlington, Vermont (in the University Green Historic District)

R. and F. Cheney Building, Hartford

City Hall, Albany

New York State Capitol, Albany

Buffalo State Hospital, Buffalo

Emmanuel Episcopal Church, Pittsburgh

Allegheny County Buildings, Pittsburgh

Benjamin H. Warder house, Washington, D.C.

Bagley Memorial Drinking Fountain, Detroit

J. J. Glessner house, Chicago

Ames monument, Sherman (Buford)

Geographical Index
by Zip Code

(D) after a project indicates that it has been demolished.

MA (Massachusetts)

01040 **Holyoke**
Connecticut River Railroad Station
Lyman Street at Bowers Street

01069 **Palmer**
Boston & Albany Railroad Station, Palmer
Depot Street

01103 **Springfield**
Church of the Unity
209 State Street

Hampden County Courthouse
37 Elm Street

01105 **Springfield**
Western Railroad Offices (D)
236 Main Street

Agawam National Bank (D)
233 Main Street

North Congregational Church
18 Salem Street

Benjamin F. Bowles house (D)
School Street at Union Street

01608 **Worcester**
Worcester High School (D)
Maple Street at Walnut Street

01701 **South Framingham**
Boston & Albany Railroad Station, South
Framingham
Waverly Street at Concord Street

01801 **Woburn**
Winn Memorial Library
88 Montvale Street

01915 **Beverly**
Ephraim W. Gurney house
6 Greenwood Avenue

02025 **Cohasset**
Dr. John Bryant house
150 Howard Gleason Road

02111 **Boston**
Hayden Building
681 Washington Street

F. L. Ames Wholesale Store (D)
Bedford Street at Kingston Street

F. L. Ames Store, Washington Street, remodeling (D)
515–521 Washington Avenue

F. L. Ames Store (D)
30 Harrison Avenue

02116 **Boston**
Benjamin W. Crowninshield house
164 Marlborough Street

Brattle Square Church
Commonwealth Avenue at Clarendon
Street

Trinity Church
Copley Square

Rectory for Trinity Church
233 Clarendon Street

Bridge in Fenway Park (D)
Charlesgate East

Bridge in Fenway Park
Boylston Street

Stony Brook gatehouse
Fenway Park

F. L. Higginson house (D)
274 Beacon Street

02118 **Boston**
Boston & Albany Dairy Building (D)
Castle Street (between Tremont Street and
Shawmut Avenue)

02135 **Boston**
Boston & Albany Railroad Station,
Brighton (D)
Brighton Center

02138 **Cambridge**
Sever Hall
Harvard University

Austin Hall
Harvard University

Mrs. M. F. Stoughton House
90 Brattle Street

02146 **Brookline**
H. H. Richardson studios (D)
25 Cottage Street

Dr. Walter Channing house (D)
Chestnut Hill Avenue near corner of
Boylston Street

02148 **Malden**
Converse Memorial Public Library
36 Salem Street

02154 **Waltham**
Robert Treat Paine house
577 Beaver Street

02155 **Medford**
Grace Episcopal Church
160 High Street

02158 **Newton**
Immanuel Baptist Church
187 Church Street (at Center Street)

02161 **Newton**
Boston & Albany Railroad Station, Eliot
(D)
Circuit Avenue

02166 **Newton**
Boston & Albany Railroad Station, Auburndale (D)
Auburndale Center

Boston & Albany Railroad Station,
Woodland
1897 Washington Street

02167 **Newton**
Boston & Albany Railroad Station, Chestnut Hill (D)
Hammond Street

02168 **Newton**
Boston & Albany Railroad Station, Waban
(D)
Woodward Street at Beacon Street, Waban
Square

02169 **Quincy**
Thomas Crane Public Library
40 Washington Street

02181 **Wellesley Hills**
Boston & Albany Railroad Station,
Wellesley Hills
339 Washington Street

02215 **Newton**
Doctor H. J. Bigelow house
474a Brookline Avenue

02356 **North Easton**
Oliver Ames Free Library
53 Main Street

Oakes Ames Memorial Town Hall
1 Barrows Street

Old Colony Railroad Station
80 Mechanic Street

F. L. Ames gate lodge
135 Elm Street

F. L. Ames gardener's cottage
149 Elm Street

02738 **Marion**
Reverend Percy Browne house
Front Street

RI (Rhode Island)

02840 **Newport**
F. L. Andrews house (D)
Maple Avenue, Coddington Point

William Watts Sherman house
2 Shepard Avenue

E. F. Mason house alterations (D)
Rhode Island Avenue and Bath Road

VT (Vermont)

05401 **Burlington**
Billings Memorial Library
University of Vermont

CT (Connecticut)

06103 **Hartford**
Phoenix Fire Insurance Company Building
(D)
64 Pearl Street

R. and F. Cheney Building
942 Main Street

06320 **New London**
Union Passenger Station
27 Water Street

NY (New York)

10003 **New York**
Century Association alterations (D)
42 East Fifteenth Street

All Souls Church alterations (D)
245 Fourth Avenue

10010 **New York**
Brunswick Hotel alterations (D)
225–231 Fifth Avenue

10016 **New York**
George E. Stone house alterations (D)
12 East Thirty-seventh Street

Jonathan Sturges house (D)
38 Park Avenue

Frederick Sturges house (D)
40 East Thirty-sixth Street

H. B. Hyde house alterations (D)
11 East Fortieth Street

Reverend Henry Eglington Montgomery
memorial
Church of the Incarnation
209 Madison Avenue

10036 **New York**
Francis M. Wild house alterations (D)
58 West Forty-fifth Street

Joseph H. Choate house alterations (D)
50 West Forty-seventh Street

10305 **Staten Island**
H. H. Richardson house
45 McClean Avenue

12204 **Albany**
Pruyn monument
Albany Rural Cemetery

12207 **Albany**
City Hall
Eagle Street at Maiden Lane

12210 **Albany**
Grange Sard, Jr., house
397 State Street

12224 **Albany**
New York State Capitol
State Street

14202 **Buffalo**
William E. Dorsheimer house
438 Delaware Avenue

14209 **Buffalo**
William H. Gratwick house (D)
776 Delaware Avenue

14213 **Buffalo**
Buffalo State Hospital
400 Forest Avenue

PA (Pennsylvania)

15212 **Pittsburgh**
Emmanuel Episcopal Church
North Avenue at Allegheny Avenue

15219 **Pittsburgh**
Allegheny County Buildings
436 Grant Street

DC (District of Columbia)

20003 **Washington**
Alexander Dallas Bache monument
Congressional Cemetery

20006 **Washington**
N. L. Anderson house (D)
1530 K Street at Sixteenth Street N.W.

Benjamin H. Warder house (partially
rebuilt)
1515 K Street N.W.

John Hay and Henry Adams houses (D)
800 Sixteenth Street and 1603 H Street,
N.W.

OH (Ohio)

45202 **Cincinnati**
Cincinnati Chamber of Commerce (D)
Fourth Street at Vine Street

MI (Michigan)

48226 Detroit
Bagley Memorial Fountain
Campus Martius

Bagley Memorial Armory (D)
42–44 Congress Street

IL (Illinois)

60603 Chicago
American Merchants Union Express Company Building (D)
21 West Monroe Street

60606 Chicago
Marshall Field Wholesale Store (D)
West Adams Street at South Franklin Street

60610 Chicago
Franklin MacVeagh house (D)
103 North Lake Shore Drive (at Schiller Court)

60616 Chicago
J. J. Glessner house
1800 South Prairie Avenue

MO (Missouri)

63106 St. Louis
J. R. Lionberger house (D)
Vandeventer Avenue

63108 St. Louis
I. H. Lionberger house
3630 Grandel Square

63112 St. Louis
Henry S. Potter house (D)
5814 Cabanne Avenue (at Goodfellow Boulevard)

WY (Wyoming)

82052 Buford
Ames monument
(Sherman)

Argentina
Exhibition building (D)
Cordova

England
Professor Hubert Herkomer house (fragment remains)
43 Melbourne Road
Bushey, Hertfordshire

Index